# Developing Early Literacy 0 to 8

# Developing Early Literacy 0 to 8

## from theory to practice

edited by

# Virginia Bower

Los Angeles | London | New Delhi
Singapore | Washington DC

Los Angeles | London | New Delhi
Singapore | Washington DC

SAGE Publications Ltd
1 Oliver's Yard
55 City Road
London EC1Y 1SP

SAGE Publications Inc.
2455 Teller Road
Thousand Oaks, California 91320

SAGE Publications India Pvt Ltd
B 1/I 1 Mohan Cooperative Industrial Area
Mathura Road
New Delhi 110 044

SAGE Publications Asia-Pacific Pte Ltd
3 Church Street
#10-04 Samsung Hub
Singapore 049483

Editor: Amy Jarrold
Editorial associate: Miriam Davey
Production editor: Thea Watson
Copyeditor: Michelle Clark
Proofreader: Katie Forsythe
Indexer: Bill Farrington
Marketing manager: Catherine Slinn
Cover design: Wendy Scott
Typeset by: C&M Digitals (P) Ltd, Chennai, India
Printed and bound in Great Britain by Ashford
Colour Press Ltd

Editorial arrangement, Chapter 5 and Chapter 8 © Virginia
Bower, 2014
Chapter 1 © Kathy Goouch, 2014
Chapter 2 © Joanna Palmer, 2014
Chapter 3 © Michael Green, 2014
Chapter 4 © Karen Vincent
Chapter 6 © Virginia Bower and Verity Hill, 2014
Chapter 7 and Chapter 11 © Tracy Parvin, 2014
Chapter 8 © Susan Barrett and Virginia Bower, 2014
Chapter 9 © Caroline Tancock
Chapter 10 © Roger McDonald
Chapter 12 © Susan Barrett

First published 2014

**Library of Congress Control Number: 2013957880**

**British Library Cataloguing in Publication data**

A catalogue record for this book is available from
the British Library

ISBN 978-1-4462-5532-2
ISBN 978-1-4462-5533-9 (pbk)

# Contents

This book is for my very favourite young learners – Sienna, Darcey, George and Alfie

# Acknowledgements

The authors would like to thank all the schools, colleagues, parents and children who helped with the material for this book.

# About the editor and contributors

## The editor

**Virginia Bower** is a senior lecturer in primary education at Canterbury Christ Church University. She teaches on both the undergraduate programme and on the full-time PGCE English course and is also part of the team teaching the Masters in language and literacy course. Virginia is very keen to promote a love of literature in both children and university students and convenes a reading group for undergraduate trainee teachers where children's literature is shared, studied and enjoyed. She is currently undertaking a doctoral study focusing on supporting children with English as an additional language.

## The contributors

**Susan Barrett** is a senior lecturer in the Department of Primary Education at Canterbury Christ Church University, where she teaches undergraduate and postgraduate English and professional studies courses. This follows a classroom teaching career of 23 years, first as a secondary English teacher and later an upper Key Stage 2 teacher and deputy headteacher. She has a keen interest in children's literature, poetry in particular, and its use in the classroom.

**Kathy Goouch** is a reader in education and currently works in the Research Centre for Children, Families and Communities at Canterbury Christ Church University, where she specialises in the early years of education and care. Her research interests are in the care and educational experiences of babies and very young children, as well as the care and professional development of practitioners and teachers in the field of early childhood. Kathy has been involved with a number of research and development projects, with a specific focus on professionalism and professional development in the early years of education, early literacy development and, more recently, babies and children under two years of age.

**Michael Green** is the Programme Director for the undergraduate degree in primary education at Canterbury Christ Church University. He teaches a number of modules on the programme, including one focusing on learning outside the classroom. Prior to joining Initial Teacher Education (ITE), Michael worked as an assistant headteacher in a primary school in Medway. His current research interests include using the potential of outdoor learning opportunities for children and digital literacy practices.

**Verity Hill** is currently working as a SENCO and Key Stage 2 class teacher. Since qualifying as a teacher in 1997, Verity has worked in several schools in Kent, teaching both in mainstream and special needs classes. For some years she worked in a hearing impaired unit and has completed British Sign Language levels 1 and 2. Verity is committed to unlocking, for the children, the limitless world of reading via carefully chosen texts that will feed their vocabulary, widen their imagination and send shivers of excitement down their spines!

**Roger McDonald** has been a primary school teacher for 14 years, latterly as a deputy headteacher in a school in Medway. Having joined the English team at Canterbury Christ Church University as an associate tutor, he found that he relished the challenge and enjoyed teaching in higher education. Most recently he has moved to the University of Greenwich, where he is a senior lecturer in primary education. Roger's main research interests, in addition to picture books, are in the fields of drama, emotional engagement and speaking and listening.

**Joanne Palmer** is a senior lecturer in primary education at the University of Northampton, where she teaches English and professional studies on both the undergraduate and PGCE programmes. Previous to her move to Northamptonshire, Jo was on secondment at Canterbury Christ Church University, where she taught on the undergraduate primary education course alongside teaching in primary schools in the Medway area. Jo is currently engaged in developing international research opportunities with members of the Initial Teacher Education team at the University of Northampton.

**Tracy Parvin** worked as a primary school teacher for 14 years, gaining experience in EYFS and Key Stages 1 and 2. She has worked in ITE for five years and is a senior lecturer in primary education at Canterbury Christ Church University. She teaches on both the undergraduate programme and on PGCE English courses. Her current research interests are focusing on the development of early reading teaching practices alongside children's responses to picture books.

**Caroline Tancock** is a senior lecturer in the Department of Primary Education at Canterbury Christ Church University, where she is a member of the BA (Hons) primary education management team. She teaches many modules on the undergraduate programme, including English and educational and academic studies, in addition to teaching on the full-time PGCE English course. Prior to joining the university, Caroline worked in a primary school in the Medway area. Her current research interests include cultural influences on reading experiences and attitudes.

**Karen Vincent** worked as a teacher in Early Years, primary and secondary education for 17 years before taking up a post as a senior lecturer in the Department of Primary Education at Canterbury Christ Church University in 2010. She teaches across a range of primary teacher training programmes, specialising in Early Years education. Her research interests include young children's perceptions of learning, the transition between Reception and Year 1 and pedagogies of teacher education. She is Programme Director for the Primary Education Progression Route.

# Introduction

Excellent literacy practices should begin at birth and can set young learners on an exploratory journey from the very beginning of their lives; a journey that allows them to discover the power of language – both oral and written – and develop effective communication skills, enabling them to succeed in a range of settings. Working with babies and young children carries a huge responsibility, as we strive to promote curious, motivated learners who are able to collaborate and cooperate with others, working towards a common goal and, at the same time, having the confidence and ability to work independently where necessary. Support from more able others, high-quality resources and well-planned environments all play a part in the development of these young learners. Practitioners need to combine their knowledge of relevant research and their own experience with working with children in order to ensure that settings provide these elements. We owe it to every child we meet to be well informed, up-to-date with our knowledge of child development and prepared to continually improve our practice by talking with colleagues, doing extensive reading and being prepared to take well-judged risks to promote exciting and innovative learning environments and opportunities for all children.

Every contributor to this book has worked or is still working in primary schools. In our roles as class teachers, literacy leaders, senior management and university lecturers, we have engaged in hundreds of conversations with colleagues and trainee teachers. This book has emerged from those conversations, wherein practitioners have identified particular aspects of early literacy learning that interest them or raise issues. As we explored the nature of those interests and issues, it became apparent that particular themes were recurring and these themes have become the basis for the structure of this book. The themes of the four parts of the book are 'Environment', 'Provision for all', 'Promoting language' and 'Inspiring readers and writers'. Within each part there are three chapters and the contents of these are summarised below.

In writing the book, we were aware there are already many excellent texts available that discuss the nature and importance of early literacy, but felt none of these were based specifically on the direct everyday concerns of practitioners. We hope, with this book, to address some of these concerns and raise an awareness that all of us who wish to see our children learning and having fun in inspiring environments with knowledgeable and caring practitioners are in this together and, by sharing our knowledge, experience and understanding, can successfully achieve these goals.

To this end, this text is a combination of evidence-based discussion and practice-based case studies. Each chapter begins with a list of objectives and topics covered, which provide an overview of the intentions of the author and an outline of the chapter's structure. The chapters then go on to examine the research-informed literature relating to the subject matter and present a range of viewpoints and opinions. Ideas and issues are raised and case studies are presented that illustrate some of these, followed by discussion to attempt to examine the concepts and implications relating to the practice described. A summary is included at the end of each chapter to draw the ideas together and hopefully provoke your own thoughts and lead to conversations with colleagues. Each chapter includes ideas for further reading, providing a brief explanation of why these particular texts might prove useful, and all finish with a reference list, which might be useful as a starting point for your own follow-up reading.

Although the book is divided into four parts, the chapters are designed so that they can be read in any order, depending on your current need or interest. However, links are sometimes made between chapters, particularly if a certain idea is discussed in more depth in another chapter. Below is a summary of the contents of all the chapters.

# Part 1: Environment

## Chapter 1: *Baby rooms* Kathy Goouch

This chapter centres on a research-informed discussion supporting the idea that babies arrive in the world curious, predisposed to learn and already experienced in tuning in to the sounds and patterns of their mother tongue. Kathy discusses how these early dispositions can be acknowledged, celebrated, supported and embedded and how rich literacy practices with babies can be promoted to support their natural development. There is a strong emphasis within the chapter on the importance of environment on babies' very early literacy development. The author uses examples from *The Baby Room* project (Goouch and Powell, 2012) to provide the contexts for discussion.

## Chapter 2: *Role-play areas for EYFS (ages zero to five), Key Stage 1 (ages five to seven) and beyond* Joanne Palmer

This chapter begins with an examination of different types of play. The discussion then moves on to consider role-play areas and how these might be used to enhance and develop children's language and literacy skills in the Early Years Foundation Stage (EYFS) and Key Stages 1 and 2. Joanne includes case studies that are examples from her own practice, where she has used role-play areas with different year groups to enhance the children's language and literacy skills. The role of the teacher is identified and suggestions are made relating to how this role is vital when setting up and monitoring role-play areas to ensure that the children can have fun and develop into independent learners, but receive effective intervention from the practitioner when needed.

## Chapter 3: *Getting outside* Michael Green

This chapter presents an argument for embedding children's development as literate language users within meaningful contexts outside the classroom, placing demands on children to express themselves in a variety of ways and in a variety of modes – spoken, written and visual. Michael explores both the particular benefits of outdoor environments as learning contexts and considers the possibilities afforded by visits to local and cultural settings, such as museums, art galleries and historic buildings. There is a particular focus on non-fiction and how children's interest and learning in this area might be promoted by provision of learning opportunities outside the classroom. The case studies are drawn from the author's own experiences, utilising a range of environments outside the classroom in order to maximise the potential for enhancing the learning and teaching of early literacy.

# Part 2: Provision for all

## Chapter 4: *Seamless transition from the Foundation Stage to Year 1 (ages three to six)* Karen Vincent

This chapter explores what good practice in literacy transition between the Foundation Stage and Year 1 might look like. It examines the sources of transition tension generally and in terms of literacy and discusses how these may be overcome. Karen provides a range of case studies to offer an insight into literacy and transition for four- and five-year-olds and raise awareness of some of the potential issues that might occur for young children as they encounter the different aspects of early literacy.

## Chapter 5: *Supporting learners with English as an additional language* Virginia Bower

In this chapter, the author aims to raise awareness of the fundamental role of language in relation to early literacy learning and highlight strategies that can support children with English as an additional language (EAL) in relation to literacy. Discussion is included relating to the importance of routines, classroom layout, grouping and promoting dialogic talk and case studies are used to demonstrate how this might look in practice. The importance of strong home–school links is emphasised in relation to providing the best possible early literacy support for EAL pupils.

## Chapter 6: *Literacy and diversity*
## Virginia Bower and Verity Hill

It is not the intention of the authors in this chapter to explore specific literacy-related special educational needs, such as dyslexia. Instead, while recognising and acknowledging that specific and individualised support may well be needed for pupils with particular educational needs, the aim is to provide examples of classroom literacy practices that can motivate, inspire and empower *all* pupils. To this end, the authors discuss a range of strategies that might support children's diverse learning needs in early literacy, with a particular emphasis on making literacy real and enabling children to make links with their own lives. The case studies include examples using literature and film and there is an examination of a range of pedagogical strategies, including the use of paired and group talk, shared reading and writing frames.

## Part 3: Promoting language

## Chapter 7: *Diverse approaches to language development*
## Tracy Parvin

This chapter examines different theories and pedagogy associated with language development and their importance in ensuring children's ability to communicate their ideas in a range of forms. Two case studies of schools are utilised to show how two EYFS settings approach language development, using very different strategies to encourage speaking and listening skills. Discussions follow the case studies, exploring the implications of these two different approaches. Within these discussions, the themes of home and school literacy and language, the importance of resources, parental involvement, embedded practices and knowledge of child development emerge.

## Chapter 8: *Rhythm, rhyme and repetition*
## Virginia Bower and Susan Barrett

This chapter aims to highlight particular aspects of rhythm, rhyme and repetition and how they can be effectively used to support both teachers and learners with early literacy. The first section focuses on rhythm, in relation to both poetry and prose, and then the authors move on to explore the idea of rhyme and how rhyming texts can support early literacy learners in a multitude of ways. Particular issues and challenges that might occur when exploring rhyme are identified and these are illustrated by a case study. The final section explores repetition and this is examined through three separate lenses: reading and rereading stories; storytelling and the retelling of stories; and learning and playing with songs and rhymes. Throughout the chapter, texts and/or poets and authors the authors have found to be useful resources in relation to early literacy in general, and rhythm, rhyme and repetition specifically, are recommended.

## Chapter 9: *Tales and the oral tradition* Caroline Tancock

In this chapter, Caroline focuses on the power of traditional tales and the impact they can have on young children's development of language and attitudes to reading. The author explores the idea that tales can teach children about the diversity of language by means of their repetition, rhythms and rhymes and that, by supporting children in making connections between their oral use of language and the written word, we can promote an excitement about using language as a powerful tool. The oral tradition of tales is explored to show how the spoken patterns, narrative structures and memorable story language can inspire and excite young learners and promote an enjoyment of reading. Case studies are utilised to illustrate how tales have been used to motivate and involve children in their use of language and the effects on their social and emotional development and early reading skills.

## Part 4: Inspiring readers and writers

### Chapter 10: *Picture books* Roger McDonald

This chapter investigates the complex world of picture fiction, focusing on the inter-relationship between the words and the pictures, as well as addressing the question of how children reflect and respond to these texts in a range of situations. The vital place picture books have in early literacy is explored, examining the rich literature available and relevant to children, whether they are babies, pupils in the EYFS or those moving on to Key Stages 1 and 2. The power of the pictures is analysed and questions are raised regarding the differences between a child's imaginative world and that of an adult's. Using a range of case study material, the author describes how well-chosen books can open up a range of reading and writing experiences for children and teachers alike, inspiring a deeper conversation and an engaged response, culminating in a shared emotional connection with texts.

## Chapter 11: *'This is how we teach reading in our school'* Tracy Parvin

This chapter provides a detailed overview of government initiatives that have led to the introduction of systematic synthetic phonics as the prime approach to developing early reading. The author then goes on to examine different perspectives on the teaching of early reading, the difference between decoding and reading and how reading for meaning needs to be embedded in our teaching of early reading. Two case studies are offered that describe the approaches to early reading taken by two different schools and readers are offered the opportunity to consider the implications of the diverse approaches schools might take to this aspect of early literacy.

## Chapter 12: *Empowering young writers* Susan Barrett

Sue begins by discussing the theories relating to the writing process in order to provide a background against which the question as to how children's writing can be affected by particular pedagogies and assessment strategies can be examined. The idea of 'school' writing is introduced, with reference to a specific approach used in many schools, and the implications of such an approach are discussed in some detail. Using two very powerful case studies, Sue illustrates particular issues relating to writing, leading to suggestions as to how we might empower young writers.

# Part 1
# Environment

# Baby rooms

Kathy Goouch

 **Chapter Objectives**

- to identify how rich literacy practices with babies can be promoted to support their natural development
- to understand the importance of environment on babies' development of very early literacy
- to explore the importance of appropriate levels of knowledge and understanding about literacy and language for those working with babies.

## This chapter will cover:

- research supporting the idea that babies arrive in the world curious, predisposed to learn and already experienced in tuning in to the sounds and patterns of their mother tongue
- how these early dispositions can be acknowledged, celebrated, supported and developed
- the potential of home and daycare environments to shape babies' and very young children's literacy learning.

### CASE STUDY 1

'Where do you get them words from?'

A class of six-year-olds were given their Monday morning task. On the flipchart was written, 'At the weekend I went to ...'. As a result, the most advanced of the young literacy learners wrote fairly low-level sentences, including examples such as, 'At the weekend I went to my nan's'; 'At the weekend I went to the shops'. The next group wrote, 'At the weekend I went to ...' and thought they had completed the task; the rest were not engaged and tended to become distracted. One child made his way to the observing adult, who was recording the difficult situation, and asked, 'What are you doing?' She said 'I'm writing'. The child asked, 'Are you copying from the board?' When the adult replied that she wasn't, he said, 'Well, where do you get them words from, then?'

This salutary tale, a very real incident, is still disturbing some ten years or more after the event. This child's lack of knowledge of the relationship between words, language and literacy, his world and his own power to create text by using oral and written language, is a valuable lesson regarding what needs to be achieved if children are to be inducted into the richness and joy of language and literacy experiences throughout their lives.

Where we 'get' words from might depend very much, it seems, on our cultural beginnings. It is claimed that 'the average young middle-class child hears 32 million more spoken words than the young underprivileged child by the age of five' (Wolf, 2008: 20). Of course, as with all research, the details of this kind of claim need to be questioned, but, nevertheless, it offers at least an indication of the issues to be faced. While there is clearly a need, an urgent one, to scrutinise claims that children from so-called 'non-privileged' families are set to fail as they are perceived to be linguistically deprived, recent research suggests that, while material disadvantage is not in itself a reliable predictor of poor attainment in school, the range and extent of the infant's early communicative experiences is a clear factor (Roulstone et al., 2002).

International research and literature across disciplines provide evidence that babies arrive in the world curious and predisposed to learn and they learn from the people, routines, behaviours and customs surrounding them. How such predispositions and early infant learning can be acknowledged, celebrated, supported and developed in relation to literacy will be helpful in national plans to improve teaching practices in literacy and learning outcomes for all children. Although, in England, national 'benchmarking' of two-year-olds will acknowledge difference in children in developmental terms, this is already rather late in terms of acknowledging the kinds of lived language experiences and early linguistic capabilities of these infants. What it seems is needed is a relatively seamless journey for babies and their families, the creation of sensitive pedagogical links and a literacy curriculum to consolidate, reconcile, support, enrich and enhance early infant experiences, for their intrinsic value and also their foundational uses. This chapter will discuss how rich literacy practices with babies can be created to support their natural development.

A further fact to consider is that, while some babies spend their babyhood predominantly at home, with parents, family or other carers, many babies and young children (from about 6 weeks' old upwards) now spend as many as 45 hours a week in daycare settings – baby rooms – while parents return to work. In this chapter, therefore, reference will be made to a research project that has been undertaken in the UK – *The Baby Room* (Goouch and Powell, 2013) and these dedicated environments and the underpinning principles informing literacy practice with the babies spending their time there will be considered.

Evidence from *The Baby Room* project suggests that the political and commercial interests now dominant in the Early Years sector in England and in some other English-speaking countries may introduce tensions about care and education and these will be discussed in relation to the potential for literacy to be foregrounded, or neglected, in the early lives of babies and young children. Additionally, there is the troublesome notion to consider that all services provided before school, even for the youngest infants, are simply in existence to 'ready' children for the specific demands of nationally designed school curricula. Before considering these issues, however, it is important to acknowledge babies and babyhood, who babies are and what they are capable of in their early literacy journey.

## Babies, babyhood and literacy

Research evidence has demonstrated that, before birth, after birth and in the first days and weeks of babies' lives, they are already processing information about the sounds and patterns of their mother's language (Karmiloff and Karmiloff-Smith, 2001; Blakemore and Frith, 2005). Babies are predisposed to develop knowledge of the tunes and patterns of sounds around them – that is, babies have a genetic predisposition to become attuned to tones, patterns and structures of language, even before birth. When babies are born, they emerge into a wild cacophony of sounds, including spoken language, and, incredibly, from this babies are each able to distinguish the particular sound of their own mother's voice – the voice most familiar to them. Attuning to the sounds coming from people – voices rather than sounds made by objects – is evident moments after birth (Murray and Andrews, 2000) and it is this attention to and special interest in 'people sounds – the sounds of language ... [which enables babies] to become perceptually tuned to the phonological, prosodic and morphologic elements categorising their native language' (Goswami, 2002: 4).

The demonstrable brilliance of babies at tapping in to the human voice and, further, one voice in particular, supports subsequent developmental experiences. That is, intimate interactions with significant adults in their environment ensure that children's speech sounds imitate those of the speech sounds around them. They also learn the power of articulated sound to fulfil immediate needs and that sound articulation provokes responses.

The fascinating world of linguistic, cognitive and neurosciences, combined with psychological and educational studies, have enlarged and exposed understandings of how, through experience, exploration and experimentation, babies are able to develop their own highly culturally specific sounds in the first weeks of life (see, for example, Gopnik et al., 1999; Karmiloff and Karmiloff-Smith, 2001; Blakemore and Frith, 2005). In these first weeks, babies are learning to 'map' both the sounds they hear and the sounds they are making themselves through the development of a 'mouth to sound' map, culturally filtered to mirror the sounds heard (Gopnik et al., 1999). Through a whole range of experiences, very young babies demonstrate the ability to learn by watching, listening, exploring, experimenting, playing, rehearsing, but, most importantly, the intimate events with significant people around them.

The success of these early encounters, measured by the attention and responsiveness of people who matter to them, is the propulsion needed to launch babies into the symbolic world around them, where names and language stand for something meaningful to them. It is from such representations that later vocabulary ranges and competence in literacy evolve, as sounds develop importance in their attachment to meaning and meaningful actions (Vygotsky, 1986).

In his exploration of theories of the development of thought and language, Vygotsky (1986: 48) discusses the essentially social nature of the emergence of language in the growth of 'communication between the consciousness of a child and the consciousness of others'. Throughout this vibrant, fast-moving early stage of language growth, the influential presence and responses of significant adults matter as 'one of the most powerful influences on development is what happens between people' (Hobson, 2002: 7), in the families and communities in which babies grow and learn. This begins when babies are first welcomed into the world and continues as they are inducted into family lives, routines and patterns of behaviour; into the sounds and rhythms of home life; into the cultural narratives of families. Indeed:

> learning to read begins the first time an infant is held and read a story. How often this happens, or fails to happen, in the first five years of childhood turns out to be one of the best predictors of later reading. (Wolf, 2008: 20)

Stories are central in mediating culture and cultural practices, in transmitting values and traditions, initiating and shaping beliefs and behaviours and in gifting a vocabulary to babies and young children as story collaborators. In fact, as well as vocabulary memorised from told narratives, 'words from books will be one of the major sources of the 10,000 word repertoire of many an average five-year-old' (Wolf, 2008: 87), gained from years of listening to, co-constructing, retelling and rereading familiar stories until that age. Wolf (2008: 90) also claims that, 'as children gain familiarity with the language of books, they begin to develop a more subtle awareness of the visual details of print' and, as stated above, the time spent affectively listening to stories told and read is a key predictor of later reading:

> The full sum of this tacit knowledge – the similar sounds in 'hickory, dickory, dock'; the multiple meanings of 'bear', the fearful thoughts of Wilbur the pig – prepares the young child's brain to connect visual symbols to all that stored knowledge. (Wolf, 2008: 223)

Researchers, including Wolf, acknowledge that such tacit learning does not begin in school or in instructional sessions, but, instead, has its roots firmly in infancy – in intimate, affective encounters and interactions situated in intimate, affective relationships. The inclusion of books and other print-related material resources in home and daycare environments is frequently considered to be a measure of the status ascribed to literacy.

So, at this early stage of human development, the key essential ingredients for building on genetic predispositions towards the development of language so essential to later literacy development seem to be:

- an environment in which babies are immersed in ambient language
- close attention from interested others
- one-to-one, face-to-face rewarding interactions with people who matter to them.

Early oral language experiences are an essential element in a child's 'evolving understanding of words and their multiple uses in speech and in written text' (Wolf, 2008: 85) and the environment that surrounds them is key to this.

## Home environments

The environments that babies encounter are considered to be crucial to brain development (Greenfield, 2000) and therefore crucial to the development of literacy. While babies' brains are busy doubling in size during the first year of life, the kinds of experiences and encounters that are enriching their lives are helping them to create and revise their understandings of the words and worlds surrounding them (Goswami, 2002).

The research undertaken during the last 30 years and even in the last decade has indicated that, while preference for the human face has been duly noted, babies frequently begin to move towards peripheral patterns at one month, patterned objects at two to three months and then, 'at four months, infants have the ability to attend to and discriminate between visual symbols reliably such as those that might exist in environmental print' (Neumann et al., 2012: 234). The suggestion by researchers is not that babies are 'schooled' or instructed towards print at such an early stage but simply that we should be aware their early experiences are, as with speech, being filtered and mapped by them through positive and rewarding encounters in social contexts and it is helpful to both acknowledge and support this very early part of children's literacy learning journeys. Thus, via the most straightforward and common print encounters with, for example, food packaging, soap and washing labels, mediated in their everyday lives, babies are collecting both language and print information from visual stimuli and verbal interactions. As 'infants prefer to imitate people ... coupled with a probably innate propensity to attend to and interact with people' (Goswami, 2002: 2), the nature of any engagement with print in the environment needs to emerge from, and be embedded within, the close sociocultural contexts in which they live rather than be superimposed artificially. In this way, the natural curiosity and explorative tendencies of babies can be supported in authentic and situated daily events, such as feeding, changing, washing and sleep times.

The implicit danger in acknowledging the power of these very early months and years to shape the architecture of the brain (Greenfield, 2000; Gopnik, 2009) is in the potential for impatient parents and other adults to hurry along the process of learning – a problem evident in some Western, and perhaps predominantly English-speaking, countries. The weight of these arguments is part of David's discussion of what early childhood is for and she concludes:

> In the end I came to the conclusion that if we behave as we would in everyday life we are simply exposing the children to the way we live in a print-dependent society and that because these events and activities really are part of life, the children want to be able to take part too. So, the fact that we make notes, read newspapers, letters, bills, adverts, programmes, notices and books, write cards, shopping lists, diaries ... means we are modelling literate behaviour to the children who share our lives. (David, 2007: 15)

Within the gradually increasing world of babies' experience, they are both shaping and being shaped by sharing in human communication events and social engagement; the language and language practices of home; people's literate actions, attitudes and behaviours; and by situated symbols and symbolic action.

It is important to note here that babies are neither sponges nor passive recipients of others' information, nor can they simply be imprinted. Rather, babies' brains are actively responding, shaping and reshaping according to surrounding environmental information, as well as actively creating contexts, introducing sounds and sound explorations and initiating conversations. Not only are adults and siblings naming the babies' worlds and conversing with and around them, but they are also rewarding the kind of self-initiating and imitative behaviour that Meltzoff's (2002) fascinating research has demonstrated as occurring from the very earliest stages. Even by the end of their first year, infants have been observed recreating adult behaviours, such as pressing the buttons on a phone and holding it to their ears to 'chat'. Appropriating language and language behaviours develops from innately being attuned to people who matter and those people's actions and behaviours. So, language and literacy are born out of cultural worlds where babies find, store, conceptualise and recreate language and literacy use.

What is unfolding here is a naturally forming, yet needing to be sensitively supported, propensity of babies and infants to learn and use language, including attention to print as it occurs in familiar contexts and situations.

Social class, cultural experience and economic disadvantage have, however, each been named as significant in relation to early literacy practices in homes and families. Some claims have been made that it is these factors which impinge on the ability of children from particular communities to achieve academic success in currently defined educational terms and that early interventions are required. Further, it has been claimed that children from 'disadvantaged' or 'non-privileged' families are preset to fail as they are deprived linguistically and begin school without language (Field, 2010; Allen, 2011). Indeed, in one report it was claimed that 'by age 5, children from the poorest fifth of homes in the country are already on average nearly a year behind when measured by their expected years of development' (Washbrook and Waldfogel, 2010: 7). These arguments are shaped to inform a 'school readiness' debate, currently pervading the field of early childhood education and care (ECEC), and the nature of the measures and tests used to score children in relation to the acquisition of vocabulary needs to be very carefully scrutinised.

Contrary to this kind of deficit position, others point to the problems associated with the simple accusation that 'children from low-income, minority and immigrant families are literacy impoverished' (Grieshaber et al., 2012: 115). A simple causal connection between low income and poor development of literacy is not easily proven. Instead, the situation of home literacy experiences is found to be more complex, but some clear assertions can be made:

- the level of print resources found in the home is not related to family income
- how print resources are used in the home is not related to income
- the level of use of print resources is not related to the number of print resources in the home. (Grieshaber et al., 2012: 133).

The core claim of this research, that 'there seems to be much more to home literacy support than income alone' (Grieshaber et al., 2012: 134), challenges some of the often made assumptions by politicians and others of there being a simple solution to the problem of underachievement in literacy and points to some of the difficulties of simply attempting to *quantify* home experiences when the *quality* of the encounters is infinitely more important.

Equally, the notion that there is a simple and single pathway to school readiness and school literacy appears to be a false assertion. Other research indicates that 'children's vocabulary size has been related to phonological awareness, a critical aspect of emergent literacy and school readiness' and developed via mother–child conversations, language play and shared narratives (Cristofaro and Tamis-LeMonda, 2012: 85). Thus, spoken language encounters – rather than material resources – seem to provide both intrinsic worth to babies and opportunities for foundational learning. For babies to learn language and its power and significance in their lives, the essential requirement is an 'interplay between factors inherent in the child and factors within the environment' as they learn 'the symbolic and referential power of words' (Waxman, 2002: 107, 125).

What is evident is that children's developing abilities in language and literacy do not occur in a vacuum, but, instead:

> All are based on underlying changes in the developing brain, the child's growing conceptual knowledge, and the particular contributions made by each child's developing emotions and understanding of other people. All these factors are either nurtured or neglected by the child's environment. (Wolf, 2008: 85)

# Other environments, other carers

It is significant that, in England in 2012, almost half of all babies up to the age of 18 months of age were cared for by people other than their parents during the working week (Goouch and Powell, 2012).

There is statistical evidence now that, while some babies and young infants spend the first years of their lives cared for in their own homes by parents or family members or in informal out-of-home contexts by extended family, many are now cared for in formal daycare settings – in baby rooms. Additionally, international research has demonstrated that the majority of members of staff in childcare services may have only a one-year, post-16 vocational qualification or are women with no qualifications in this field (OECD, 2006). Embedded within this provision are assumptions that babies, those under 18 months in particular, require little other than the basic ingredients of being fed, changed, cleaned and allowed to sleep, which it is within almost anyone's capabilities to provide. The reality is somewhat different, however.

Neuroscience provides us with evidence that enriched environments stimulate more 'branching of the brain cells' (Greenfield, 2000: 21) and 'there is a threshold of environmental richness below which a deprived environment could harm a baby's brain' (Blakemore and Frith, 2005: 33). Further, we learn that:

> no infant under 6 months can gain confidence and understanding in a large group of infants with a small proportion of caregivers. Infants require consistent and close adult attention, for rest, protection and nurturance and to benefit from playful communication. (Trevarthen et al., 2003: 41–2)

While quality in relation to baby rooms in daycare is often measured by physical space and resources – both of which are important – there is also a powerful argument for

Acknowledging the incredible sophistication and brilliance of the first years of life may help teachers of older children to realise that they are only influencing one part of a child's literacy 'lifecourse project' and the more connections are made, with and for children, the more easily transitions can be managed. All of those involved with the literacy education of children, as we help them to not only 'get' words but to enrich and indulge in language, must begin with the knowledge of 'the fetus's growing sensitivity during its last months in the uterus to the particularities of its mother's voice and rhythms of its native language', plus the fact that 'from the moment of birth onward, the infant is continually processing the speech that fills his world'; also, that 'well before the child produces his first words we now know that he has been actively processing the sounds, rhythms and basic building blocks of the words and grammar of his mother tongue'; and that 'the child does not simply reproduce what he hears, but actively creates language, experimenting with the rules that he has extracted from input' (Karmiloff and Karmiloff Smith, 2001: vii). Armed with this and other invaluable research information regarding the brilliance of a baby's brain and ability to learn, it behoves us all to ensure that we join with babies and young children to ensure their literacy experiences, literacy encounters and literacy interactions in which we engage are worthy of such beginnings.

## Further reading

Moss, P. (ed.) (2013) *Early Childhood and Compulsory Education: Reconceptualising the relationship*. Abingdon: Routledge.

Traditionally, one of the problems besetting the care and education of children, here and in other Western societies, has been the fragmentation of services for children and families. This is particularly evident in the divide between early childhood education (ECE) and compulsory school education (CSE) and comes sharply into focus now that new political discourse is focused on 'school readiness'. This book challenges assumptions and draws together colleagues from Belgium, France, Italy, New Zealand, Norway, Sweden and the United States to debate some of the complex issues surrounding infants and young children and their families as children encounter institutional care at an ever younger age. Discussions in this text support the notion that there should be 'meeting places' between stages rather than contested spaces. This chapter has demonstrated the power of very early learning in relation to literacy and stresses the importance of the acknowledgement of prior learning, family and community practices as well as the awesome ability of babies and young children to access language and print literacy. Moss' book reminds us of the importance of bridging artificial gulfs in educational structures and centring efforts on support for children and families.

Goouch, K. (2007) 'Understanding educational discourse: attending to multiple voices', in K. Goouch and A. Lambirth (eds), *Understanding Phonics and the Teaching of Reading: A critical perspective.* Maidenhead: Open University Press.

This text is relevant to the central argument in this chapter as it includes case study material of a child entering the world – a literacy-rich world – and focuses attention on what children are learning, can see and hear as they are born into families, communities and cultures. The child in question is fortunate in her 'literacy community' at home and a range of opportunities is presented to her to gently nudge and nurture her towards becoming literate. The challenge presented in this study is that of the potentially uneasy relationship between her early experiences from birth and those presented in school. Little attention is given, in research, political or policy terms, to the range of 'voices' heard by children as they struggle to learn, manipulate language and literacy, achieve control but also please those around them. It is a short step to extrapolate lessons from this study of a literacy-'advantaged' child to help us understand the lived literacy lives of others, in other families and communities.

## References

Allen, G. (2011) *Early Intervention: The next steps: An independent report to Her Majesty's Government.* London: Cabinet Office.

Blakemore, S.J. and Frith, U. (2005) *The Learning Brain: Lessons for education.* Oxford: Blackwell.

Cristofaro, T.N. and Tamis-LeMonda, C.S. (2012) 'Mother–child conversations at 36 months and at pre-kindergarten: Relations to children's school readiness', *Journal of Early Childhood Literacy,* 12 (1): 68–97.

David, T. (2007) 'What is early childhood for?', in K. Goouch and A. Lambirth (eds), *Understanding Phonics and the Teaching of Reading: Critical perspectives.* Maidenhead: Open University Press. pp.9–22.

Edwards, C., Gandini, L. and Forman, G. (1998) *The Hundred Languages of Children* (2nd edn). Greenwich, CT: Ablex.

Field, F. (2010) *The Foundation Years: Preventing poor children becoming poor adults.* London: Cabinet Office.

Goldschmied, E. and Jackson, S. (1994) *People Under Three: Young children in day care.* London: Routledge.

Goouch, K. and Powell, S. (2012) 'Orchestrating professional development for baby room practitioners: Raising the stakes in new dialogic encounters', *Journal of Early Childhood Research,* 11 (1): 78–92.

Goouch, K. and Powell, S. (2013) *The Baby Room: Principles, policy and practice.* Maidenhead: Open University Press.

Gopnik, A. (2009) *The Philosophical Baby.* London: The Bodley Head.

Gopnik, A., Meltzoff, A. and Kuhl, P. (1999) *How Babies Think.* London: Phoenix.

Goswami, U. (2002) 'Infancy: The origins of cognitive development', in U. Goswami (ed.), *Blackwell Handbook of Childhood Cognitive Development.* Oxford: Blackwell. pp.5–9.

Greenfield, S. (2000) *The Private Life of the Brain.* London: Penguin.

Grieshaber, S., Shield, P., Luke, A. and Macdonald, S. (2012) 'Family literacy practices and home literacy resources: An Australian pilot study', *Journal of Early Childhood Literacy*, 12 (2): 113–138.

Hobson, P. (2002) *The Cradle of Thought: Exploring the origins of thinking*. London: Pan.

Karmiloff, K. and Karmiloff-Smith, A. (2001) *Pathways to Language: From fetus to adolescent*. Cambridge, MA: Harvard University Press.

Moss, P. (2013) 'The relationship between early childhood and compulsory education: A properly political question', in P. Moss (ed.), *Early Childhood and Compulsory Education: Reconceptualising the relationship*. Abingdon: Routledge. pp.2–51.

Meltzoff, A.N. (2002) 'Imitation as a mechanism of social cognition: Origins of empathy, theory of mind, and the representation of action', in U. Goswami (ed.), *Blackwell Handbook of Childhood Development*. Oxford: Blackwell.

Murray, L. and Andrews, L. (2000) *The Social Baby: Understanding babies' communication from birth*. Richmond: The Children's Project.

Neumann, M.M., Hood, M., Ford, R.M. and Neumann, D.L. (2012) 'The role of environmental print in emergent literacy', *Journal of Early Childhood Literacy*, 12 (3): 231–58.

Nutbrown, C. (2012) *Foundations for Quality: Review of early childhood qualifications*. Runcorn: DfE. Available online at: www.education.gov.uk/nutbrownreview (accessed 18 December 2013).

OECD (2006) *Starting Strong II: Early childhood education and care*. Paris: OECD.

Peeters, J. (2008) *The Construction of a New Profession*. Amsterdam: SWP.

Rogoff, B. (1990) *Apprenticeship in Thinking: Cognitive development in social context*. Oxford and Richmond: Oxford University Press and The Children's Project.

Roulstone, S., Loader, S., Northstone, K. and Beveridge, M. (2002) 'The speech and language of children aged 25 months: Descriptive data from the Avon Longitudinal Study of Parents and Children', *Early Child Development and Care*, 172 (3): 259–68.

Trevarthen, C., Barr, I., Dunlop, A.-W., Gjersoe, N., Marwick, H. and Stephen, C. (2003) *Supporting a Young Child's Needs for Care and Affection, Shared Meaning and a Social Place: Review of childcare and the development of children aged 0–3: Research evidence, and implications for out-of-home provision*. Edinburgh: Scottish Executive. Available online at: www.scotland.gov.uk/Resource/Doc/933/0007610.pdf (accessed 18 December 2013).

Vygotsky, L.S. (1986) *Thought and Language*. Cambridge, MA: MIT Press.

Washbrook, E. and Waldfogel, J. (2010) *Cognitive Gaps in the Early Years: A summary of findings from the report 'Low income and early cognitive development in the UK'*. London: The Sutton Trust.

Waxman, S.R. (2002) 'Early word-learning and conceptual development: everything had a name and each name gave birth to a new thought', in U. Goswami (ed.), *Blackwell Handbook of Cognitive Development*. Oxford: Blackwell. pp.180–208.

Wolf, M. (2008) *Proust and the Squid: The story and science of the reading brain*. Cambridge: Icon Books.

# Role-play areas for EYFS (ages zero to five), Key Stage 1 (ages five to seven) and beyond

Joanne Palmer

 **Chapter Objectives**

- to develop an understanding of different types of play and how they can be used effectively in your literacy teaching
- to recognise that role-play areas can be used to enhance and develop children's language and literacy skills in the EYFS and Key Stages 1 and 2
- to identify the role of the teacher when setting up and monitoring role-play areas.

## This chapter will cover:

- theories relating to play and different types of play
- how role-play areas can be utilised to enhance children's literacy learning
- extending accepted and excellent Early Years practice into later age phases
- case studies that describe role-play areas across the age phases.

It would be unusual to *not* see role-play areas within Early Years settings. Often these are wonderfully designed, colourful spaces that are sometimes co-constructed by adults and children. These areas usually reflect a topic that is under study at the time, such as the seaside, dinosaurs or robots, or they might be based on a real-life setting, such as a post office, hospital or veterinary surgery, or sometimes they are based on the works of a particular author whom the children are engaged with, such as Julia Donaldson, Martin Waddell or Allan Ahlberg. Whatever the origins of their genesis, these role-play areas are usually designed to promote imaginative play, enable the children to interact and learn how to engage with others collaboratively and constructively and, if well-planned and with suitable resources, develop children's literacy and language skills at the same time that they are having fun.

The philosophy underpinning this chapter is that play is an essential aspect of all children's lives and the best practice seen in Early Years classrooms might usefully be replicated (albeit with appropriate alterations according to age groups) across the primary phases. First, I shall explore notions relating to play and how play and literacy can be usefully combined and then briefly examine different types of play, to provide a context for the later focus on the use of role-play areas to promote literacy for both younger and older children.

# Play

Play is a vital component of life, but particularly for primary-aged children. This has been highlighted, for younger children, with the introduction of the updated Early Years Foundation Stage (EYFS) Framework, which states that:

> Each area of learning and development must be implemented through planned, purposeful play and through a mix of adult-led and child-initiated activity. (DfE, 2012: 7)

The documentation also makes explicit the fundamental role that play has in a young child's development as a learner, through the prime areas of learning and development:

- communication and language
- physical development
- personal, social and emotional development.

*Development Matters* (Early Education, 2012) – the non-statutory guidance to support practitioners in their implementation of the EYFS – reinforces play and exploring as two of the key characteristics of learning for children in the Early Years.

This is not new – within Early Years classrooms, there is a long-established history of high-quality play being used to enhance and develop children's learning experiences:

> play is a medium for learning, and practitioners who acknowledge and appreciate this can, through provision, interaction and intervention in children's play, enhance progression, differentiation and relevance in the curriculum. (Moyles, 2010: 10)

The collaboration that children are exposed to during play enables them to 'develop their knowledge, language and social skills' (Briggs and Hansen, 2012: 23). It creates opportunities for children to explore real-life situations, construct imaginary worlds and allow unrealisable desires to be realised (Vygotsky, 1978). Within a literacy context, teachers can use play as a teaching tool to enhance children's vocabulary as well as providing opportunities for:

> using connecting language, for experimenting with narrative and characters, revisiting songs and rhymes and stories, making alternatives using familiar rhymes, rhythms and alliteration, and collaborating with others in order to work as a team and bring about a satisfying play scenario. (Bruce and Spratt, 2011: 19)

Play can take many forms and, next, I will examine some examples commonly seen in Early Years settings.

## Different types of play

There are many different types of play, but the examples explored in this chapter are those that I feel link directly to role-play areas and could benefit children with their learning, including:

- exploratory play, where the child explores both known and unknown objects and situations in depth
- directed play, where the child is initially guided by an adult
- free-flow play, where the child's play relies on the use of imagination.

### Exploratory play

Exploratory play gives an individual child or, indeed, a group of children the opportunity to explore an object or situation, allowing them to become familiar with it and develop an understanding of its purpose as the object is put into a context in the course of the playful activity. Such play allows children to take on the role of an explorer or investigator, discovering the outcomes of trial and error (Briggs and Hansen, 2012), using play as a means to learn and obtain life skills and develop an understanding of the world in which they live. In this way, children begin to develop an understanding of how to deal with situations and scenarios and, throughout this journey of familiarisation, a sense of calm can be established and any anxieties linked to the object or scenario may well fade and be replaced with enjoyment. After all, 'role play is nothing more than a rehearsal' (Blatner, 1995).

In relation to literacy teaching, introducing the children to ICT opportunities in an exploratory way allows them to find out about new technologies within a literary context. The following case study describes how a class teacher of six- and seven-year-olds trialled such exploratory play within the role-play area over a series of lessons to develop the children's knowledge and understanding of vocabulary and storytelling. Previously, during whole-class lessons, the children had been taught about story structure. The overall theme was 'outer space' and one of the stories that the lessons had been based on was *Way Back Home* by Oliver Jeffers (2007). Other books with the same theme were studied during the course of the unit and the role-play area was designed to match this topic. During the period of a week, an exploratory activity was planned where the children were to use iPads. The iPads had recently had a storymaking app downloaded on to them – Story Patch – and the class teacher informed the children that each time their group entered the role-play area, they needed to explore the new app. She advised them that they would be taking on the role of an author writing a story about being in space and the new iPad app would be used to do this. The children were then left to explore using it independently.

## CASE STUDY 1

Two boys (aged six) entered the role-play area, keen to take on their roles as authors. Immediately one of them picked up the iPad and accessed the storymaking app.

Child 1:   I am going to try using this storymaking app.

Child 2:   I want to use that, too. Do you know how it works?

Child 1:   Not yet. I have worked out how to start a new story. I want to put a background in.

Child 2:   What about this?

Child 1:   Oh, we have to put the writing in first. How shall I start?

Child 2:   Once upon a time?

Child 1:   Yes, once upon a time.

After spending some time using the iPad to create a story, the children decided that they would use the role-play area to retell their tale. This proved useful for the

*(Continued)*

*(Continued)*

boys as the setting of the role-play area (a space scene) enabled them to make improvements that otherwise they may not have considered.

Child 1:    I'm changing some of the story now.

Child 2:    What bit?

Child 1:    This bit. I put 'Jack stepped out of the spaceship.' I'm going to change it to, 'Jack peered out of the door of the spaceship before stepping out on to the strange orange planet.'

The case study above demonstrates the two-fold nature of the learning taking place. The children not only had discussions that involved accessing their existing knowledge of stories but also talked about the app and how they could use it successfully. They demonstrated to each other ways of doing things and explored the differing features of the app. This was echoed by the other members of the class as they all came to have opportunities to explore the role-play area too. Through this exploration, the children were able to create a range of stories, all of which were different. Due to the task having been presented to them in a playful way, the children initially focused more on the exploration of the app than on the completion of the task. As the week progressed, however, the children became more and more familiar with the app and were able therefore to focus their attention on aspects of narrative.

It was at this point that the teacher made the decision to intervene and ensure that elements she would expect to see in their stories were present. By the end of the week, all the children had successfully created a story using the app. This is an activity that was focused on the initial exploration of something new with very little teacher intervention; the direction from the teacher came later. This shows how exploratory play can be exploited by the teacher in a positive way.

## Directed play

Moyles (1989) states that exploratory play should be used alongside directed play. That is because exploratory play allows children the opportunity to identify two aspects – what they can do with an object/setting and what the object/setting can do for them. If this is then followed by directed play, where the teacher demonstrates how the object/setting can be manipulated or used, the child's knowledge and understanding is enhanced. The cycle of exploratory play and directed play can then be repeated. Moyles (1989) further argues that this creates a spiral of learning, which develops into the accommodation of an object and the mastery of its use.

To illustrate this, I shall return to the setting depicted in Case Study 1 and describe what happened next.

## CASE STUDY 2

The children were very excited and enthusiastic about the new app and wanted to tell the class teacher all about it. By means of questioning, the teacher directed the children's next steps in the role-play.

Teacher: Who can tell me what they have found out about the new app, Story Patch?

Child 1: We found out that you need to put your writing in first before the pictures.

CT: Good. So if we need to put our writing in first, what is the first thing we need to do?

Child 2: We need to know what we want to write.

Child 3: We need to plan the story first.

After the children had acknowledged this, the class teacher discussed and modelled how to plan a story, including how an author might borrow ideas from other authors and make them his or her own. She also modelled how to use the app to create a first page after further discussion with the children. The children were then set the task of planning their stories and, once their plans were complete or nearing completion, the children could once again enter the role-play area in the role of author and continue to use the app for their story writing.

Child 1: How are you starting your story?

Child 2: Erm, 'Once upon a time' – I've heard that in stories Miss X has read to us before.

Child 1: Oh yeah, I forgot that one. I'm going to use that, too.

Child 3: I'm going to start 'On a dark, dark, night.' You know, like Funnybones and *It's Dark in Space*.

Child 2: Oh, maybe I'll change my starter to, 'We're going on an alien hunt!' That would be good.

Here the children used the direction from the teacher to begin their planning, using ideas from favourite stories and adapting them to suit the setting of their own stories. Exploratory talk (Corden, 2000) was evident as the children discussed their ideas, considered possibilities and made decisions based on collaborative examination of different options. The role-play area provided the ideal context for the children to engage in exploratory and dialogic talk, but this was only possible because of their existing knowledge of a range of stories and narrative structures. This is where the role of the practitioner is crucial, ensuring that children have a wealth of experience of high-quality literature on which they can draw when needed.

### Free-flow play

This form of play can also be referred to as 'imaginative play', 'fantasy play', 'pretend play' and 'ludic play' (Bruce, 1991). Although much of the experience might be make believe, free-flow play involves children bringing their own life experiences to the play and this not only allows them to take their places within society but it also enables them to contribute to it, with vision, imagination and competence (Bruce, 1991). Ultimately, this form of play allows children to put into practice what they already know and use their knowledge of a situation or object competently. Free-flow play allows children to develop social skills that are required for 'real-life' scenarios, such as setting and following rules, and the focus of the play is entirely in their hands, undirected by adults, giving them both the benefits and the challenges of autonomy.

Observing free-flow play provides practitioners with opportunities to assess particular aspects of literacy. You may find children playing skipping or clapping games on the playground, which involve the use of rhymes and songs, or they may decide they are going to retell a favourite story or play a game that involves characters from their favourite television programme.

What kinds of literacy skills and competencies might the children be experiencing and developing when engaged in these types of free-flow play and how might your assessment of these influence how you design a role-play area or go on to organise directed play? The types of play discussed above tend to be associated with very young children, but this chapter seeks to suggest that play and role-play areas can support children not only within the EYFS but also across Key Stages 1 and 2 in their literacy development. The following section illustrates how this might be accomplished and how play might enhance the experience of literacy for children who have moved beyond the Early Years classroom.

## Role-play areas

The knowledge that role-play is used with such success in the Early Years made me consider how professionals might incorporate it with equal success for older children.

After all, the fundamental benefits of role-play areas (listed below) are relevant to all learners. Not only this but, by incorporating aspects of the EYFS classroom into later age phases, we might also reduce the negative effects of the transition from one key stage to another (see Chapter 4, Seamless transition from the Foundation Stage to Year 1 (ages three to six), for more discussion of this). As professionals seeking to provide children with the best possible learning experiences, mirroring some of the practices that they are familiar with will, ultimately, allow the transition to be more natural and productive, as well as permit their continued development, particularly in relation to literacy.

Role-play areas offer opportunities for children to:

- model life experiences
- develop social skills, such as sharing, cooperation, empathy and effective communication
- develop imagination
- use technical and specialised vocabulary
- develop confidence
- develop their expertise in curriculum areas such as reading and writing in informed ways.

The above list (adapted from Beardsley and Harnett, 1998: 30–1) was compiled by a group of teachers working with six- and seven-year-olds after they had witnessed each of these aspects of learning taking place a number of times in their own role-play areas. As a teacher of older children, I find this list illuminating, as these are all aspects that we aspire to develop within *all* pupils' learning, although with older children this is often attempted through more formal methods of teaching. This list suggests that these mutual areas of learning for younger *and* older children can be approached through the successful use of role-play areas, but for older children we need to consider more specifically what we hope to gain from their use.

As the focus of this book is on literacy, I will next explore briefly two of the points from above to demonstrate how literacy and role-play areas might be combined effectively.

## Use of technical and specialised vocabulary

Role-play areas give children the opportunity to sequence narratives by re-enacting familiar stories and creating new narratives of their own. This in turn leads to building a store of relevant vocabulary, the children developing crucial 'lexical sets' relating to a range of real-life scenarios. 'Lexical sets' are groups of words that are connected in some way, such as hospital, nurse, doctor, ambulance, stethoscope. Developing these lexical sets enables children to engage in dialogue appropriate to the setting and promotes the need to use connecting words, such as but, so, even if, despite; prepositions, such as in, under, behind, next to, and so on; and other linguistic elements, such as adverbs, adjectives and appropriate pronouns. As stated by Briggs and Hansen:

> Pretend play helps children develop storytelling skills, imagination and grammar for English. (2012: 41)

Role-play areas might allow children to contextualise the more formal learning of grammar – an aspect of the literacy curriculum that has taken on new significance with the introduction of an English spelling, punctuation and grammar test at Key Stage 2 from May 2013.

## Developing expertise in reading and writing

Role-play can be used to support children in their knowledge and understanding of reading and writing. Research carried out by Welsch (2008) showed that using play within the context of a story allowed children to:

> investigate social relationships and interactions, encouraging personal responses as well as enhanced comprehension of the literature. (Briggs and Hansen, 2012: 34)

Initially, it may appear that children can make sufficient progress with reading and writing as they move through the first years of school without having opportunities for role-play and the exploration that inevitably accompanies it. Results from a study carried out by Ragnarsdottir (in Bruce and Spratt, 2011) showed, however, that later, at the age of nine, such children had difficulty in a test situation with reading comprehension. This might indicate that providing the children with opportunities to explore and investigate literature through play has benefits for learning beyond that of an understanding of society and self. It is about:

- developing vocabulary through extended discussions and interactions with others
- reading and writing in a range of contexts
- developing attributes such as empathy, the ability to reflect and the determination to work through any difficulties.

All of these contribute to children's reading and writing success.

## Introducing role-play areas to older children

The most obvious way to introduce a role-play area to older children is by making a link to a topic or a text being studied, in the same way that this is done in many Early Years classrooms. In this way, as opportunities for role-play and drama emerge in more sophisticated forms, children are able to appreciate and explore the characterisation and dilemmas that may occur within a text (Beardsley and Harnett, 1998). Older children can, however, have more of a leading role in the planning, organisation and construction of the role-play area, thereby taking ownership of their environment and making relevant links with the literacy curriculum – they might create posters, labels, instructions or information booklets that link to the theme of the role-play area, for example. These literacy-based 'props' could be initiated by the children after a taught session, where they have been inspired to do something. The teacher might also use items produced in the role-play area as a starting point for planning whole-class sessions, if the children do not have full understanding of what they have attempted in the role-play area.

Some examples of role-play areas that have been constructed in my class of seven-year-olds include:

- a hardware shop – linked to a topic on electricity
- a chocolate factory – linked to the topic 'chocolate' and the book *Charlie and the Chocolate Factory* by Roald Dahl
- a smoothie stall – linked to a 'healthy eating' topic
- a museum – based on work on the Romans
- an outside garden centre/conservation area – linked to the topic 'our changing environment' and the book *Window* by Jeannie Baker.

Role-play areas that have been constructed with other year groups include:

- an air raid shelter (nine- and ten-year-olds) – linked to a World War II topic
- a market stall (nine- and ten-year-olds) – tackling misconceptions linked to mathematics/money
- a pirate ship (10- and 11-year-olds) – linked to the book *Treasure Island* by Robert Louis Stevenson
- a travel agent (seven- and eight-year-olds) – linked to the topic 'India'.

The following case study describes the experiences of a class of seven-year-olds as they explored a role-play area designed as a chocolate factory. The children had read *Charlie and the Chocolate Factory* and had studied the characters of Charlie and Willy Wonka in detail, as well as the problems and dilemmas that other characters in the story face. The children had also used many drama activities, including hot seating and freeze frames, to explore the feelings and personalities of the characters. Further, instructions and advertisements had been a focus of literacy lessons and the children had followed instructions to make chocolates and then wrote their own. The children also created their own radio advertisements and jingles and designed packaging after in-depth analysis of real-life products. Through these activities they began to appreciate the important role that word play has within advertising.

**CASE STUDY 3**

When in the chocolate factory role-play area, the children would frequently draw on their real-life experiences. For example, there was usually a shopkeeper in the retail area. The child taking on this role would price up chocolates, ensure the display was tidy, take charge of the till and speak to customers.

Within the roles taken on by the children in the role-play area, they began to draw on knowledge they had acquired during literacy lessons. For example, children playing the role of a chocolatier pretended to follow instructions when making their chocolates or wrote their own instructions for others to follow. Sometimes the children would create posters showing a special offer or an advertisement to put in the shop window. This was something that the children had explored in more formal contexts and they were transferring this knowledge to support their activities in the role-play area.

A more complex element to the children's play was the creation of their own problems using past experiences. During one of our science lessons, we had used a microwave to melt different foods. When we tried to melt chocolate, it burnt as it was heated for too long. During one session, two of the children used their knowledge of this problem as the basis for their unfolding story in the role-play area.

Teacher:   How are the chocolates going?

Child 1:   The chef burnt the chocolate buttons.

Teacher:   Oh no. What happened?

Child 2:   They got too hot. We need to start again – or get a new chef.

Child 1:   Or a second chef?

Teacher:   How will you go about finding a new chef?

Child 1:   Erm, an advert. People find jobs by seeing adverts.

Child 2:   Let's go to the boardroom and write an advert for a new chef.

The children then used the knowledge of advertising that they had acquired in lessons to make the decision to find a new chef by advertising for one and they created the following advert:

WANTED!

A chocolate chef.

> Must be able to melt chocolate without burning it.
>
> Will be able to design new chocolates that are very tasty.
>
> Can work with others without arguing.
>
> Pay – £8 per hour.

From this case study, it is clear to see that the children accessed, practised and applied their literacy knowledge within a particular context. By setting the chocolate shop area up in the classroom and engaging in role-play, the children had the opportunity to put into practice the following literacy skills:

- using specific linguistic devices, such as imperative verbs in instructions, alliteration, rhyme and persuasive language
- rehearse the order of instructions to ensure that they are effective
- use word play to engage listeners or readers
- discuss possibilities, listen to the views of others, negotiate and compromise.

Opportunities for writing arose in a natural way, such as when the children realised that they would need to advertise for another chef. The advertisement they produced is very basic, but the children used techniques that linked to previous literacy lessons. They clearly understand the tone and register needed for this type of text, as the advertisement is direct and to the point, providing the reader with the necessary information. From this the teacher could see that the children had a good understanding of this text type, but needed support with how a positive 'spin' could be put on the content, to encourage people to apply. Thus, the teacher used this as a starting point for a lesson focused on persuasive writing and how an advertisement might persuade someone to apply for a job.

## The role of the teacher

When using play and role-play areas for educational purposes, it is important to obtain a balance between child-initiated activities and teacher interventions or direction:

> Children need to be offered more than just time to play as play can so easily become unchallenging if they are left to their own devices. (Fisher and Williams, 2006: 94)

An educator's role is to challenge the children, stretching their capabilities and exposing them to problems that require careful consideration in order to solve them. After all, it is the challenge that brings with it new learning opportunities.

In order to move children's learning forward, opportunities are needed for old skills to be practised and new ones to be discovered. Such progress can only occur with an element of well-timed teacher intervention alongside a considerable degree of professional judgement:

> By introducing an element (though not an over obtrusive element) of structure into play, the teacher renders children's learning less haphazard and therefore more efficient. (Fontana, 1995: 41–42)

This clearly links to Vygotsky's (1978) 'zone of proximal development' (ZPD), where children are supported by a more able other to move beyond their 'comfort zone' and develop their thinking.

The creation and management of role-play areas can enable teachers to provide this support in a number of ways, while ensuring that children have the opportunity to take risks, make mistakes and develop their own strategies for effective learning. Below are two ways that teachers can intervene or influence learning in role-play areas, with specific reference to literacy.

- *Questioning* The teacher can, for example, take on a role within the role-play area and ask questions to support the children in their understanding of the task. 'Teacher in role' (TIR) is a common technique used in drama. If used in a role-play area, it involves the teacher becoming part of the drama or play. Using characterisation, the teacher can guide the children and question them by also engaging with the play.
- *Changing objects within the role-play area and setting problems to be solved* This is a useful way of encouraging discussion among the children. The teacher can place things such as letters, bills or a scenario for children to tackle in their play. Alternatively, by means of TIR, the teacher can enter the role-play area in character and present a problem verbally.

These two techniques for teacher interventions could be described as 'co-construction learning' (Scarlet et al., 2005), as the teacher becomes actively involved in the play and the learning. Of course, co-construction can also occur within groups of children. An example of when children are actively involved in the learning is during the 'mantle of the expert' approach (Heathcote and Boulton, 1995), which is when the children take on the roles of experts in different situations. In the case study below, we see a group of eight- and nine-year-olds who have been studying the Romans and been given the role of expert archaeologists. The children had previously watched a short video that showed them how an archaeologist works. They were then provided with tools and told there was a site that needed their expert help as there was thought to be Roman treasure hidden there. The site was the school garden, where the teacher had earlier buried some coins, crockery and jewellery.

## CASE STUDY 4

The children, in their small archaeology team, discussed the film that they had watched and how they should start the hunt, then chose the relevant tools to help them. The teacher entered the area in the role of the person who had called on the children's expertise:

Teacher: Thank you so much for coming at short notice. I really do hope that this dig can be completed in a reasonable time as my builders are due back in a few days to complete my extension.

Child 1: Once we have located the area, we should be finished in that time.

Child 2: It is important that we do not rush, though. There may be important and rare objects here.

Teacher: How will you record what you have found? How will I know what items have been buried in my garden?

Child 2: Hmmm, we will write a list of what we find.

Teacher: But what if you find a coin, for example – there may be more than one. How will you document their similarities or differences?

Child 1: We will have a member of our team who will write a description of each object that we find. Description and notetaking are important skills for archaeologists you know.

Here, the teacher, in role, used carefully planned questioning designed to guide the children to respond appropriately and informatively in their roles as archaeologists. Their knowledge regarding recording information is something that the children had absorbed from the video. They were then able to use their skills in descriptive writing and notetaking to support their archaeological dig. These were then used later to write a report about the excavation of the site.

Leading on from this idea of co-constructed learning and taking on the mantle of the expert, it is important for teachers to recognise the importance of good planning and preparation. The final case study gives an example of how successful planning and intervention like this by the teacher can enable learning to take place and provide the practitioner with opportunities to assess the pupils.

A class of seven- and eight-year-olds were given a problem to solve via a letter. We had looked at letterwriting during the previous term, so I was interested to see how the children would react, if they would draw on previous knowledge of this genre and to what extent teacher intervention would be required. The setting, once again, was the chocolate factory role-play area.

**CASE STUDY 5**

The situation was that a letter of complaint had been received from a customer. It had been posted and was addressed to 'The Manager'. The customer was extremely unhappy with a new chocolate flavouring that the factory had put on the market.

The children began their role-play by trying to create a new chocolate and were busy mixing new combinations of flavours. They were exploring ideas for possible amalgamations of flavours that we had discussed and sampled during our lessons, therefore bringing previous experience into play. In-depth discussion took place regarding possible changes that could be made to the flavour, but, although the children responded to the letter proactively, they did not identify the importance of replying to the customer, explaining what was being done to rectify the problem, so at this point I decided to intervene.

On entering the children's play, I asked if everything was OK as I had noticed a sense of panic in the factory. The children then began to explain the problem and showed me the letter that they had received. It was at this point that I initiated some direction by asking them what they might expect to happen if they had written a letter of complaint to somebody. Most children in the group said that they would want the problem to be resolved, while some of the more able children identified the fact that a response to their letter would be the expectation.

After this discussion and teacher intervention, the group split into two smaller groups, with some still working on new flavours for the chocolate and some sitting in the 'boardroom' writing a reply to the original letter.

This activity highlighted the different capabilities of the children and that the concept of receiving and then responding to letters required further exploration during lesson time. Teacher intervention highlighted gaps in the children's knowledge and understanding of a particular situation and the specific expectations that arose from this. The directed teaching of how to respond to letters that followed enabled them to practise newly learned skills with more confidence on their next visit to the role-play area.

It is quite a step for children to go from exploring and manipulating a given object that might be found in a role-play area to then developing the literacy skills and understanding to act and react appropriately in a given situation. Careful planning can provide practitioners with invaluable opportunities to guide learning and assess the children's reading, writing and speaking and listening in different contexts.

In the case study above, the ZPD allowed the children to work at a higher level than they usually would. Thus, teachers planning to use play and playful activities in their teaching should pitch the child's play and learning experiences above that of their mastered capabilities, as long as there is the opportunity for teacher intervention and support if it is needed. In this way, we can work towards ensuring that children are suitably challenged, allowing for progression in their learning.

## Summary

Within and outside most EYFS classrooms there will be different areas allowing children the opportunity to explore via playful activities. Such areas might include sand, water, large construction, small construction, small world and role-play areas. Each area provides children with the opportunity to explore the materials provided and play and manipulate them in an imaginative way. As well as being able to explore, children are also encouraged to communicate in a range of different ways, by talking, drawing, markmaking, construction, and so on. I believe that there is the potential for practitioners working with older children to adapt these methods to support the development of literacy skills at their level, too.

This might require us to be more flexible in our approach to the curriculum and think about ways in which we can meet our children's needs by means of play-based activities. In his review of reading, Rose (2006) states that, in order for children to develop confidence, self-belief and positive attitudes towards reading, they should be exposed to a language-rich environment. An environment rich in vocabulary is something that can be achieved by having a role-play area, wherein the children have the opportunity to use vocabulary in context, in both oral and written forms. Children can use role-play to explore and discuss characters from texts, settings, plots, and so on, as well as engaging with real-life scenarios and linking these with their studies of non-fiction.

In 2008, the *Talk for Writing* documentation was released by the DCSF, as it was then known (now DfE). In it, teachers were encouraged to use talk as a means of developing a child's understanding and knowledge, giving them more ownership of their learning. This document highlights the importance of 'independent pupil talk', where children communicate verbally, independent of teacher intervention. In these situations, children have the opportunity to develop their own voice and begin to use it more confidently in order to learn how to communicate their ideas and views with an audience in mind. As the *Talk for Writing* project promotes the use of speech as a starting point for children's writing, it would be a good opportunity for teachers to exploit role-play areas across the primary phases, giving children a place where they can practise the communication of their ideas both orally and in writing in a more informal setting than whole-class work.

*(Continued)*

*(Continued)*

In order to become successful learners, children need to develop confidence to take risks as well as recognise that mistakes can be made, reflected on and this can be used to then change the way in which a problem is approached in the future. It is clear to me that role-play areas can provide children of all ages with these opportunities, in a multisensory learning environment, and this, arguably, makes the literacy curriculum accessible to all learners as they explore language in context.

## Further reading

Ackroyd, J. and Barter-Boulton, J. (2012) *Drama Lessons: Ages 7–11*. London: David Fulton. This text by Ackroyd and Barter-Boulton is one of two – the other aimed at four- to seven-year-olds. It is full of lesson ideas in which drama is used as a stimulus, with many activities involving the teacher being in role and directing the learning.

Briggs, M. and Hansen, A. (2012) *Play-based Learning in the Primary School*. London: Sage. This is useful as it discusses play across both Key Stages 1 and 2. Briggs and Hansen discuss in some depth the issues that have been raised in this chapter, such as the different types of play, the role of the adult, as well as aspects I have not had the opportunity to explore, such as the assessment of play-based learning.

## References

Beardsley, G. and Harnett, P. (1998) *Exploring Play in the Primary Classroom*. London: David Fulton.

Blatner, A. (1995) 'Drama in education as mental hygiene: A child psychiatrist's perspective', *Youth Theatre Journal*, 9 (1): 92–6.

Briggs, M. and Hansen, A. (2012) *Play-based Learning in the Primary School*. London: Sage.

Bruce, T. (1991) *Time to Play in Early Childhood Education*. London: Hodder & Stoughton.

Bruce, T. and Spratt, J. (2011) *Essentials of Literacy from 0–7* (2nd edn). London: Sage.

Corden, R. (2000) *Literacy and Learning Through Talk*. Buckingham: Open University Press.

DCSF (2008) *Talk for Writing*. Runcorn: DCSF.

DfE (2012) *Statutory Framework for the Early Years Foundation Stage*. Runcorn: DfE.

Early Education (2012) *Development Matters*. London: Early Education.

Fisher, R. and Williams, M. (2006) *Unlocking Literacy* (2nd edn). London: David Fulton.

Fontana, D. (1995) *Psychology for Teachers* (3rd edn). Houndmills, Basingstoke: Palgrave Macmillan.

Heathcote, D. and Boulton, G.M. (1995) *Drama for Learning: Dorothy Heathcote's mantle of the expert approach to education*. London: Heinemann.

Jeffers, O. (2007) *Way Back Home*. London: HarperCollins.

Moyles, J. (1989) *Just Playing: The role and status of play in early childhood education*. Buckingham: Open University Press.

Moyles, J. (ed.) (2010) *The Excellence of Play* (3rd edn). Maidenhead: Open University Press.

Rose, J. (2006) *Independent Review of the Teaching of Early Reading*. Nottingham: DfES Publications.

Scarlett, W.G., Naudeau, S., Salonius-Pasternack, D. and Ponte, I. (2005) *Children's Play*. Thousand Oaks, CA: Sage.

Vygotsky, L.S. (1978) *Mind in Society: The development of higher psychological processes*. Cambridge, MA: Harvard University Press.

Welsch, J.G. (2008) 'Playing with and beyond the story: Encouraging book-related pretend play', *Reading Teacher*, 62 (2): 138–48.

## Children's literature referred to in the text

Baker, Jeannie (2002) *Window*. London: Walker Books.

Dahl, Roald (2007) *Charlie and the Chocolate Factory*. London: Penguin Books.

Stevenson, Robert Louis (2013) *Tresure Island*. London: Usborne Publishing.

# Getting outside

## Michael Green

 **Chapter Objectives**

- to examine the philosophies and approaches to using environments outside the classroom to enhance early opportunities for literacy
- to link learning outside the classroom to key principles and practices relating to the teaching and learning of early literacy
- to demonstrate how learning within meaningful contexts can provide opportunities for children to express themselves in a variety of ways and via a range of modes.

## This chapter will cover:

- the debate regarding the effectiveness of different types of 'experiences'
- the decline in children's engagement with settings and experiences beyond home and the classroom
- what the literature and research tell us about the benefits of children engaging in opportunities to learn beyond the classroom
- how to explore non-fiction in experiences beyond the classroom.

Every young person should experience the world beyond the classroom as an essential part of learning and development. (DfES, 2006: ii)

Over the last decade, a plethora of research studies have been undertaken into learning outside the classroom and its resultant benefits on pupils (Rickinson, 2001; Gould, 2003; Dillon et al., 2005; Peacock, 2006; Malone, 2008). This chapter examines the philosophies and approaches to using environments outside formal education and care contexts for children from birth to the age of eight. Woven throughout are principles and practices related to the teaching and learning of speaking, listening, reading and writing and how these can be developed in contexts outside the usual 'classroom' or care environment.

The chapter will present an argument for embedding children's development as literate language users within meaningful contexts outside the classroom, thereby placing demands on children to express themselves in a variety of ways and using a variety of modes – spoken, written and visual. This will include an exploration of the particular benefits of out-of-classroom environments as learning contexts, as well as a consideration of the possibilities afforded by visits to local and cultural settings, such as museums, art galleries and historic buildings. There will be a particular focus on the genre of non-fiction and how children's interest and learning in this area might be promoted.

## What do we mean by learning outside the classroom?

The term 'outside' is somewhat ambiguous as it can of course include *outdoor* experiences, but also *indoor* experiences *outside* the classroom. This chapter will be considering both examples, but, first, it is useful to understand what others believe this entails.

Rickinson et al. provide a useful definition of *outdoor* learning as:

learning that accrues or is derived from activities undertaken in outdoor locations beyond the school classroom. (2004: 9)

They consider this to include:

- projects in the school grounds or within the local area surrounding the school
- outdoor adventurous education
- fieldwork or visits to nature centres, farms, parks, and so on.

Malone provides a broader definition, describing it as any opportunity:

initiated by teachers and/or students to engage with alternative learning settings to complement and/or supplement the formal indoors classroom curricula. (2008: 7)

The range of possible settings that exist outside the classroom – both indoor and outdoor – are considerable and include playgrounds, the school grounds, museums, libraries, outdoor and adventure settings, zoos, art galleries and urban spaces, but, according to Rebar (2009), whatever the setting used, common characteristics are shared which are distinct from what he terms the 'formal classroom setting'. In general, out-of-classroom settings are associated with being more informal, learner-driven and learner-centred (Waite and Pratt, 2011). There is also the strong belief that the learning which occurs within these settings is more open-ended, interactive and flexible (Dillon et al., 2005). Such settings, whether around the pond in the school grounds or the coastal cliffs of Dover, are also unique in that the learning is characterised as being context-embedded and rooted in 'real-world' experiences (Rea, 2008) – something, as shall be discussed in due course, possibly lacking in many primary schools and, yet, key to the successful teaching and learning of early literacy.

The revised framework for the Early Years Foundation Stage (EYFS) (DfE, 2012) puts a strong emphasis on the three prime areas considered essential for children's development and well-being – communication and language, physical and personal, social and emotional development – and, for practitioners working with these young children, 'getting outside' should enable them to embrace these areas of learning in real and exciting settings. Interestingly, the language used in the revised EYFS Framework is pertinent to both outside learning and literacy – and children's learning beyond the Early Years. Some of the phrases include, 'to experience a rich language environment', 'providing opportunities for young children to be active and interactive', 'to develop their co-ordination, control and movement' and 'to have confidence in their own abilities' (DfE, 2012: 5). All of these goals might more readily be achieved outside the classroom and are very relevant to literacy for all ages, as children need to learn about language in environments where they can be actively involved and feel safe, while also being able to take risks. As will also be discussed, however, best practice in the teaching and learning of early literacy should focus on a seamless integration between outdoor and indoor learning.

## The debate regarding types of experiences

With educationalists and researchers alike making the distinctions expressed above, it opens up the argument regarding whether some learning experiences are more beneficial than others. Hirsch (1996), for example, is one such critic, who argues that some of the learning experiences mentioned above should not be accepted uncritically. He contends that 'bookish hard work' (Hirsch, 1996: 76) is equally, if not more, important and it is through drill and practice that results are yielded, rather than an holistic approach to learning, which, he contends, is an 'insecure way of learning' (Hirsch, 1996: 86). Indeed, he goes on to argue that 'specialized drill and practice' is 'essential' in teaching and the emphasis should not constantly be on creating 'lifelike, meaning-ful contexts' (Hirsh, 1996: 86).

In stark contrast, there is a growing body of thought that schools actually achieve nothing more than to distance children from the real world (Austin, 2007). The National Advisory Committee on Creative and Cultural Education (NACCCE, 1999), for example, rightly asserted that 'schools alone cannot provide all the educational experiences that children need', implying 'bookish hard work' (Hirsch, 1996: 76) is not enough on its own. In fact, others would argue that our current school system removes children from the real world and 'offers them a constrained environment in which to learn which regularly fails to make connections with their experiences' (Austin, 2007: xi). Moreover, Vare (1998) earlier raised the important question of what learning children actually miss out on by going to school. School-based learning can, according to Resnick (1987), often be solitary, divorced from real-world experiences and have little or no connection with real life. Indeed, Bentley (1998: 47) – writing some 11 years after Resnick, argues that:

> One of the most telling criticisms of school education is that it can insulate pupils from the outside world and one of the most important failures is that knowledge gained in school is not transferred or applied successfully in contexts beyond the classroom.

This, though, is not a new argument; Illich (1971: 73), writing in the early 1970s, made the case that learners need to engage with the real world 'instead of continuing to funnel all educational programmes though the teacher'. Illich's vision of children engaging more with the world beyond the classroom is one that we need to hold on to, particularly in this current educational climate of accountability and the need to have measurable outcomes driven by targets. This chimes with Hayes (2007), too, who, when problematising the 'over-formalised' curriculum driven by learning objectives, suggested that learning outside the classroom would be the alternative to this. How, then, does this relate specifically to early literacy?

Cognitive development in relation to out-of-classroom education can be linked to decision-making skills, problem-solving ability, affective knowledge, environmental awareness and understanding, acquisition of knowledge and skills and attitudes to learning (Malone, 2008), all of which are relevant and useful with regard to early literacy. Whitehead (2010: 163) believes that children's early experiences of oral and written communication are directly influenced by 'the stimulation they find in their personal and cultural situations' and, arguably, this stimulus needs to come partly from experiencing a range of environments, including outside the classroom. Bearne (2002: 30) writes that the setting for writing should be an 'environment of possibility' with 'an atmosphere where risks can be taken with writing' and, once again, different environments need to be part of these possibilities and risks. Working outside will provide natural opportunities for children to engage in exploratory talk and solve problems via discussion, interaction and negotiation. They will engage with reading – not just signs, labels, instructions or other manmade reading materials but also other people's expressions and body language. All of these literacy experiences could be said to occur within the classroom environment, but my argument would be that, by providing alternative learning environments, we are extending the children's experiences and offering them the increased freedom that 'getting outside' suggests.

So, if the benefits of literacy learning outside are so considerable, what, then, is the current situation with regard to learning outside the classroom in the United Kingdom?

## The current climate for learning outside the classroom

Over the last decade, there have been considerable developments in promoting out-of-classroom education. Examples include the establishment of a House of Commons Select Committee enquiry into education outside the classroom in September 2004, the launch of the *Learning Outside the Classroom Manifesto* in November 2006 by the DfES, the creation of a quality badge for providers of learning outside the classroom in October 2008 and the £5 million investment by the DfES in the Council for Learning Outside the Classroom between 2006 and 2010.

Such developments reflect the previous government's and others' strong beliefs in the broad range of benefits associated with learning outside the classroom, but also the growing concerns about the marked decline in the opportunities being afforded to children to learn away from more formal settings (Dillon et al., 2003; Rickinson et al., 2004). While it is difficult to quantify the amount of learning that *does* occur beyond the classroom every year, it is clear that there has been a decline in the opportunities given to primary-age children. The reasons for the decline are well documented in the literature (Clare, 2004; Rickinson et al., 2004; Peacock, 2006; Malone, 2008; Bilton, 2010; Sangster and Green, 2010; Waite, 2011) and have been attributed to a number of key issues, including:

- the perceived concerns regarding health and safety (not helped by adverse media headlines)
- lack of teacher confidence in relation to skills and knowledge
- pressures of the curriculum and the school timetable
- cost
- union guidance – in particular, the NASUWT's statement in 2004 advising its members to not take children on school trips
- bureaucratic demands on teachers.

Given such daunting obstacles to education beyond classroom walls, the question that has to be asked is why such provision is receiving so much positive attention and support from all quarters, including at government level? Indeed, what does learning outside the classroom offer teachers and their pupils that classroom contexts may lack? What does educational research tell us about the contribution that this type of learning experience can have on pupils and teachers and how strong is the evidence that this type of provision is beneficial?

The following section will explore the benefits of learning outside the classroom, with specific reference to children learning about non-fiction in literacy. A case study will be introduced to illustrate the power of learning outside the classroom and how it impacts children's literacy learning.

## Learning outside the classroom and non-fiction

Some children have very few opportunities to experience life outside of their home and school, other than through images on the television (Waite, 2007). This 'divorcing' of children from real-life experiences was illustrated by Owens (2004), who found that, even though children could name a range of television characters, they struggled to name wildlife, such as birds or flowers.

According to Medved and Medved (1998), this lack of children's engagement with the outdoors can partly be attributed to popular culture, television watching and technological advancements, such as spending time in the online world rather than the outside world. Arguably, aspects of the outside world can be powerfully experienced through television programmes and Internet sites, so adults working with young learners need to ascertain what experiences the children have had, in both the real and virtual worlds. Many children do enter the classroom with a rich understanding and experience of the world around them (Barnes, 2007) and such experiences should be sought out and shared so that all the children might benefit. The world outside the classroom can provide the perfect stimulus for eliciting such experiences from the children. This is of particular importance when considering how to engage and motivate children to be confident readers and writers of non-fiction.

Children's personal interests need to be recognised and exploited to provide an authentic and meaningful context for their writing of non-fiction. The outside environment provides this context for emerging and developing writers:

> Outdoor play is an equally strong context for encouraging all kinds of print. Boys in the nursery years seem particularly motivated to write when their role play is out of doors and centres on familiar locations like garages, plant nurseries and builders' yards. (Mallett, 2003: 8)

The following case study describes the literacy learning planned for by a class teacher linked with a learning experience outside the classroom at a stately home and gardens.

### CASE STUDY 1

The children (aged eight) were learning about the Tudors and, as part of the unit of work, the children were due to visit Penshurst Place in Kent. The teacher identified several writing opportunities that could arise from the children's visit to the stately home and gardens, one of which included a non-chronological report about life in the Tudor times. As part of the teacher's planning, he had visited Penshurst Place and spoken in advance with the education officer to carefully plan the day and consider how the trip could be integrated into the unit of work.

In the days leading up to the trip, the children learnt about the history of the house and its historical significance so that they had some existing knowledge and understanding prior to their trip. In their literacy lessons, the children had been looking at a range of non-chronological texts and identifying the language and organisational features, as well as exploring effective notetaking techniques. The primary purpose of the trip was to provide the stimulus for the children to apply their learning and produce a non-chronological report about life in Tudor times.

Keen for the trip to have maximum impact on the children's learning, it was purposely planned to coincide with Penhurst Place's annual 'living history' week, providing a hands-on, practical, experiential learning opportunity for the children with skilled musicians, actors and actresses recreating characters and the daily life of the period.

Keen not to overload the children with worksheets to complete, the teacher adopted a more open-ended approach, providing groups with 'tuffcams', audio recording equipment, digital cameras and mini sketchbooks to capture their experiences.

Prior to arriving, the teacher had explained to the children that, during the day, they would be required to apply their prior learning about notetaking to record their learning experiences while also making effective use of ICT as a tool to further support this recording.

Throughout the day, the children were immersed in a range of activities that actively involved them in experiencing for themselves what life during the Tudor period was like. They were aware that they would be expected to use their notes and other evidence when they returned to the classroom to work on their non-chronological reports.

In the case study above, the teacher used literacy lessons as the vehicle for expanding on other areas of the curriculum, creating meaningful contexts in which the children could apply their reading, writing, speaking and listening skills. It has been argued that cross-curricular approaches within the primary classroom provide great motivation for children (Barnes, 2007) and, as Palmer (2001) points out, if children have become 'experts' on a particular topic, it makes sense to link their writing to cross-curricular learning. Further, the combination of the cross-curricular approach with the real-life experience of the trip provides a very powerful learning experience for any child.

I would at this point, however, like to look more carefully at this case study with regard to literacy and young learners through the lens of Wray and Lewis' (1997) EXIT model. The EXIT model (extending interactions with texts) examines ten stages that children can usefully go through in order to support their literacy learning. These stages are:

1. activation of previous knowledge
2. establishing purposes
3. locating information
4. adopting an appropriate strategy
5. interacting with text
6. monitoring and understanding
7. making a record
8. evaluating information
9. assisting memory
10. communicating information.

Prior to the trip, the children were given opportunities to learn about the historical site they were going to see and were able, therefore, to access this knowledge when they arrived at the setting (1). They had already begun to explore the genre of non-chronological reports and were aware that they would ultimately be producing a report about life in Tudor times (2). During their visit, the children were able to interact with and find out relevant information from a range of sources and use a variety of methods to record their findings (3, 4 and 5). The children's understanding of the information they had learned and their ability to put this into an appropriate written format enabled the teacher to monitor their understanding (6 and 7). Because they also had electronic and pictorial evidence from their trip, they were able, once back in the classroom, to evaluate their findings, remember the details and share these with others (8, 9 and 10).

Thus, this experience outside the classroom gave the children plenty of opportunities to extend their interactions with a range of texts and embed their learning within useful and relevant processes. The ten stages explicated by Wray and Lewis (which do not necessarily have to be followed in the above order) provide a very valuable framework to use when planning and teaching a non-fiction unit of work with children of all ages, particularly when children are visiting alternative learning sites, where the wealth of opportunities to interact with texts needs to be exploited.

## Learning outside the classroom: some things to think about when planning a trip

If you are going to use a trip as a stimulus for literacy learning, you may want to heed the following considerations.

- Remember to look at what is available on your doorstep! Trips do not have to involve lengthy journeys. Look at your local area and your school grounds and consider how these can be incorporated into your literacy and language curriculum and what texts are available with which children can interact.
- Do your homework – ensure that you visit the venue. Often if a venue is aware in advance that you are undertaking a preliminary visit for a planned school trip the cost of entry will be waived. Visiting will ensure that you can maximise all the literacy learning opportunities available.
- Think carefully about how you are going to incorporate your trip/visit within your unit of work. A mistake made by many is that they plan a trip towards the end of a unit as a 'treat'. This can make it difficult to follow up any of the learning that occurs as a result of the experience and so often reduces its impact. Likewise, having it too early can also cause an issue if the children are not adequately prepared in advance. In the example in the case study above, the teacher was keen to prepare the children before the trip and also use the outing as a stimulus for some follow-up activities and therefore planned the trip partway through the unit. Mallett (2003: 8) suggests that, initially, children might look at 'texts, diagrams and pictures' relating to a topic before then going outside and making links between what they have discovered in print-based and electronic texts and the things they find in the new environment.
- Think carefully about what you want the children to do while on the trip. Another common mistake is to provide the children with countless worksheets to complete. Completing worksheets can detract from many of the rich learning experiences that can occur. That is not to say mere exposure to the environment beyond the classroom will be enough to support effective learning, however. Consider how you can draw on ICT as a way of capturing the children's learning and experiences so that you can refer back to it when in the classroom. A productive activity with younger children is to let them take photographs of the trip so that when they return to the classroom, they can use these to support recounting, both orally and in writing, the events of the day.

Opportunities to learn outside the classroom by taking trips are an excellent way to get children away from the normal school and classroom environment, but, of course, these cannot form part of the day-to-day experiences of the child and are likely to take place just once or twice a year. It is important, therefore, to ensure that other opportunities to 'get outside' are provided as part of everyday practice. The next section explores how this might be promoted using role-play.

## Role-play outside the classroom

Having direct engagement with and experience of a variety of settings beyond the four walls of a classroom can provide opportunities for children to interact effectively with language – a crucial aspect of early literacy, as children are beginning to access a range of forms of communication and find their oral and written voice in the world. As Cotton (2011: 69) highlights, if children have little opportunity to experience the outside world, they will find it 'hard to model the spoken and written language' appropriate to different settings. Mindful of this warning, it is essential that authentic learning experiences are provided to support children's language development within a range of learning contexts, including the outside environment, so children are exposed to speaking and listening, reading and writing in meaningful contexts and can begin implicitly to realise how language and literacy can empower them (Neaum, 2012).

The role-play area can provide the ideal opportunity to not only build on young children's existing experiences of the world around them but also help them reflect on and make sense of their world and these experiences. The EYFS Framework recommends play as a language-learning opportunity. When identifying how the role-play area can support young children's understanding of non-fiction, you might consider organising the area around real-life situations and bring the outside into the classroom. Potential examples include visits to the doctor, dentist, vets, travel agents, bank, post office, supermarket, or restaurant. All of these situations provide the creative teacher with an opportunity to provide real, purposeful opportunities to promote speaking and listening, writing and playing with language. Where possible, however, although it is beneficial to have an indoor role-play area, also take role-play outside of the classroom.

The following case study describes the experiences of a class of five- and six-year-olds as they gave new and exciting meaning to the idea of a role-play area by creating their own garden centre within the school grounds. In this way, role-play and reality became interlinked so as to create as authentic an experience as possible.

### CASE STUDY 2

The children were learning about plants and how they grow as part of their science topic at school. Within literacy, the children were focusing on instructional texts and lists, labels and captions. Recognising that the role-play area does not have to be confined to the classroom, the teacher, keen to create an authentic learning experience, decided to develop a cross-curricular 'real-world' garden project with her class, combining the science and literacy units of work.

*(Continued)*

*(Continued)*

Many of the children had never visited a garden centre before and the nearest centre to the school was a considerable distance away, so the teacher arranged a visit from an employee from the garden centre. He wore his uniform and brought into school packets of seeds, pots, planters, watering cans, plant labels and an assortment of pictures of the garden centre.

The class, inspired by the visit and what they had learned, decided to create their own garden centre within the school grounds, which would culminate in a plant sale to raise money for new playground equipment. The children set about asking for further donations of other plant and vegetable seeds from parents and people from the local community. Several enthusiastic parents were keen to support the class and worked with the children to prepare some raised beds and plant a whole host of different fruit, vegetables and flowers. The children were thoroughly engaged with the growing and tending of the plants and the employee from the garden centre visited regularly to check on progress.

Inside the classroom, the children busily produced labels for their plants and wrote instructions for how to grow and care for the various plants. Science lessons became focused on the class 'garden centre', with the children observing the plants as they grew, drawing and labelling their findings, measuring their height and watering and tending to the plants.

The culmination of this term-long project was the official opening of the garden centre and the plant sale where the children could put into practice the speech patterns they were familiar with from their own visits to shops – 'That'll be £1 please' and 'Would you like a bag for that?'. Every lunchtime, the school opened its gates to allow parents to visit the garden centre and the children took it in turns to staff the shop and sell their produce to parents.

The creative teacher will not limit role-play to the 'corner' of a classroom, but seek to use other settings to support children's literacy and language development. In the above case study, the children were immersed in a rich, meaningful and, perhaps most importantly, authentic context, making use of the outside space to bring role-play alive. This cross-curricular unit of work actively promoted the use of the four language skills. The children were required to adapt and modify their spoken language to real-life situations and contexts and the patterns of speech that were utilised indicated to the practitioner that the children were able to respond to settings and situations. Writing was given a real purpose – the labelling of plants and the writing of instructions provided a purpose and 'real' audience for the children. Such authentic learning experiences are essential. Mallett (2010) highlights the importance of children who are developing their early literacy being active learners and having the opportunity for first-hand experiences as a stimulus for instructional writing. Importantly, though, the garden centre experience not only enabled the children to learn about language but also language in this context provided a valuable medium for learning, as the children expanded their understanding about settings beyond the classroom. The opportunities afforded from such an experience for new language to be acquired, practised and new ideas and understandings developed were endless. Hopefully, as you read the above case study it raised your awareness of how alternative settings can be used as an extension to the classroom.

An important principle that the teacher in the above case study wanted to reinforce was the equal weighting that should be given to both learning inside and beyond the classroom. Bilton (2010: 85) reinforces this, pointing out that, within the EYFS provision, both environments need to be combined to avoid the outside environment being perceived as an 'add-on' that has a lower status than the classroom, 'where the important schooly stuff happens'.

## Learning outside the classroom: key considerations regarding effectiveness

In order to further maximise the effectiveness of children learning outside the classroom, Dillon et al. (2003) identified the need to make links between learning inside and outside the classroom and the necessity of follow-up activities to maximise the learning experiences. This, too, was highlighted by Ofsted (2008) as one of the key contributing factors influencing the effectiveness of out-of-classroom provision. Dillon et al.'s (2003) research also identified the need to take into account the wide range of perceptions and experiences that learners from different backgrounds will bring to the setting.

While the overwhelming majority of research concurs that opportunities to learn outside the classroom provide a range of experiences which classroom contexts cannot offer, it is important to acknowledge, as Rickinson (1999) has done, that there is a possibility such experiences may be unproductive for some children. Individual children favour different pedagogical strategies and, as Semper (1990) reminds us, learning is a highly individualised thing. In addition, the plethora of benefits, highlighted earlier may be lost if, as Waite (2011: 204) warns, 'classroom norms and practices are simply taken outside with the class'. It seems, therefore, that the novelty of the setting is not enough; it also requires teachers to adopt a different pedagogical approach. These concerns were raised in an earlier study by Ballantyne and Packer who concluded that:

> the use of worksheets, note-taking and reports were all unpopular with the students and did not appear to contribute greatly to their learning. (2002: 228)

Ricketts and Willis (2001) and Rea (2008) likewise argue that if there is an insistence on practitioners seeking to extract learning from each outside experience, it runs the risk of disengaging children. There is evidence (Rea, 2006) indicating that children are capable of engaging in reflective thought independently and construct meaning from these experiences without the need for teachers to facilitate this reflection process in a formalised way.

## Summary

In an education climate driven by accountability and measurable outcomes, it can be tempting to revert to 'drill and skill' approaches to teaching and learning. It is hoped that this chapter has provided an alternative pedagogical approach. Making use of the 'outside' as an extension of the four walls of a classroom can promote learning within an authentic, active, hands-on, meaningful context, whereby the children are fully involved. Nixon et al. (1996) argue that learning actually depends on motivation – without the motivation to invest the time and effort, no learning will occur. They go on to suggest that traditional teaching and learning methods, as seen in many of our primary schools, bring about apathy towards learning, decrease motivation and the 'standards agenda' can create anxiety instead of joy. This is of particular relevance and importance for our young learners, who need to acquire the ability to communicate in a range of settings with an array of people, using a variety of media to reflect the world they live in, in the twenty-first century. Our commitment to offering innovative and motivational experiences is crucial if we are to ensure that young children see learning as fun and relevant to their lives.

## Further reading

Bilton, H. (2010) *Outdoor Learning in the Early Years: Management and innovation*. Abingdon: Routledge.
This comprehensive text provides a thorough exploration of working outdoors in the Early Years and explains the centrality of outdoor play for children's development. A whole range of topics are explored, providing practical advice on setting up the outdoor area.

Waite, S. (ed.) (2011) *Children Learning Outside the Classroom: From birth to eleven*. London: Sage.
An excellent text aimed at bridging the gap between theory and practice concerning learning outside the classroom. The authors explore how environments beyond the classroom can provide the context for learning for children from the EYFS to the end of Key Stage 2.

# References

Austin, R. (ed.) (2007) *Letting the Outside in: Developing teaching and learning beyond the Early Years classroom*. Stoke on Trent: Trentham Books.

Ballantyne, R. and Packer, J. (2002) 'Nature-based excursions: School students' perceptions of learning in natural environments', *International Research in Geographical and Environmental Education*, 11 (3): 218–36.

Barnes, J. (2007) *Cross-Curricular Learning 3–14*. London: Paul Chapman.

Bearne, E. (2002) *Making Progress in Writing*. London: RoutledgeFalmer.

Bentley, T. (1998) *Learning Beyond the Classroom: Education for a changing world*. London: Routledge.

Bilton, H. (2010) *Outdoor Learning in the Early Years: Management and innovation*. Abingdon: Routledge.

Clare, J. (2004) 'Union tells teachers to end all school trips', *The Daily Telegraph*, 19 February.

Cotton, H. (2011) 'English and language outside the classroom', in S. Waite (ed.), *Children Learning Outside the Classroom: From birth to eleven*. London: Sage.

DfE (2012) *Statutory Framework for the Early Years Foundation Stage*. Runcorn: DfE.

DfES (2006) *Learning Outside the Classroom Manifesto*. Nottingham: DfES Publications.

Dillon, J., Rickinson, M., Sanders, D., Teamey, K. and Benefield, P. (2003) *Improving the Understanding of Food, Farming and Land Management amongst School-age Children: A literature review*, Research Report RR422. Nottingham: DfES Publications.

Dillon, J. Morris, M. O'Donnell, L. Rickinson, M. and Scott, W. (2005) *Engaging and Learning with the Outdoors*. Bath: Centre for Research in Environmental Education.

Gould, H. (2003) *Settings other than Schools: Initial teacher training placements in museums, libraries and archives*. Leeds: YMLAC.

Hayes, D. (2007) 'What Einstein can teach us about education', *Education 3–13*, 35 (2): 143–54.

Hirsch, E.D. (1996) *The Schools We Need and Why We Don't Have Them*. New York: Anchor.

Illich, I. (1971) *Deschooling Society*. Harmondsworth: Penguin Education.

Mallett, M. (2003) *Early Years Non-fiction*. London: RoutledgeFalmer.

Mallett, M. (2010) *Choosing and Using Fiction and Non-fiction 3–11*. Abingdon: Routledge.

Malone, K. (2008) *Every Experience Matters*. Stoneleigh Park: Farming and Countryside Education.

Medved, M. and Medved, D. (1998) *Saving Childhood: Protecting our children from the national assault on innocence*. New York: HarperCollins.

NACCCE (1999) *All our Futures. National Advisory Committee on Creative and Cultural Education*. Available online at: http://sirkenrobinson.com/skr/pdf/allourfutures.pdf (accessed 18 December 2013).

Neaum, S. (2012) *Language and Literacy for the Early Years*. London: Sage.

Nixon, J., Martin, J., McKeown, P., Ranson, S. (1996) *Encouraging Learning: Towards a theory of the learning school*. Buckingham: Open University Press.

Ofsted (2008) *Learning Outside the Classroom: How far should you go?*. London: Ofsted.

Owens, P. (2004) 'Researching the development of children's environmental values in the early school years', *Researching Primary Geography*, 1 August: 64–76.

Palmer, S. (2001) *How to Teach Writing Across the Curriculum at Key Stage 2: Developing creative literacy*. London: David Fulton.

Peacock, A. (2006) *Changing Minds: The lasting impact of school trips*. Exeter: The Innovation Centre, University of Exeter. Available online at: www.peecworks.org/PEEC/PEEC_Research/0179ABED-001D0211.0/Peacock%202006%20field%20trip%20effects.pdf (accessed 18 December 2013).

Rea, T. (2006) '"It's not as if we've been teaching them …"': Reflective thinking in the outdoor classroom', *Journal of Adventure Education and Outdoor Learning*, 6 (2): 107–20.

Rea, T. (2008) 'Alternative visions of learning: Children's learning experiences in the outdoors', *Educational Futures*, 1 (2): 42–50.

Rebar, B.M. (2009) 'Evidence, explanations and recommendations for teachers' field trip strategies'. Unpublished PhD thesis, Oregon State University, Corvalis, OR.

Resnick, L.B. (1987) 'The 1987 presidential address: Learning in and out of school', *Educational Researcher*, 16 (9): 13–19.

Ricketts, M. and Willis, J. (2001) *Experience AI: A practitioner's guide to integrating appreciative enquiry with experiential learning*. Chagrin Falls, OH: Taos Institute Publications.

Rickinson, M. (1999) 'People–environment issues in the geography classroom: Towards an understanding of children's experiences', *International Research in Geography and Environmental Education*, 8 (2): 120–39.

Rickinson, M. (2001) 'Learners and learning in environmental education: A critical review of the evidence', *Environmental Education Research*, 7 (3): 207–320.

Rickinson, M., Dillon, J., Teamey, K., Morris, M., Choi, M., Sanders, D. and Benefield, P. (2004) *A Review of Research on Outdoor Learning*. Shrewsbury: Field Studies Council.

Sangster, M. and Green, M. (2010) 'The value of an alternative placement experience primary initial teacher training students'. Paper presented at the European Educational Research Asssociation Conference, Helsinki, 25–27 September. Available online at: www.eera-ecer.de/index.php?id=421&Action=showContributionDetail&conferenceUid=3&contributionUid=4328&cHash=21044039e25bea14b03152e7cba216fe (accessed 18 December 2013).

Semper, R.J. (1990) 'Science museums as environments for learning', *Physics Today*, 43 (11): 2–8.

Vare, P. (1998) 'Schooling for transition: Whither or wither?: A view from environmental education'. Paper presented at the Bristol Conference on International Education, University of Bristol, January.

Waite, S. (2007) 'Memories are made of this: Some reflections on outdoor learning and recall', *Education 3–13*, 35 (4): 333–47.

Waite, S. (ed.) (2011) *Children Learning Outside the Classroom: From birth to eleven*. London: Sage.

Waite, S. and Pratt, N. (2011) 'Theoretical perspectives on learning outside the classroom: Relationships between learning and place', in S. Waite (ed.), *Children Learning Outside the Classroom: From birth to eleven*. London: Sage.

Whitehead, M. (2010) *Language and Literacy in the Early Years 0–7* (4th edn). London: Sage.

Wray, D. and Lewis, M. (1997) *Extending Literacy: Children reading and writing non-fiction*. London: Routledge.

# Part 2
# Provision for all

Part 2

Provision for all

# 4

# Seamless transition from the Foundation Stage to Year 1 (ages three to six)

Karen Vincent

---

**Chapter Objectives**

- to explore what good practice in making the transition in literacy between the Foundation Stage and Year 1 might look like

- to examine the sources of tension around this transition generally and in terms of literacy and discuss how these may be overcome

- to use case studies to provide an insight into the transition in literacy for four- and five-year-olds.

---

This chapter will cover:

- the complexities of making this transition for young children
- how the transition in literacy between the Foundation Stage and Year 1 can be managed effectively with regard to speaking and listening, reading and writing
- three case studies that show examples of good practice and issues that might arise if the transition in literacy is not carefully managed.

Transitions are part of life. As we grow, learn and develop, we acquire an ability to adapt, respond in new ways to new people and become increasingly competent, until the next transition in our lives when the cycle is repeated. There are many transitions in an educational context and this chapter will focus on one of the most challenging – that from the Foundation Stage to Year 1, where the EYFS Framework meshes with the National Curriculum.

Children (and parents and carers) at this stage will already have experienced the transition from home to school and the assumption can sometimes be made that now the child is at school, the rest should be straightforward. For many children, however, *each* transition is a real challenge. So, as teachers of young children, we want to ensure that this stage in their education is as smooth and anxiety free as possible. To this end, the aim of this chapter is to explore what good practice in making this transition may look like, as well as examine some of the challenges that this particular phase may bring. There will be discussion of transition issues, specifically with regard to literacy, and three different case studies will highlight how three children experienced the transition from Foundation Stage to Key Stage 1 and the impact this had on their development in terms of literacy.

## Transition

During the first transition – starting school – many settings work hard to ensure that the children and parents feel supported and understand how school systems work (Yeboah, 2002). There are visits to school with familiar adults, perhaps a storytime with the new teacher and consultations with parents about their children's interests and needs. Discussions are encouraged about favourite stories and interest in books and often the Reception class teacher makes a visit to each child's home. This teacher may also visit each child in their preschool settings and so relationships begin to develop months before the children enter the daily routine of school. The preschool and school teachers will liaise with regard to each child's achievements, which may take the form of written records or photographs that illustrate particular moments of attainment. Many of these practices support the children's ability to link their home literacy experiences with the new world of school literacy learning. Bruce and Spratt (2011) emphasise the importance of making links between rhymes, poetry, real-life and meaningful experiences and, if children realise that the nursery rhymes, songs and stories they have explored at home have a place within this new and sometimes frightening environment, then their transition from home to school literacy can be less hazardous.

Although many schools and families make considerable efforts in these and other ways to smooth the transition between home and Early Years settings, this is not always replicated for the transition between Foundation Stage and Key Stage 1 (Ofsted, 2004; Alexander, 2010). This might be attributed to the fact that the EYFS finishes its involvement at the end of the Reception year and the National Curriculum begins in Year 1. In Wales, this is not such an issue as, there, the Foundation Phase has been developed, taking children from birth to the age of six. In England, however, the fact that the National Curriculum starts in Year 1 has meant the ideals and foundations laid down in the first year of school are, in some cases, at odds with the rigid expectations of the National Curriculum.

Children are not legally required to be in school until the term after they reach the age of five, yet many begin Reception class before this, at the age of four. This is often due to parents feeling that they would like their child to continue their education with their peer group or, perhaps, perceived pressure from the school due to a lack of places available.

Schools, following the Foundation Stage, need to ensure that the children learn through play, with access to the outside for prolonged periods of the day where possible. The children need to be encouraged to think for themselves, problem-solve, make decisions – all good foundations for their later literacy-learning lives. In an ideal world, children would progress seamlessly from the Foundation Stage into the first year of school. Their literacy development would not be hampered by a change of teacher, pedagogy, classroom or different friendship groupings. They would continue to learn in ways appropriate to their needs, in ways that support good early learning dispositions and nurture and develop their creativity. In many schools this is the case. The move from the Foundation Stage to Year 1 can, however, sometimes pose challenges to all concerned – children, parents and teachers and:

> The transition from one level of education to the next puts each time new demands for adjustment that cause critical psychological strains and conflicts in the relation between the child and the school. (Kakavoulis, 1994 cited in Yeboah, 2002: 54)

In order to counter these demands, strategies can be implemented to ease the transition for young children. The first case study below addresses this, describing how one school manages the transition from Reception to Year 1. Following the case study will be a discussion relating to general aspects of this transition and, then, a more focused analysis of how the strategies implemented might support children's development in speaking and listening, reading and writing as they move from Reception to Year 1.

## CASE STUDY 1

Four-year-old Mathias started in his Reception class along with his friends from pre-school. He had spent the year in Reception forming friendships and learning the routines of being in school. From his class teacher's observations, it was clear he understood the routines associated with coming into school in the morning: he put his book bag in a particular place, along with his coat, and understood that he

*(Continued)*

*(Continued)*

needed to stick his name on either the school dinner or packed lunch board before he could select an activity which had been put out. He knew that when a bell sounded, it meant he needed to stop what he was doing and sit on the carpet. He understood the routines for lining up for lunch and the routine for the end of the day.

During the summer term a few changes occurred. Mathias began to be introduced to his next (Year 1) teacher in the afternoons, who visited for storytime. Gradually, she began to be present for small group activities, too. His teachers also explained to the class that the gate between the Reception playground and the Key Stage 1 playground was to be deliberately left open each day so that the children could venture out and play with the five-, six- and seven-year-old children if they wished. Mathias stated that 'he enjoyed playing with his sister and her friends'. This was noted by his teacher.

Mathias' teacher also arranged for time to be spent visiting the Year 1 classroom while the Year 1 children were out practising for sports day on the field. Mathias enjoyed using the different pens and pencils he found in the 'mission control' role-play area and using the digital microscope and magnifying glasses to look more closely at the different materials that were on display. He discussed animatedly what he saw with his teacher and friends. His teacher noted that he was very able at connecting up the digital microscope and navigating the interactive whiteboard to share his 'finds' with his classmates. It was also observed that he enjoyed using the different resources in the construction area and selecting the themed boxes to take outside to the sandpit where he could act out stories with his friends. The children were also invited to watch the Year 1 assemblies, which were based on their favourite stories.

Mathias felt confident that Year 1 was not going to be so different from the educational setting that he had already come to know and enjoy. His parents stated that 'Mathias is really looking forward to being in Year 1 and using the digital microscope'. Mathias said to his Reception class teacher that he 'was really pleased that he will be able to play out of doors in Year 1, too'. As Mathias had begun to build a relationship with his new teacher while still in his Reception class, his parents were also invited to visit to meet with her during the latter part of the term.

When Mathias began in Year 1, his Reception class teacher joined the class, too, working in small groups, just as his Year 1 teacher had in his Reception class. She read stories to the children and was available during playtimes. Gradually, her presence decreased as the children settled in and the demands of her new Reception class took over.

## For reflection

- How did Mathias' Reception class teacher ensure that a positive relationship with his prospective Year 1 teacher was built gradually over time?
- How did Mathias' new teacher get to 'tune in' to his development with regard to speaking and listening, reading and writing?

# What is good practice when making the transition from the Foundation Stage to Key Stage 1?

With reference to the case study, this section will look at what constitutes good practice in transition *generally* before moving on to specific good practice in relation to transition in terms of *literacy*. The two are, of course, inextricably linked, as children's competence and confidence as literacy learners will be influenced by how safe and secure they feel within a new environment.

Good practice when it comes to making this transition should be seen as 'a process and not as an event' (Sanders et al., 2005), one involving all parties associated with the child, which was exemplified in the case study above. The gradual and increasing presence of Mathias' prospective Year 1 teacher meant that she became a known adult and began to develop a relationship with him while he was still in the familiar surroundings of his Reception class. This is vital as such relationships are of fundamental importance in the Foundation Stage. Mathias' teachers showed that they recognised the value of giving him opportunities to forge new relationships at his own pace and in a setting that he knew well. The frequency of these encounters was also increased as the term moved on. Laevers (2000) stresses the importance of a caring and familiar adult in enabling young children to learn effectively (see Chapter 1, Baby rooms, for more discussion of this). By spending this time with him, Mathias' teacher was able to become highly tuned in to his needs and so provide effective support.

In addition, providing Mathias with the opportunity to choose how he spent time out of the classroom meant that he was able to make his own decisions about where and with whom he wanted to spend his time outside. Many children find playtimes particularly difficult (Fabian, 2005), but this strategy meant that if Mathias felt uncomfortable with any aspects of being in 'the big playground', he was able to take himself back to safe and familiar territory. Fostering independence is a key emphasis in the Foundation Stage and the developing ability to make decisions is built on in Year 1.

Increasingly regular visits to the Year 1 classroom during periods when the existing children in the class were not there (PE, sports day practice, ICT lessons, assemblies, and so on) gave Mathias the opportunity to get to know the layout of the classroom and the resources contained within it ahead of his first day there full time.

Mathias' Year 1 teacher showed that she understands the importance of learning through play as we saw her classroom was deliberately set up to facilitate this. Like

Mathias' Reception teacher, she had arranged her room into areas of learning, together with access to an outdoor area to enable children to take their learning outside. These areas of learning were designed to promote speaking and listening, reading and writing, providing the security of familiar settings alongside the challenge of more complex literacy practices. One of these settings was the 'mission control' role-play area, which Mathias loved. There he could use the digital microscope to examine objects. This microscope was connected to the interactive whiteboard and Mathias was able to use this resource to show his friends what he had found and discuss his discoveries. Doing this helped him to embed in his mind what he had learnt as he expressed himself orally through talk, thus engaging in speaking and listening activities relevant to specific National Curriculum learning objectives, but in an EYFS atmosphere. Alexander (2010: 306) discusses the 'true potential of talk', which happens when it is:

- *collective* children and adults working and talking together
- *reciprocal* listening and responding to the ideas of others
- *supportive* children are able to express their thoughts and ideas in an atmosphere that promotes individuality
- *cumulative* building on the ideas of others to extend one's own thinking
- *purposeful* activities are designed to promote dialogic talk that enables particular objectives to be achieved.

The 'mission control' role-play area and ensuing activities enabled the teachers in Mathias' school to exploit this 'true potential of talk' via a collective, reciprocal, supportive, cumulative and purposeful environment.

As time went on, Mathias' teacher recognised his growing confidence in the interactions with both her and his peers and introduced several books to encourage his emergent interest in the plants that he had found outdoors. She supported this interest by taking photographs of Mathias with his newly found objects and as he demonstrated what he saw through the digital microscope to his friends. Encouraging Mathias to make these into a book of information about plants provided him with the chance to use the range of pens, rulers, staplers and hole punches in the environment, thereby using these tools to make meaning in written form. On occasion, he also painted some images that he had seen through the digital microscope to put on the wall for all to see. Once again, this approach by the teacher demonstrates the best practice of the EYFS, combined with an ability to introduce elements of the Year 1 literacy curriculum with its greater demands on children's writing and recording in order that they might be assessed against specific level descriptors. For Mathias, though, this transition was invisible. He entered the world of Key Stage 1 literacy, with its attendant pressures of assessment and accountability, yet the pedagogies employed ensured that this could take place in a familiar and secure environment.

This case study showed Mathias going through processes that led to the realisation for him that Year 1 was going to be fun and was going to support his interests in very similar ways to those with which he had become accustomed in his Reception class. Hopefully, this careful planning by the practitioners will ensure that Mathias can move as smoothly into the next primary phase, thus enabling him to confidently access the literacy curriculum:

> Successful transition appears to be positively correlated with performance in the first few years of primary school, if not the entire primary education phase. (Yeboah, 2002: 52)

## The challenges of making the transition

While Mathias' experience of making the transition between classes was smooth, thanks to his teachers' careful planning and use of resources, it must be acknowledged that there are significant challenges when addressing the issue of transition between the Foundation Stage and Year 1. It cannot be ignored that there can be distinct differences in terms of pedagogical approach between the EYFS Framework and the National Curriculum in Year 1:

> early childhood education encourages children to initiate their own learning activities through play, while learning is more structured in the primary school with the teacher determining what the children do and learn. (Yeboah, 2002: 56)

Alongside informing parents of their child's development during the Foundation Stage, two of the primary uses of the EYFS Profile (DfE, 2013) data are to support a smooth transition to Key Stage 1 by informing the professional dialogue between EYFS and Key Stage 1 teachers and help Year 1 teachers plan an effective, responsive and appropriate curriculum that will meet the needs of all the children. The effect of assessing children at the end of the Reception year, however, accompanied by pressure to achieve good results in the standard attainment tasks (SATs) at the end of Year 2, can mean that Year 1 teachers feel 'sandwiched' between two assessment systems. That is, the Foundation Phase is based on a developmental model that seeks to take account of the whole child. Planning is based on a sound understanding of that development and knowledge of each child's interests, in recognition of the importance of motivation for their learning and nurturing these early learning dispositions. Teachers can be responsive to children's interests and take a flexible approach. Many Year 1 teachers also try to capture these interests in their planning, but there are constraints that mean this is far more challenging to achieve in reality.

One possible reason for learning perhaps being more structured in Year 1 than in the Foundation Stage could be the time allocated to each subject in the National Curriculum. The legacy of the Literacy and Numeracy Strategies is a formalising of learning, with many teachers adopting a literacy hour at the end of the Reception year in order to prepare their children for a new way of working in Year 1 and implementing more teacher-directed learning. Although, in 2001, the then new Government announced that the former strategies and frameworks would no longer apply, many schools still use this approach to the teaching of literacy and numeracy.

The EYFS is based on a model that places the child very much at the centre of their learning rather than being led by programmes of study, but this is more difficult to achieve in Year 1 because the planning and the curriculum direct the learning that takes place. Sometimes, there can be a mismatch between the expectations relating to a task, the expectations relating to the National Curriculum and the developmental level of a child. In these instances, teachers are trying to 'juggle' the provision for those children who are working within the National Curriculum and those who are still very much developing within the Foundation Stage areas of learning.

In addition to this, timetabling the provision over the course of a week can mean that much of the 'flow' throughout the day and opportunities to become absorbed in learning may be missed. Inevitably, in Year 1 there is less of an emphasis on learning outdoors and:

> The transition from choosing to learn inside or out, to interrupt their learning to go outside to play, can be quite strange to children when they first begin school. (Fabian, 2005: 5)

The idea of stopping their learning to go outside to play does not feature in many Reception classrooms, where children have access to a play-based curriculum, both indoors and out. Year 1 practitioners understand the benefits of this, where children learn in an active and collaborative way, but they also feel the pressure of ensuring that children meet reading and writing targets. This has been compounded by the introduction of the 'phonics check' for six-year-olds, conducted in the summer term. Although the government insists that this is not a test, merely an instrument to enable teachers to assess the decoding skills of the pupils, schools are under an obligation to report the results to parents and, as with all standardised testing, children are expected to be at a certain level, regardless of the differing developmental stages they may be at.

The following case study demonstrates some of the issues that might occur with early reading and phonics as children move from home to Reception and then to Year 1.

## CASE STUDY 2

Francesca came to school with a particular view that school was where she was going to learn how to read and write. This view was largely influenced by her parents, who were very keen for her to learn.

Francesca's parents did all that they could to support her, buying toys with the alphabet on and books with the alphabet in. They wrote out letters of the alphabet for her to copy and she spent time playing 'schools' with her younger sister. Once Francesca started school and got to know her teacher, she was keen to demonstrate that she could write her name. She also enjoyed playing 'schools' with her friends and using the whiteboard to 'write' on for the children to copy.

While the Year 1 teacher was pleased Francesca understood that marks have meanings and different letter shapes make different sounds, she was anxious for Francesca to use the sounds of each of the letters rather than their names, as she had been taught to do at home. She also made it clear that Francesca needed to be able to write in lower case rather than upper case, which was something she had seen her parents do at home. Thus, during her phonics lessons each day, Francesca found that she struggled to relate the sounds to the lower-case letters that her teacher was referring to. She did not understand what the 'new to her' letter shapes looked like or how they sounded. This had the effect of knocking her confidence and meant that instead of playing 'schools' during child-initiated time, as she had enjoyed doing previously, she began to play in the role-play area instead. She became reluctant to write during teacher-initiated activities and constantly asked for support with each word that she wrote. Sometimes she copied her friend's work if the teacher and teaching assistant were busy with other children.

## For reflection

- Why did Francesca's confidence decrease?
- What could have been done to prevent Francesca feeling a failure at school?
- How could the situation be remedied?

## Making links between home and school literacy to support transition

Ofsted (2004) acknowledges that the development of the Foundation Stage as a separate phase has highlighted differences between pupils' early experiences. It has also drawn attention to the differences in approaches to teaching and learning taken in the Early Years and the later primary phases, which affect the success of making the transition between them. O'Connor and Angus (2012) see entering into formal learning too soon as being a disruption in children's learning and a play-based environment as more conducive to children's education. In Francesca's case, she enjoyed learning through play and initially felt confident in her ability to write. Her early positive literacy experiences at home were appreciated and built on in the Reception classroom and her growing understanding of the connections between letters and sounds enabled her to enjoy taking on the role of teacher within her friendship group. The change in teacher and pedagogy meant that she no longer felt valued for these abilities and utilising her existing knowledge became too much of a risk to take. It was then easier to only write when she felt that she knew that she was correct.

Since the Rose Review of reading (2006), there has been an increased emphasis on the use of systematic synthetic phonics when teaching early reading (see Chapter 11, 'This is how we teach reading in our school', for a detailed examination of this). Discrete phonics lessons are part of the daily diet of children in the Reception year and throughout Key Stage 1 and, because of the rigid formality of this pedagogy, there is little opportunity to acknowledge the existing experience and understanding children bring to the classroom:

> literacy programmes of this kind push all children along at the same pace and do not consider individual developmental differences. (Whitehead, 2010: 141)

This is evident from the case study above, where Francesca brought a wealth of knowledge and understanding of reading and writing from her home literacy experience, all of which became irrelevant – if not a hindrance – as she fell victim to a 'one size fits all' approach to early reading and writing. By this very early stage of her literacy education, Francesca came to see that it is not worth taking risks and writing as a potentially 'dangerous' activity. Perhaps this could have been avoided if Francesca had been supported in making links between her existing understanding of letters and sounds, reading and writing and the expectations of school.

So far, I have provided one example of a smooth and effective transition from Reception to Year 1 and another showing how children's literacy development can be impeded when this transition process goes awry. The next section looks at particular considerations that need to be explored in order for children's progression in literacy to be supported by safe and effective transition from one stage to another.

## The relevance of the curriculum to children's literacy lives

From a very young age, most children will scribble, make marks and express themselves in their drawings. Anning (2004) alerts us to the importance of encouraging children to draw in their journeys towards becoming literate. She argues that their freedom to express themselves by drawing is then transformed into a more focused view founded on the need to express themselves in the written, symbolic forms. When children are given the opportunity to do this in ways that they choose, they are experimental and continue to express themselves using a range of means. Her argument is that we should value this and capture this flexibility. We should enable children to bring the experiences they have outside of school into school and value this rather than restrict literacy to the '"high status" versions of language and graphicacy associated with learning to read and write' (Anning, 2004: 32).

Kress (1997) argues that multimodality is an essential feature of young children's lives as they combine speech, action, drawing and sound in their activities. By the time they begin school, many (although not all) children will have shared books with parents and carers at home, listened to stories, rhymes and songs and have experienced the joys of picture books, the wealth of information on the Internet and been exposed to films, television programmes and electronic games. When they enter the culture of schooling, much of this experience is not valued. You are not supposed to sing while you draw or move around while you compose stories or use the characters from your favourite electronic game in your storytelling or whistle your favourite television theme tune while you read.

This change is often a feature of learning as it becomes more formalised. If learning is formalised too soon, however, children's natural development can be affected, leading to demotivation and a lack of engagement in school-based activities. During the transition to Year 1, therefore, practitioners need to be aware of what literacy experiences children bring from home and from their time in the Foundation Stage and the more links they can make between these experiences and the requirements of the curriculum, the more successful this transition will be.

## Literacy, play and transition

Play is a complex and highly contentious area of education. There are many differing views and everyone has their own theories and perceptions. There is no doubt, however, that, for young children, it is integrated with their learning experiences. Play is essentially an exploration of a process or an object as the 'player' is attempting to fit the new knowledge into an existing mental framework. Play gives children the opportunity to 'play out' their internal thought processes physically. It allows them to create and influence the process and, ultimately, the end product. Deep intrinsic desire drives the action and an environment that supports the learning of new skills and ideas will nurture early learning dispositions.

Think about how you respond to tasks. If you are told how to do something and asked to replicate it, your motivation will possibly not be as high as it would be for a task that you had initiated yourself, based on a real and driving curiosity to find out more about something. David (1999), states that activities stemming from the child's interests, which, therefore, are intrinsically motivating, are likely to lead to effective learning. Early learning dispositions need to be nurtured so that young children develop flexibility of thought, understand symbolic representation and foster persistence and success. These are all key aspects of being a learner. Young children do not own play, but they play more because more in the world is new to them. This, combined with their innate curiosity, means that they naturally seem to be open to new experiences.

Children in the Foundation Stage have plenty of opportunities to engage in play. Themed role-play areas are a common sight in EYFS classrooms (see Chapter 2, Role-play areas for EYFS (ages zero to five), Key Stage 1 (ages five to seven) and beyond, for more discussion). Although these practices are sometimes seen in Key Stage 1 classrooms, too, there tends to be more of an emphasis on formal learning and less on play-based learning. The following case study describes a role-play area in a Reception class. As you read it, think about the literacy skills that are being developed as the children engage in their role-playing and how these might be extended as children make the transition into Year 1.

## CASE STUDY 3

A group of boys are playing 'building sites' during child-initiated time. One child – The Boss – has assigned roles to the rest of the group who are busy negotiating what their roles entail. Once they have agreed, the 'workers' set to it, using the tools they have collected from the shed. They have spades, forks, soft blocks for bricks, buckets, metre rules and string. They cordon off the area to ensure that the site is 'safe' and a no go area for casual passers by.

The site manager (The Boss) decides that he needs to make a note of what his workers are doing so they can be paid at the end of the day's work. His teacher notices the action that is taking place in the corner of the outside area and goes over to observe. Hearing a conversation between the site manager and one of the workers about whether he is going to help them or not, the teacher asks what his role is in the play. He explains that he is 'in charge' and he needs to check they are doing their work properly.

The teacher, seeing an opportunity, suggests that it may be helpful for him to note down whether the work is being done correctly or not and supports the site manager in recording each of the names of the workers. A laminated sheet of letters is helpful in relating the initial letter sound of each name to its shape (graphical representation). The teacher is careful not to set the level of challenge too high and, noticing the effort required in writing each of the names, sensitively suggests that he tick or put a cross by the names of the workers who need to be paid at the end of the day.

Having a clipboard clearly defines this child as the boss and soon the teacher notices that some of the other children have also gone in search of a clipboard so that they too can participate in this prestigious role.

## For reflection

- In what other ways might the teacher have supported the children with writing during this episode?
- Consider how you set tasks for children. Are they tasks to be done for the teacher or are they 'territories to be explored'?

- Do you see play as something that only very young children should engage in?
- Do you think that Key Stage 1 (five- to seven-year-olds) should incorporate more play-based approaches and how might this enhance their literacy skills?
- Do you consider play to be inseparable from and infused with learning – play is learning and learning is play – or do you see it as a means to an end, such as a way of occupying children until you can spend some 'quality teacher time' with them?

## Building on EYFS literacy practice

Bruce and Spratt (2011: 18) believe that 'literacy has its beginnings in social relationships, movement and the senses, communication and language' and it is clear from the case study above that all of this is going on as the children forge relationships within the role-play area. They move around and use their senses and both oral and written communication to solve problems and respond to their environment.

So how might this excellent Foundation Stage practice be built on in a Year 1 classroom, so that children's literacy development is supported and nurtured to make the transition a smooth one?

Take the first part of the case study as an example, where the children are negotiating roles within the setting and deciding what each role entails. This is the perfect foundation for learning how to work in a group in a collaborative and cooperative manner, as 'children need to learn the ground-rules for group work' (Corden, 1999: 38). Also, group work has the potential to enable young children to 'use talk to aid understanding and enhance critical thinking' (Corden, 1998: 27), but, in order for this to be effective, they need to learn how to negotiate, listen to others, compromise, initiate ideas and become active participants. The very beginnings of all these skills, and many more, can be explored initially via role-play, before the children are introduced to more formalised groupings and roles.

The next element of good practice exemplified in the case study above is the promotion of writing for a purpose. If children realise from an early age that writing is useful and powerful, they are more likely to develop a desire to write competently and effectively:

> The inspiration for writing arises partly from children's perceptions of it as a high-status activity – something that is done by significant people in their social world. (Whitehead, 2010: 173)

Many Year 1 classrooms may still have a role-play area wherein these opportunities to write for genuine reasons and for real audiences can be exploited fully. If this is not the case, however, practitioners need to find suitable times to incorporate similar pedagogies. This can be organised across the curriculum, but, of course, literacy teaching is the natural time to promote writing.

The obvious way to make the transition from writing within role-play areas to writing in a more formal environment is to continue the role-play, but within whole-class and group literacy activities. Exploring characterisation via drama techniques such as hot seating, freeze frames and a conscience corridor can provide children with ideas for their writing and is a continuation of their natural role-play experiences in their Foundation Stage role-play areas.

Writing can also be promoted as one aspect of group work, linking with the ideas for collaborative talk noted earlier. In the case study above, one child had nominated himself as the chief 'writer' as this was a significant aspect of his role and this can be replicated in small group work as the children can take it in turns to be the scribe, while other members of the group take on different roles.

These are just a few ways in which the often observed practices of Foundation Stage classrooms can be continued in later years, thus softening the transition from one year group to the next. Communication between practitioners, creative and innovative literacy planning and teaching and a determination to place the children at the centre of their learning are all vital requirements if we are to provide the best possible opportunities for children to enjoy and succeed in developing their literacy.

## Summary

Fisher (2011) compares the experiences of five-year-olds in Year 1 with five-year-olds still in the Foundation Stage. The children in Year 1 were being offered a teacher-dominated model of practice that included the setting of objectives for a whole class of children, while the teachers of the five-year-olds still in the Foundation Stage were being encouraged to follow the children's own interests and plan for individualised learning based on the uniqueness of each child. This difference between the teaching styles, pedagogy and expectations of these two classes can prove too challenging for many children and may have long-lasting consequences for their development, particularly in relation to literacy because of the way in which this subject is central to so many of the other subjects in the curriculum.

This chapter has identified both good practice in relation to literacy when children make the transition from the Foundation Stage to Year 1 and issues that might arise and have a negative impact on the process by means of several case studies. These highlighted how communication between Reception and Year 1 teachers can enhance the process of transition and developing literacy for young children and how, by continuing to employ what have proven to be excellent practices in the Foundation Stage in later years, we can support children as they move through their primary school lives.

## Further reading

Dunlop, A. and Fabian, H. (2007) *Informing Transitions in the Early Years*. Maidenhead: Open University Press.
This book includes a wealth of perspectives on transitions made during the Early Years from a range of settings and authors.

Fisher, J. (2010) *Moving on to Key Stage 1*. Maidenhead: Open University Press.
This book focuses particularly on the transition between Reception and Key Stage 1 and is written in an easily readable style by a very well-respected author. It contains lots of practical guidance to support transition practice.

Trodd, L. (2013) *Transitions in the Early Years*. London: Sage.
This book focuses on a range of different transitions in children's lives and includes perspectives such as transitions for children with special educational needs and children who have been bereaved.

## References

Alexander, R. (2010) *Children, their World, their Education: Final report and recommendations of the Cambridge primary review*. Abingdon: Routledge.

Anning, A. (2004) 'The role of drawing in young children's journeys towards literacy', *Education 3–13*, 32 (2): 32–8.

Bruce, T. and Spratt, J. (2011) *Essentials of Literacy from 0–7*. London: Sage.

Corden, R. (1998) 'Talking into literacy', *Reading*, 32 (3): 27–31.

Corden, R. (1999) 'Reading and talking into writing', *Education 3–13*, 27 (1): 34–41.

David, T. (1999) *Young Children Learning*. London: Sage.

DfE (2013) *Early Years Foundation Stage Profile Handbook*. Available only online at: www.education.gov.uk/schools/teachingandlearning/assessment/eyfs/a00217599/eyfs-handbook (accessed 18 December 2013).

Fabian, H. (2005) 'Outdoor learning environments: Easing the transition from the Foundation Stage to Key Stage 1', *Education 3–13*, 33 (2): 4–8.

Fisher, J. (2011) 'Building on the Early Years Foundation Stage: Developing good practice for transition into Key Stage 1', *Early Years*, 31 (1): 31–42.

Kress, G.R. (1997) *Before Writing: Rethinking the paths to literacy*. London: Routledge.

Laevers, F. (2000) 'Forward to basics!: Deep-level learning and the experiential approach', *Early Years*, 20 (2): 20–9.

O'Connor, D. and Angus, J. (2012) 'Give them time: An analysis of school readiness in Ireland's early educations system: A Steiner Waldorf perspective', *Education 3–13*, 41 (5): 1–10

Ofsted (2004) *Transition from the Reception Year to Year 1: An evaluation by HMI*. Reference 2221. London: Ofsted.

Rose, J. (2006) *Independent Review of the Teaching of Early Reading*. Nottingham: DfES Publications.

Sanders, D., White, G., Burge, B., Sharp, C., Eames, A., McEune, R. and Grayson, H. (2005) *A Study of the Transition from the Foundation Stage to Key Stage 1*. DfES Research Report SSU/2005/FR/013. Nottingham: DfES.

Whitehead, M. (2010) *Language and Literacy in the Early Years 0–7* (4th edn). London: Sage.

Yeboah, D. (2002) 'Enhancing transition from early childhood phase to primary education: Evidence from the research literature', *Early Years*, 22 (1): 51–68.

# Supporting learners with English as an additional language

## Virginia Bower

---

 **Chapter Objectives**

- to raise awareness of the fundamental role of language in relation to early literacy learning
- to highlight strategies to support children with English as an additional language (EAL) in literacy
- to make links between home and school literacies and how this can help us to support children.

---

## This chapter will cover:

- theories relating to EAL learners, in order to contextualise current practices and provide a theoretical underpinning for the decisions we make when we support children who are learning to learn in a language other than their first
- literacy in the classroom, emphasising the fundamental role of language and how it is not just a means to communicate but also a tool to 'mediate cognition' (Swain et al., 2011: 43)

- the value of classroom routines, including the use of verbal and non-verbal strategies
- classroom layout, grouping and promoting dialogic talk
- links between home and school literacies.

Although it is generally accepted that inner-city schools are likely to have a wider range of ethnic groups and spoken languages than schools in more suburban or rural areas, it is also becoming clear that primary schools outside of these urban settings are increasingly involved with supporting pupils whose first language is not English. Some settings may contain isolated learners who are the only pupils with a particular first language and they will need specific support, socially, academically and linguistically. Other schools may have groups of pupils from certain countries, due to their proximity to military bases or sea ports, for example.

These very different situations require innovative and flexible approaches to the teaching of literacy, to ensure the children are able to engage with the whole curriculum and develop their understanding of English to the point that they are able to learn in this new language. Teachers need to be aware of a range of strategies that might be used in order to ensure the pupils can engage with the key aspects of primary literacy – speaking and listening, reading and writing.

Many would say that language within contexts is the key here and, indeed, the philosophy underpinning this chapter is based on this premise – that we need to move away from looking at individuals in an isolated context and see the necessity for supporting pupils in the social context of the classroom, wherein they can experiment with and be immersed in language – both their first language (L1) and English (L2) – while taking into consideration their home background and existing knowledge and experience.

## Learning English as an additional language

Theories and viewpoints relating to bilingualism and intelligence levels have undergone radical transformation since the mid-twentieth century. Until the 1960s, the general belief was that learning an additional language would have negative effects on intelligence. Research was conducted that indicated bilingual students were at a disadvantage and intellectually confused and bilingualism would adversely affect the brain. From the 1960s onwards, however, opinions began to change. Research began to reflect the idea that being bilingual may induce more positive traits. It was suggested that bilingual learners had a more flexible mental attitude, improved abstract thinking, the ability to adapt to a range of environments and the potential to transfer linguistic skills from one language to another. Since then, bilingual children have been found often to have a 'more highly developed linguistic and social awareness as well as a cognitive and intellectual flexibility' (Gregory and Williams, 2000: 6) exceeding that of monolingual peers. Brain imaging techniques show 'increased activation in the dorsolateral prefrontal cortex (DLPFC), a brain region associated with cognitive skills like attention and inhibition' (Marian and Shook, 2012). Cummins (2001: 4), however, emphasises that L1 still has to be a high priority, not be replaced by L2, stating that 'bilingualism is associated with enhanced linguistic, cognitive and academic development *when both languages are encouraged to develop*' (my emphasis).

When children are learning L2, they will potentially bring to bear all the literacy skills they have learnt for L1, which might include an understanding of how particular texts are read, a range of cueing strategies for reading and an appreciation of the fact that writing can be used to communicate ideas. Children will also bring their existing experience and knowledge of the world to their learning, which, for younger pupils, might be fairly limited, but, for older children, who might be starting a new school as EAL learners, will be quite considerable. Children may not, however, automatically make links between L1 and L2 and may not realise that their existing knowledge and experience of the world can help them in this new setting. It is the role of the teacher to ensure that pedagogies employed within the classroom environment provide opportunities and catalysts to enable the children to make such links between their existing knowledge of L1 and English. That way, the child 'learns to see his native language as one particular system among many, to view phenomena under more general categories, and this leads to awareness of his linguistic operations' (Vygotsky, 1962: 110).

Even if the two languages are not linguistically similar, the learners will still be able to use this existing knowledge. The extent of the effectiveness of this will depend on their level of competence in L1, their attitude to the learning and their own cognitive ability:

> Success in learning a foreign language is contingent on a certain degree of maturity in the native language. The child can transfer to the new language the system of meanings he already possesses in his own. The reverse is also true – a foreign language facilitates mastering the higher forms of the native language. The child learns to see his native language as one particular system among many, to view phenomena under more general categories, and this leads to awareness of his linguistic operations. (Vygotsky, 1962:110)

If bilingual learners have already achieved a degree of proficiency in literacy in L1, they are more likely to be successful literacy learners in L2, as they will have an innate knowledge of grammar and an awareness of the fact that language has a structure, rules, and so on. If the languages are similar, this effect is due more to linguistic similarities between the two than proficiency. Equally, however, if the orthography of the languages being learnt are very different, this can be challenging as far as reading and spelling are concerned. Children need to become 'language detectives' (Cummins,

2001: 20), looking at similarities and differences between the languages, noting connections and discussing their findings with others. This will lead to enrichment and critical language awareness.

Cummins identifies two schools of thought:

- the more time that is spent being immersed in the second language (English) the better
- there needs to be an interdependence, where EAL learners are transferring knowledge and understanding back and forth between L1 and L2, using their experience of language structures, grammar, sentence construction, and so on in their first language and making links where possible with their new learning.

In the latter example, a pupil's first language is seen as an asset and an advantage:

> When bilingualism and biliteracy develop under these additive conditions, children experience demonstrable metalinguistic, academic, and possibly cognitive advantages. (Cummins, 2001: 178)

Kelly (2010: 87) realised with the children in her study (nursery age) that hearing and using their first language was essential for the pupils, not just for comfort and security but also 'to ensure their learning and development would not be restricted by a language that was emerging.'

In some schools, I have witnessed children being reprimanded for using their first language in the classroom, yet its use is permitted in the playground. The irony of this is that, in play, children are more likely to engage in social discourse, wherein they will quickly develop an ability to use L2, yet, in the classroom, with its focus on academic, complex lexis, they are more likely to benefit from some use of L1. There is, of course, the argument that, with the curriculum being delivered in English, then the children need to hear and speak English as much as possible. The other side of this, however, is the need to recognise that the children are in school five days a week, six hours a day, listening to the teacher speaking English and, therefore, particularly with very young children, the need for some respite and the comfort of a conversation in L1 is often crucial to their mental well-being.

This leads on to thinking about language within a context. In this instance, the context is school. Language proficiency and cognitive functioning cannot be separated from the context – they are always culturally and socially situated. For example, the children need to become aware of what is expected in an educational context and learn the language associated with that context. It is not, however, that straightforward.

Within the setting, the children will encounter the language of the playground, where relationships are formed and developed and within which there are social and cultural norms and expectations. For most of each school day, however, they will be immersed in the language of the classroom and will need to develop what Cummins refers to as 'academic language proficiency', defined as 'the language knowledge together with the associated knowledge of the world and metacognitive strategies necessary to function effectively in the discourse domain of the school' (Cummins, 2001: 67). The related idea of 'registers' is also vital – particular groups use certain registers and, again, children need to identify and take command of both the oral and written registers of school. Cummins uses the two terms 'basic interpersonal communication skills' (BICS) and 'cognitive academic language proficiency' (CALP) to describe this dual aspect of learning language in school for our EAL pupils.

BICS are more easily achieved for a number of reasons. First, these skills tend to be developed in collective situations where social conventions and the context of the conversation support understanding. Often additional communicational devices are utilised – facial expressions, hand gestures, posture – and the level of the language used tends to be less complex, presenting less cognitive demand. High-frequency, 'popular' vocabulary is often used and, whereas academic language moves on as we grow older and learn more, conversational skills can be embedded in the Early Years and do not undergo dramatic changes.

CALP is not so easily achieved, however, and proficiency in communication skills (BICS) does not mean that there is automatically academic proficiency as well. As Cummins (2001: 79) states, 'The lexicon used in English conversational interactions is dramatically different from that used in more literate and academic contexts'. Because of this, EAL pupils need to read a lot of written text (with academic language) and talk to peers and teachers about their reading, promoting higher-order thinking skills, thereby engaging with academic language and improving their comprehension of what has been read. We need to be aware that, just because a pupil with English as an additional language appears to be happy and settled, has fitted into the class and made friends and is observed using an appropriate everyday L2 lexicon, this may not mean that he or she has also developed CALP. Our classroom and curriculum language needs to be adjusted accordingly, as does the approach to teaching – using drama, visual prompts, tangible objects, and so on 'to make abstract concepts comprehensible' (Cummins, 2001: 83).

As well as the issue of BICS and CALP, some children will be constrained by what Tabors (1997: 35) describes as the 'double bind', which is when communicative competence and social competence are barriers for children and, because they are inextricably linked, children can have problems. In a study undertaken by Kelly (2010: 71), one of the young EAL pupils found the whole business of school 'an exhausting and demanding business' and he sought respite in listening to audiotapes in his first language.

For all these reasons, it is vital that we use our day-to-day formative assessment to gauge whether children with EAL need support cognitively, linguistically or socially – or, indeed, a combination of some or all of these.

It is also important to consider the ages of the children and their stages of development. As far as learning a language is concerned, there are aspects that are covered early on in life and have a finite learning lifespan, such as the phonological code. For most children, this is 'cracked' in the Early Years and this knowledge can be automatically accessed when it is needed. Lexical knowledge, however, is infinite, as we continue to develop our knowledge and use of vocabulary according to the settings and situations in which we find ourselves.

What are the implications of this for EAL pupils? For children entering school at the age of four or five, with a typical lexicon in L1 for their age, their average English-speaking peers will know around 2000 words (although many children will not yet have this range of vocabulary). As a non-English speaker, therefore, they will be 2000 (English) words behind. If, however, EAL learners enter school in the latter years of primary school, their peers will have a much broader lexicon – for both social and academic purposes – and these can be difficult gaps to breach.

If we look at this from a different angle, although four- or five-year-old EAL pupils would seem to have it easier, having less language to 'catch up' on, they would also have the disadvantages of limited knowledge and understanding of their first language, so would have fewer previous linguistic experiences that they could carry over to learning L2. Older children have a more in-depth knowledge of how language works, grammatical structures, registers, sentence construction and an understanding of the power of language, which could prove useful when tackling the learning of L2.

Classrooms tend to be 'strongly assimilationist and normative', despite 'policy and practitioner discourses of multiculturalism and diversity' (Walters, 2007: 99). Pupils may often be supported to 'fit in' and be like other pupils rather than to help them with language and learning. In this way, primary classrooms may be 'complicit in the reproduction of educational (and therefore social) inequality, in the achievement and underachievement of particular pupil groups' (Walters, 2007: 99). This tends not to be deliberate, but it happens. Our role as primary practitioners is to provide a secure, safe environment where children realise that all languages are valued, while also ensuring that support is given to enable children to make progress in the language of the curriculum.

Hopefully, from this discussion it can be seen that there are many factors to take into consideration with regard to supporting children who have English as an additional language. Their backgrounds, levels of cognitive competence in their first languages, social skills and, of course, the level of support available, will all have an impact on what happens in the classroom. The next section will look at the practical implications of all this.

# Classroom literacy

Kelly (2010: 1) sees literacy as 'a complex human activity rather than a set of skills to be learned'. Within a sociocultural framework, there is the idea of collaborative dialogue, where people are involved in problem-solving and building knowledge and understanding together. Underpinning this is the fundamental role of language and the idea that collaborative talk can 'mediate cognition' (Swain et al., 2011: 43). Swain et al. refer to this as 'languaging' – not just any old talk but talk that is used as a 'cognitive tool to mediate thinking' (Swain et al., 2011: 43). This section will look at the different ways in which classroom literacy practices can promote the use of language so that children can function and learn and enjoy, whether their first language is English or not.

# Daily routines

For all young children, but particularly those for whom English is an additional language, routines are vital as they are predictable and enable learners to anticipate, prepare and participate (Willett, 1995). Even with simple routines such as calling the register, assigning jobs, giving out homework, and so on, children are engaging with literacy as they begin to socialise, develop their oral responses and find an identity for themselves within this 'foreign' domain.

I say 'foreign' because, for many young children, whether they have English as their first or second language, the primary classroom is an alien environment, very different from what they may have encountered previously in their lives. Even for English children, 'school talk' may contrast starkly with the oral traditions they are familiar with at home, so it can be just as strange to them as it is to EAL pupils who are suddenly immersed in a world where their first language is not spoken and the social and cultural traditions are very different. Thus, negotiating the world of school can be daunting for all, but EAL pupils are having to learn not only the new culture of the classroom but also do so via the 'medium of a new language' (Kelly, 2010: 76).

Predictable and familiar routines can provide both a safe and secure environment for all the pupils, at the same time developing early literacy practices without putting pressure on individuals. Below is an example of an early morning routine in a Reception class (of four- and five-year-olds) in which 30 per cent of the children have English as an additional language.

## CASE STUDY 1

It is 8.35 a.m. on a chilly October morning and pupils in Year R, aged four and five, begin drifting into the classroom, most accompanied by one or both of their parents. The class teacher and a bilingual teaching assistant are on hand in case there are any queries or issues and the children put their belongings into plastic boxes, which are clearly labelled in both English and Nepalese.

The children move to their groups where practical, hands-on activities await them. The activities need no explanation as they are either self-explanatory or the children look to each other and begin to imitate their peers. Some children remember to self-register – finding their names on a prepared board and moving them on to an adjacent board.

Ten or fifteen minutes pass, at which point it appears that everyone has arrived. The class teacher switches on a piece of music that is instantly recognised by the children as the signal to tidy up and move on to the carpet. The music is taken from the film *Mission Impossible* and is dynamic so seems to promote activity.

By the time the soundtrack has finished, all the children are expected to be sitting on the carpet and the class teacher calls the register. The children reply in different ways – some say 'Good morning' others say 'Yes Mr D' and the teacher repeats 'Good morning' back to them.

In what ways does this morning routine support the children as developing literacy learners? Having the boxes and equipment labelled with both L1 and L2 enables the children to begin to make connections between languages and realise that the written word – whether English or Nepalese – conveys meaning. If we can develop in children, at an early age, a realisation of the power of the written word and that it can serve a very useful purpose, they are more likely to engage positively with writing tasks and use writing to achieve their own aims. Recognising and selecting their own names for self-registering also promotes the idea of reading and writing for a purpose.

The activities set out at the tables for the children to engage with as soon as they entered the classroom were centred on motor control, such as threading beads, connecting shapes, tracing patterns, and so on. Such activities support literacy development in two key ways: they develop and strengthen hand and finger movements and coordination, which help with future writing tasks; and they encourage talk between peers. According to Corden (2000), children use talk to investigate, hypothesise, question, negotiate, argue, reason, justify, consider, compare, evaluate, confirm, reassure, clarify, select, modify and plan. Much of this could be seen going on during this early morning activity.

When the music began to play, the children were aware of what was expected of them. Even for those children who have very little English as yet, such a signal is clear and no child is disadvantaged. In this way, the class teacher has set up an inclusive atmosphere as, by using non-verbal instructions, all the children are able to understand and be involved. Similarly, when the register was called, all the children were able to engage at their own level of linguistic competence, in a safe and secure environment where language is being modelled and repeated, offering support for their oral language development.

This is just one example of some of the regular classroom routines that can be used to support EAL learners with their literacy and, indeed, all the pupils in the class.

Routines can be developed throughout the school day, which might include access to visual timetables so that children who cannot yet decode text or understand written English can identify the structure of the day or perhaps having a habit of giving bilingual instructions to the children, if you are lucky enough to have someone to support you with this.

## Classroom layout, grouping and promoting dialogic talk

When considering classroom layout, grouping and differentiation, we need to avoid generalisations that do not help us to help the children. By grouping children according to economic status, ethnicity, language, and so on, we are not considering their individual needs (Kelly, 2010: 81). Mobility around the classroom, groupings and seating arrangements can have a considerable impact on literacy learning and the collaboration that is fundamental to this aspect of learning. Teachers' control over this can restrict communication, particularly with regard to children's first language. If children do not have opportunities to practise English or converse in their own language, most of their communication will be with the teacher and this is not the type of speech that is useful to them at their age and stage of learning – they need to hear 'peer talk'. In the current educational climate, with the pressures of testing, results and accountability, it is difficult to escape the emphasis on individualism, with children being advised to work on their own, not copy others, work it out for themselves, and so on, rather than encourage collective thoughts and ideas:

> This individualising of the children starts a process of community stratification which increasingly leads to the exclusion of some students from certain activities, practices, identities and affiliations. (Toohey, 2003: 92–3)

As children begin to grow in confidence and competence with language, early literacy needs to be underpinned by a commitment to the importance of oral communication. Providing opportunities for whole-class, group and paired talk will support all pupils, including those for whom English is an additional language. Teachers need to consider whether their questioning and conversation promote extended utterances from pupils or if it is predominantly a one-way system. If teachers ask questions to which they know the answers, EAL learners are unlikely to respond in any extensive way and are more likely to opt for the safe 'right' answer. Pupils working in peer groups are in a less 'risky' environment and so may engage in longer conversations, depending on the relationships within the group.

At other times, teachers need to promote dialogic talk by working with a group and engaging in what Dyson (1990) and Aukerman (2007) refer to as 'guided participation'. This enables us to support EAL pupils with bringing together what Vygotsky (1962) calls their 'spontaneous' knowledge (gleaned from their knowledge and understanding of the different contexts and environments in their lives) and the 'scientific' concepts of school. If links are not made between what the pupils already know and the knowledge teachers wish to impart, then the children have no 'hooks' on which to hang their new learning and it is soon forgotten. In the past, teachers tended to adopt a *didactic* stance – that is, they transmitted and the children were expected to listen and learn. *Dialogic* teachers instead listen to the needs of the children and, if the children do not appear to understand, they assume that they have not been able to link this new knowledge to the pupils' existing schemas and therefore need to find another way to teach a particular concept. Working with small groups of children allows us to support language learning within a literacy context. Below is an example of how useful this can be.

## CASE STUDY 2

I was working with a group of six eight-year-old pupils, three of whom were Nepali. As a group, we read a poem all about the natural world – animals, weather and seasons – each of us reading a verse. All the children read fluently and with effective expression and, after the reading, all the children agreed that they had really enjoyed the poem.

It was only as I began to ask them more specific questions, however, that I realised some of them had no idea of the meaning of some of the key words in the poems – 'frost', 'speckled', 'freckled', 'stumble' and 'pinpricks', for example. With some of the words, this was the case for both English and Nepali pupils, but all of the English children were familiar with most of the vocabulary.

One particular example of a word for which the Nepali children were unable to make any meaning was the word 'frost'. Now, I found it surprisingly difficult to describe frost in an effective way, so we went to the classroom computers and found images that made it clear. This led to a discussion about the difference between ice and frost and snow and how they feel different to touch.

Abstract words, such as 'pinpricks', were even harder to explain, but we turned the metaphor into a literal example with real pins and sore fingers! 'Freckled' and 'speckled' are, of course, very similar and, by using freckles on a child's face and a picture of a speckled egg, we were able to talk about their meanings. A lively and constructive discussion ensued.

It can be seen from this example that working with a small group, listening to and responding to the particular needs of the pupils and using specific resources to support their linguistic needs can be a very valuable and rewarding experience for all.

With hindsight, I could perhaps have pre-taught some of the vocabulary from the poem in advance, so that the children had a better chance of understanding the nuances of the poem. It could be argued, however, that the constructivist nature of our discussion and activities that emerged from a realisation that not all of the vocabulary was understood led to a joint construction of knowledge and empowerment for all. Links might also have been made to their out-of-school experiences. The following section explores the importance of these links.

# Home and school

This section will explore how links between home and school literacies can be one way in which we can support our pupils with English as an additional language.

One of the key messages here is that, although it is important to have an understanding of the culture and home life of our EAL pupils, it is vital we do not see the inevitable differences as deficits. Indeed, research evidence has found that 'access to contrasting literacies gives children strength, not weakness' (Gregory and Williams, 2000: 203). Gregory and Williams believe that the fact home and school literacy practices might differ considerably is a plus, as long as teachers 'tap into' it. So, how can we 'tap into' home literacy practices and how might this help us to support our EAL pupils in school?

First, we need to find out as much as possible about children's home literacy practices. Here are some questions and ideas you might want to use as an initial exploratory exercise.

- How confident are the children linguistically? It is useful to have an understanding of their ability in L1 as this ability will have an impact on how easily they begin to adapt to L2 learning.
- How have they developed their linguistic and literacy skills so far? Are the parents involved?
- Are the children/families keen to learn English?
- How do the parents view their role in their children's literacy education?
- What does literacy mean to the families?

A better knowledge and understanding of the children's backgrounds can help teachers to support them with their literacy learning. By observing children in their own homes or when interacting with parents, it is possible to ascertain their linguistic competency, even if they are conversing in L1.

One of the schools I work with has 25 per cent Nepali pupils and has developed a number of strategies to forge links between home and school. A parents' evening is held in June for the parents of those children who will be starting school in September and a bilingual teacher is there to translate. Nursery visits take place in early July alongside home visits, the class teachers being accompanied by Nepali teaching assistants, who are able to bridge the language gap. There are also two induction days where the school's family liaison officer talks to the parents alongside a Nepali teaching assistant and the teachers have the children for a short time. All of these events enable the teachers to find out about the children's home literacy and the levels of language they have acquired so far, in both L1 and L2.

It is very useful to have an idea of *how* the children have developed their literacy skills up to this point, too, and the level of engagement of the parents. Below is an example of this from my own practice.

## CASE STUDY 3

Many years ago, I was researching into reading fluency and children's and parents' perceptions of fluency in reading. I interviewed a young child (eight years old) who had English as an additional language (but who could read fluently in L1) and his mother.

On questioning his mother, I found out that this child had refused to speak until he was three years old – something that had worried her considerably at the time, but had not impeded his later cognitive development.

When I spoke to the child, I asked how he had learned to read and he said that he had taught himself, using the family Bible. Somewhat surprised by this, I asked him about his motivation for learning to read and his response was that he wanted to be as good as his older sister, with whom he had a very difficult relationship, and be able to read what she could read (there was a five-year difference in their ages). When I pushed him further regarding who had helped him, he insisted he had been responsible for his own learning (and his mother agreed that this had been the case).

As the term progressed, I noticed that the pupil's English was taking on a significant American 'twang', so I asked him why this might be. He replied that he was teaching himself English by watching *The Simpsons*!

The conversations I was able to have with this child and his mother told me a great deal about him as a learner and his acquisition of literacy. He was clearly determined and self-motivated – a strong-willed, independent learner. My challenge was to support him linguistically (initially his level of English was very limited), while challenging him cognitively. In his own country, this child would undoubtedly have been a high achiever academically, so it was important to ensure that he was able to be equally successful in his second language.

I adopted a number of strategies, particularly in literacy lessons, to try to achieve this. First, I sat him with pupils who had excellent levels of oral language, so that they were able to provide him with strong models for his own speech. Where possible, key vocabulary relating to the literacy topic at the time was pre-taught so that he was able to access the lesson and actively participate. As he grew in confidence, we used the interactive whiteboard, so that he was able to locate (using Google Earth) his home town and show his home country to his peers on a world map. Ultimately, he made a PowerPoint presentation that depicted aspects of his previous life and included examples of his own language alongside the English equivalents.

Initially, writing frames were provided (see Chapter 6, Literacy and diversity, for more discussion on writing frames), with word banks from which to select vocabulary and a bilingual dictionary on hand for his personal use. I tended to have a great deal of guided work going on in my classroom on a day-to-day basis anyway – guided reading, writing, group talk sessions – and I ensured that this child was seated with groups of children who were working at a high level and, when I sat with his group, I tried to encourage exploratory talk, with the children leading the conversations.

All of these strategies that I employed were as a result of my knowledge of this child's background and family life. It was clear that he had a supportive and caring parent, who would provide assistance at home if needed. It was also clear that he was a highly motivated independent learner who was determined to succeed! Despite the initial language barrier, it would have been a mistake to have him sit with English children who had oral language difficulties. Because I was aware that this child was highly motivated to improve his level of spoken and written English and had some understanding of his cognitive ability in L1, I was able to support and challenge him appropriately.

This child was highly motivated and able to effectively syncretise his home and school learning, but for some young children, this is not so easy. So, how do we support children in transferring learning strategies between home and school?

There are two key aspects to consider here. While taking into account and acknowledging children's home experiences, teachers need to provide tools children can use to learn how to fit into 'new functional registers or genres of language', which is important for their school lives and beyond (Cummins, 2001: 75). A balance needs to be found, however, so that children are not alienated from their own home lives, where L1 may dominate, while ensuring they can achieve to the best of their ability in L2. Inevitably, at school, English is the dominant language – certainly as far as curriculum coverage is concerned – but this needs to be carefully monitored to ensure it does not have a negative impact at home with the children's families:

> the schools' right to define what constitutes literacy and their limitation and neglect of home literacies reflect a coercive exercise of power which must be reversed by building on the linguistic and cultural resource of families. (Day, 2002: 23)

Teaching and learning literacy is the perfect place to promote this balance. Here are a few ideas of how this might be attempted.

# Ideas for practice

- Introduce projects where the children are investigating each other's languages and cultures. This might include making dual language books, where parents can be invited in to contribute and support with vocabulary and ideas. Computer programs and the Internet can be used to find images and text to support the making of fiction and non-fiction books.

- Make links between literacy and the children's lives. For example, when teaching non-fiction, it might be possible to write captions or reports focusing on key events within the cultural calendars of different nationalities or, when teaching about procedural texts, utilising recipes that children's parents use at home. When teaching poetry, encouraging children and parents to bring in examples from their own cultures and read them in the original language means that the children can hear the cadence and lyrical patterns even if they cannot understand the words. With narrative, it can be helpful to find familiar stories/fairytales where there is a range of different versions from diverse cultures. For example, there are many different versions of Cinderella (*Cendrillon* by Robert D. San Souci, a Caribbean Cinderella tale, *Abadeha: The Philippine Cinderella* by Myrna J. De La Paz and *Domitila* by Jewell Coburn, a Cinderella tale from the Mexican tradition). Introducing children to this variety enables them to explore different perspectives and recognise that the version they know so well is not necessarily the only or the 'correct' one.

- Although the families might not explicitly support their children with speaking, reading and writing in English (possibly because their own literacy levels in L1, L2 or both are not strong), they can be encouraged to provide comics, books, films, magazines for their children or accompany them on visits to the library. The school could invite parents to attend a library session with the class so that the hurdle of an unfamiliar setting can be overcome.

- Use ICT to support learning. This can be in the form of translation programmes or opportunities to link with other countries and cultures via e-mail or video conferencing. Encourage the children to use digital cameras and video equipment, too, to record their ideas, rather than always having to verbalise or write them down. Perhaps with older children it would be possible to create bilingual podcasts to share with the local community.

## Summary

In my experience, the benefits of having children for whom English is an additional language in the classroom far outweigh the challenges. Because of the potential

*(Continued)*

*(Continued)*

range of languages and cultures, literacy lessons can become opportunities to share insights into unfamiliar and exciting worlds. Speaking and listening take on whole different meanings as children switch between languages and listen out for what is familiar in order to make connections between what they know and what they are learning. Planning, teaching, differentiation, the use of resources – all these need to be addressed in innovative and exciting ways, using verbal and non-verbal language, making us more effective teachers of literacy. Hopefully, too, we can learn from our children – I shall never forget the delighted giggles of my Nepali children who were attempting to teach me their language – and engage in 'collaborative empowerment' (Cummins, 2001: 220), wherein both teachers and children are empowered by the sharing of ideas.

That is not to say, however, there are not challenges in all of this, as we attempt to ensure all the children make progress and enjoy literacy and learning. Without bilingual assistance, the language barrier can be difficult to breach and new and imaginative ways of including children who cannot yet speak the language of the curriculum need to be developed. Often this can include the use of ICT, as described above; drama, whereby the children can communicate in ways other than speech; and the use of tangible resources, such as story sacks (which usually include a text and supporting resources, such as puppets, games, worksheets), artefacts and, of course, high-quality literature (some of which might be available in dual language versions).

Another challenge is the tension between the known benefits of children working collaboratively while engaged in speaking and listening, reading and writing, and the current focus on individual excellence, driven by test results and league tables. We need to hold on to the notion that promoting 'biliteracy' and raising the profile of language in general throughout our schools can only boost children's literacy levels and, while we are devising the best possible ways to support our EAL learners, we are developing better and more innovative ways to further the progress of all our pupils.

## Further reading

Kelly, C. (2010) *Hidden Worlds: Young children learning literacy in multicultural contexts.* Stoke-on-Trent: Trentham Books.

This text explores the lives of six young children in a nursery setting, all from different cultural backgrounds. Kelly examines how the children draw on familiar home practices to help them cope with the new world of literacy learning within the nursery.

Day, E.M. (2002) *Identity and the Young English Language Learner*. Clevedon: Multilingual Matters.

This text focuses on one child and his learning related to language at home and in school. Key themes are discussed including identity, use of language, attitudes of bilingual children and the influence of home.

## References

Aukerman, M. (2007) 'When reading it wrong is getting it right: Shared evaluation pedagogy among struggling fifth grader readers', *Research in the Teaching of English*, 42 (1): 56–103.

Corden, R. (2000) *Literacy and Learning Through Talk: Strategies for the primary classroom*. Buckingham: Open University Press.

Cummins, J. (2001) *Language, Power and Pedagogy*. Clevedon: Multilingual Matters.

Day, E.M. (2002) *Identity and the Young English Language Learner*. Clevedon: Multilingual Matters.

Dyson, A.H. (1990) 'Weaving possibilities: Rethinking metaphors for early literacy development', *The Reading Teacher*, 44 (3): 202–13.

Gregory, E. and Williams, A. (2000) *City Literacies: Learning to read across generations and cultures*. Abingdon: Routledge.

Kelly, C. (2010) *Hidden Worlds*. Stoke-on-Trent: Trentham Books.

Marian, V. and Shook, A. (2012) 'The cognitive benefits of being bilingual', *Cerebrum*, 31 October. Available online at: http://dana.org/news/cerebrum/detail.aspx?id=39638 (accessed 18 December 2013).

Swain, M., Kinnear, P. and Steinman, L. (2011) *Sociocultural Theory in Second Language Education: An introduction through narratives*. Clevedon: Multilingual Matters.

Tabors, P. (1997) *One Child, Two Languages: A guide for preschool educators of children learning English as a second language*. Baltimore, MD: Paul H. Brookes.

Toohey, K. (2003) *Learning English at School: Identity, social relations and classroom practice*. Clevedon: Multilingual Matters.

Vygotsky, L. (1962) *Thought and Language*. Cambridge, MA: MIT Press.

Walters, S. (2007) 'How do you know that he's bright but lazy?: Teachers' assessments of Bangladeshi English as an additional language pupils in two Year Three classrooms', *Oxford Review of Education*, 33 (1): 87–101.

Willett, J. (1995) 'Becoming First Graders in an L2: An ethnographic study of L2 socialization', *Tesol Quarterly*, 29 (3): 473–503.

## Children's literature referred to in the text

De La Paz, Myrna J. (2001) *Abadeha: The Philippine Cinderella*. Walnut Creek, CA: Shen's Books.

Coburn, Jewell (2000) *Domitila: A Cinderella tale from the Mexican tradition*. Walnut Creek, CA: Shen's Books.

San Souci, Robert D. (2002) *Cendrillon: A Caribbean Cinderella*. New York: Aladdin.

# 6

# Literacy and diversity

## Virginia Bower and Verity Hill

 **Chapter Objectives**

- to discuss a range of strategies to support children's diverse learning needs in early literacy
- to emphasise the importance of making literacy real for children and enabling them to make links with their own lives
- to provide practical examples in the form of case studies.

## This chapter will cover:

- making literacy real in non-fiction and fiction
- using literature and film effectively to support diverse needs
- an examination of a range of pedagogical strategies, including the use of paired and group talk, shared reading and writing frames.

A major challenge for all teachers is catering for the diverse learning needs of all the pupils in a class. It is a delight to have planned and taught a lesson where all the children appear to be engaged and enjoying their learning, talking through problems, making progress and feeling a real sense of achievement. Equally, it is demoralising and frustrating (for both teachers and children) if lessons are less successful because the challenge has been too much or not enough. Teachers and children can be very critical of themselves, so it is important to promote instead a reflective attitude to teaching and learning in order to be able to recognise when and why a strategy or activity is effective and when it would have been better to have employed an alternative method.

It is not our intention in this chapter to explore specific literacy-related special educational needs, such as dyslexia. There are many texts that are devoted to these topics and they offer the depth of discussion that this chapter does not have the space to include. While recognising and acknowledging that specific and individualised support may well be needed for pupils with particular educational needs, our aim here is to provide examples of classroom literacy practices that can motivate, inspire and empower *all* our children. This is indeed a high goal to aspire to and, from our own experiences, we are aware that, despite the most rigorous and innovative planning, lessons can sometimes fail to live up to our expectations. What works so well for one group of children can be less successful with others. It is crucial, however, to aim to provide our early learners with the best learning opportunities and we hope that this chapter will offer a range of ideas to help you with this.

Somehow we need to ensure that our literacy teaching and learning is accessible to all the children in the class. Obviously activities will be differentiated and it may well be that children work in their ability groups for some of the time and in mixed ability groups at other times, depending on the nature of the task, and sometimes with support, other times working independently. This would be the case for all areas of the curriculum. This section, however, will focus on specific strategies relating to literacy and how these can help us to support the diverse needs of a class. The strategies are approached using two key themes:

- making literacy real
- using a range of effective pedagogies.

# Making literacy real

This section will look at how we can make links between children's existing knowledge and understanding and their work in school, making literacy learning more real and personal to them and providing support that takes into account their individual needs and interests.

If we are to be successful regarding our aim to engage all children in early literacy, one of the prerequisites is that we know our class really well, enabling us to tap into their existing knowledge and experience when we need to in order to support their learning. If this knowledge is lacking, it is easy to overlook many of the skills children already possess. For example, many children arrive in school with a very good understanding of what reading is all about. They can distinguish road signs and advertising slogans, they have flicked through books and magazines, they play on handheld games and iPads with frightening efficiency and they are beginning to understand that print has meaning. Underestimating what children bring to the classroom gives the message that we are not interested in what is real to them and may result in early disengagement and disinterest. We need to see literacy and the world of school through the children's eyes.

One way in which we can make literacy learning real and relevant for individuals is by choosing reading books that are relevant to their interests. This could be by providing access to non-fiction texts that reflect aspects of the children's lives, such as hobbies, pets, family members, or by selecting books about their particular interests (Bruce and Spratt, 2011). Many children like to read about the natural world and subjects such as volcanoes, hurricanes and earthquakes can encourage them to share their interest and discuss it with others. Making links with popular Internet sites that provide visual images, videos and other accessible resources (even for those who are not yet reading independently) can stimulate children to do further research. Instigating conversations relating to documentaries on the television can be an effective way to get children talking in groups and these programmes can be used as the starting point for a unit of work. The case study below gives an example of how one such film was used with a class of six- and seven-year-olds.

## CASE STUDY 1

The starting point for a non-fiction unit of work for these children was the use of the film trailer for *March of the Penguins* (available online at: www.youtube.com/watch?v=V3k-fkOtTDo). This short film – which is under two minutes long – provides a stunning insight into the world of penguins. The visual and sound effects, along with the superb voiceover, draw you in to this incredible realm and provide a stimulating starting point for discussion, further reading and all kinds of writing.

In this class of six- and seven-year-olds, we used the film to encourage the children to create their own non-fiction film about their school. The children studied the filmmaking techniques used in *March of the Penguins* and thought about the importance of camera angles, sound effects and the voiceover. They needed to consider the potential audience for the film about penguins and how it might differ from the potential audience for their own film and, linked to this, they needed to decide what the purpose of their film was, in order to work out what it needed to include.

Between them the children filmed areas of the school, interviewed teachers, children and parents and put together a short documentary. The literacy processes the children went through were many and varied, including a great deal of discussion, collaboration and cooperation, scriptwriting, research about the school, film directing and editing and reviewing and evaluating. All this from a two-minute starting point.

The children were able to take on roles that best suited their strengths, ensuring that this was a very inclusive activity and the diverse needs of the whole class were met.

It could be argued that this type of text – in the form of a film – does not make literacy 'real' for the children in that penguins are clearly not a part of these children's everyday experience. This type of film is familiar to many children, however, as they may have watched it or similar programmes at home and they can relate to the features of a documentary. Also, it is what *emerges* from this starting point that can make the learning real for the children. Think for a moment about the pedagogies employed during this project.

Initially, the children's interest was captured during the 'shared reading' of the film. Shared reading is often associated with a printed text, but, in the twenty-first century, it is vital to use a range of genres to connect with children's lived experiences and shared reading of a film allows all the children access to the 'text'. The children were then encouraged to explore this particular medium of representation – film – and analyse how, in such a brief clip, the key messages were communicated:

> Communication has always involved a number of modes; multimodal texts were present in the form of the earliest of cave drawings, or the rituals of ancient cultures. (Carrington and Marsh, 2008: 2)

As the project progressed, the children began to think about the audience and purpose associated with the film they were planning to make and the specific skills and resources they would need. Carrington and Marsh (2008: 3) see this as a vital component of children's literacy in the twenty-first century:

> In order to participate successfully in the communication landscapes between 2025–2050, individuals will need to be able to identify appropriate modes for specific purposes and understand the affordances of each mode in order to use or decode them effectively.

A project such as this, where the making of film is not simply a theory but a real practice, effectively supports the diverse needs of a class. Each child can 'play to his or her strengths' and key pedagogies, such as shared and guided reading and writing, drama and role-play and immersion in texts, become embedded within the tasks the children complete.

Making literacy real for children does not necessarily involve the kinds of reality that non-fiction texts present. Linking *fiction* to their own lives can be equally useful as, 'literature makes comprehensible the myriad ways in which human beings meet the infinite possibilities that life offers' (Rosenblatt, 1995: 6). Rosenblatt sees the influence of literature and how it is taught as being of extreme importance to young learners. They are being introduced to social, cultural, historical, philosophical concepts and 'the teacher will exert an influence through the whole framework of ideas and attitudes that he builds up' (Rosenblatt, 1995:19). Benton and Fox (1998) also believe that reading is as much about what the reader brings to the story as what the story does for the reader. Whatever we read has to fit into our existing knowledge and understanding of the world and from this combination we make a meaning that is unique to ourselves. In this way, each child's reading of a text tells us a little about them, both as human beings and readers, and enables us to make connections with what is important to them.

When children encounter a picture book such as *Giraffes Can't Dance* by Giles Andreae and Guy Parker Rees, they bring their own feelings of self-worth to the text. They can empathise with Gerald – the main character – and his seeming inability to dance and they can rejoice with him as he realises that perhaps he is not quite as inadequate as he first believed. Similarly, when they read a text such as *Meerkat Mail* by Emily Gravett, where the main protagonist, Sunny, decides that the grass must be greener on the other side and goes touring the world, only to find that life at home is perhaps not as bad as he thought, children recognise their own desire to explore aspects of the world beyond their own homes and school, while appreciating the 'safe' nature of what is familiar. Picture books typically contain universal themes that children can recognise and relate to, making links to real life through fiction.

The next section will explore the accessibility of picture books and traditional tales in more depth and provides a rationale for how these texts can support the needs of all pupils.

## Use of literature

This is a very broad heading and it would be impossible to discuss all the permutations in this short section. Because of this, we will focus on the value of picture books and traditional tales.

Picture books empower children to be able to 'read' before they can fully decode text. From the illustrations, pupils can uncover the story, share with others and enter a whole new world hitherto unknown to them:

picture books put young children into the role of active readers from the start. (Whitehead, 2012: 130)

Often the words and/or the pictures mean more than is immediately obvious and texts can be accessed at a number of levels. Some picture book authors deliberately leave gaps for the reader to fill – Anthony Browne and John Burningham are two such writers – and the reader needs to learn the 'rules' of reading in these contexts (Meek, 1988). Whether young readers access the text entirely through the pictures and are encouraged to retell the story in their own words or they have developed more sophisticated reading skills that enable them to read on more than one level, the fact is, picture books make literacy accessible to all. Reading and rereading favourite texts also enables children to absorb the cadence and prosody of the writing and have this embedded in their minds for when they begin to write their own stories. Sharing picture books with their peers, teachers and parents promotes the use of relevant vocabulary and usually results in questions being asked and answered, moving children's knowledge and understanding forward.

The picture book market is vast and there are now also picture books suited more to older children, some of which are wordless, and these present new and exciting challenges for readers as they move into the later primary years. Shaun Tan, Jeannie Baker and David Wiesner are three authors whose texts provide such challenges. It is sad to sometimes hear children being told that they are too old for picture books and they should be reading longer and 'wordier' texts. As adults, many of us thoroughly enjoy picture books and look forward to the latest publications from our favourite authors – why, then, should children of all ages not feel the same? Equally, as adults we do not always wish to read texts that stretch our reading ability – often we read because we wish to laugh or switch off or relax after a hard day.

Picture books often allow children to read at different levels because of the layers of meaning. As Whitehead (2010: 129) notes, 'The apparent simplicity of picture books is, paradoxically, the source of the considerable demands they place on the reader.' We feel very strongly that picture books should be accessible to all and they provide a 'way in' to literacy for all children. Indeed, they can be the focal point of a unit of work, particularly if a range of picture books relating to a theme can be accessed and utilised, allowing children to make connections and predictions, engage in depth with their favourites and give them a bank of texts to store for future use (see also Chapter 10, Picture books).

In the same way, traditional tales can be used to make early literacy more accessible for children. This type of literature has a lengthy and strong oral history, making it memorable and distinctive (Tancock, 2011). As mentioned above, children can get usefully caught up in the rhythms and prosody of the language patterns and this can have a positive influence on their own use of language. The universality of the themes that tend to prevail in traditional tales can enable children to make sense of their own lives and feel comforted by the idea of others having felt the same way. This is particularly useful for children from different cultures and those who have English as an additional language. Then, versions of traditional tales that are also familiar in other countries can prove very useful. There are many versions of *Little Red Riding Hood*, for example, including *Lon Po Po* by Ed Young – a story from China – *Pretty Salma* by Niki Daly – a story from Africa – and *Caperucita Roja* illustrated by Tammie Speer Lyon – a bilingual English/Spanish version of this traditional tale (see also Chapter 9, Tales and the oral tradition).

If children are focusing on writing their own versions of traditional tales – a common practice in early literacy – it might prove fruitful to use a strategy that relates this task to their own areas of interest, one of which might be comic strips. Many children read and enjoy comics and they can provide a powerful link between home and school literacies for all ages and abilities. We have found, however, that they are particularly effective for children with special educational needs or who have English as an additional language and those who find literacy – in particular writing – challenging. They are a great 'hook' to motivate the children as they often see drawing as a fun and less pressured activity. The following case study describes how traditional tales and comic strips were combined to support the learning of some six- and seven-year-olds.

## CASE STUDY 2

The unit of work began by reading and then watching the very familiar story of *Cinderella*. This familiarity relaxed the children and made them feel at an advantage from the very start. It was important to remember, however, that for the children who had English as an additional language, it could have been the first time they had heard such a story, although they may well have been familiar with the plot in their own language.

The class then discussed a variety of versions, including pantomime, traditional and Disney, giving the children the opportunity to become even more familiar with the story and providing a chance to talk about their preferences. Following this, we watched, in full, the Disney version.

We then looked more closely at a range of comic strip texts (many of the children had brought their own in from home) and discussed the layouts and how the characters were represented. Different ideas were shared about how the characters from *Cinderella* might be portrayed in a comic.

The children were provided with large pieces of paper on which boxes had already been drawn in the style of a comic strip. They then used these boxes to retell the now very familiar story of *Cinderella* in the form of a comic strip.

> Having produced a comic strip of *this* story, the children were then ready to tackle the next stage – creating their own version of another traditional tale in the form of a comic strip. Within ability groupings, the children orally devised their stories and then divided this into steps. Each step of the story was a readymade picture to go into the comic strip and each child in each group completed one box. The finished comic strips told the whole new traditional tales and the children were delighted with their collaborative efforts.
>
> Each group visited a different year group within the school to share their finished alternative tales.

A number of pedagogies and activities were employed during these lessons that effectively supported the diverse learning needs of the class. Initially, shared reading was utilised – of both printed texts and film – to ensure that all the children had access to the tale. Whole-class discussion followed this, with opportunities for the children to further explore their ideas and experiences, then the children watched the whole film. A film – especially a film in its entirety rather than just a clip – engages the children and supports them with remembering the story (albeit an alternative version) and the narrative structure so they then have an immediate point of reference to refer to as the unit of work progresses. More shared reading followed this, with a more in-depth analysis of the different texts, then the children collaborated within small groups, supported by the teacher (guided work) to produce their comic strips.

To produce a successful comic strip requires a variety of skills – imagination, sequencing, story plotting, character and plot development, to name but a few. This genre provides the children with the comfort of the familiar, but the activity also challenged them to think beyond their experiences. Working collaboratively allowed them to support each other and perhaps achieve more than they might have if they had worked alone. It is good to remember that it is not always necessary for children to produce a complete story independently – indeed, many adults would struggle with this task. It is also good practice, in this world where the visual is dominant, for teachers and children to attempt different modes of representation, not always relying on the written word. This challenges the skills of the more able, provides an opportunity for those who may struggle with writing to shine and enables children who have English as an additional language to access the activity in the same way as the other children.

## Using a range of effective pedagogies

The two case studies above have illustrated aspects of pedagogy that support the diverse learning needs of early literacy learners. This section further explores a range of pedagogies that we deem particularly effective when teaching early literacy. These include the promotion of exploratory talk in paired and group scenarios and the use of writing frames and graphic organisers. The case study that follows illustrates the use of talk, providing the context for the ensuing discussion. The section then finishes with some examples of writing frames and how these resources can support diverse needs in literacy.

## CASE STUDY 3

A class of seven- and eight-year-olds were introduced to the task of reading aloud and performing a poem, then writing their own poems in groups. We chose *Teachers* by Roger Stevens, the subject matter of which we felt would 'hook' the children in from the very start as they are always keen to find out more about us!

The poem was displayed on the interactive whiteboard for shared reading, so that those who were confident readers could read along, those less confident were supported and those who struggled with reading/English were able to follow the poem without feeling too much pressure.

The children then read through the poem with their talk partners and were asked to find any traits within the poem that their own teachers (past or present) also had. Next, the children worked in groups to act out a pre-segmented section of the poem.

The end product was for the children to be filmed performing the poem and watch the performances given by the other children. The opportunity to be film stars was fine motivation indeed. To prepare for the performances, the children were put into mixed ability groups.

Performing the poem and hearing the language being repeated by different groups provided support for the next task, shared writing. The children chose a teacher within the school to write a class poem about. They talked in pairs to come up with some words and phrases to describe the teacher. As a class, we then discussed what would/would not work and, using the original as our model, we wrote our poem. Mistakes or necessary changes were discussed and many edits were made during this shared writing time. The children then worked in the same groups as they did when performing the poem, to put together a poem of their own. The use of mini whiteboards was encouraged as children enjoy the security of writing on something that can be immediately erased if they deem it to be of inferior quality. Two of the groups were 'guided' by the class teacher and the teaching assistant, supporting the children with ideas and ensuring that issues with transcription and spelling did not inhibit their engagement and use of language.

The poems that emerged from this guided work were original and personal to the children. They felt a growing confidence in their ability to produce poems and were keen to share them with their peers. The poems were put together into a class anthology entitled 'Our teachers'.

This case study shows a range of strategies being employed to ensure that all the children were able to participate in and enjoy the activities. These activities included a great deal of talk, the use of shared and guided reading and writing and performance drama. One of these pedagogies – the use of paired and group talk – will now be explored in more depth.

## Talk partners and group talk

A small study of teacher–pupil discourse during an hour-long literacy lesson showed that the longest utterances were made by the teacher, with only two per cent of pupil utterances exceeding ten words and 90 per cent of those being no longer than five words. For children with special educational needs (SEN), nearly 90 per cent of their utterances were of one to three words and their oral contributions were far fewer than those of their peers (Lee and Eke, 2004). Although whole-class discussions can be useful, particularly when combined with a shared reading exercise, children also need further opportunities to talk about and share their own experiences.

Whole-class talk often promotes a specific pattern – that of initiation, response, feedback (IRF) – in which the teacher asks a question, one child responds and the teacher then feeds back, often with the words 'Yes, well done' or 'That's not quite what I am looking for'. Unfortunately, this sequence of IRF tends to lead to the children trying to read the mind of the teacher, to give the 'correct' answer. A more useful strategy to promote is what Mercer (2000: 1) refers to as 'interthinking', where children work together, using language to help their thought processes and 'collectively making sense of experience and solving problems'. Interthinking avoids the children searching for 'correct' answers and allows children of all abilities to contribute to the discussion.

Interthinking can be promoted in a number of ways:

- talk partners and group talk
- reporting to the class
- show and tell
- guided reading and writing
- reading conferences
- buddy talk/reading
- storytelling.

In the case study above, the children had the opportunity to explore their ideas with partners and in small groups. In this particular context, the children were encouraged to share their ideas with a partner, relating the character traits of teachers they had encountered. They were given time to discuss and encouraged to feed back what had been said.

If children are working with just one partner, the teacher needs to think carefully about the arrangement of such pairings. Sometimes it might be useful to initiate mixed ability pairings, so that the children can support each other. Often, children who struggle with writing down their ideas are very good at expressing their thoughts orally, so this is a real chance for them to excel. It might be that a child who is more confident with writing can make notes on the discussion and use these to feed back what they have been doing to a larger audience. At other times, the children could be put into similar ability pairs and the starting points for discussion could then be differentiated according to the needs of those pairings.

After paired discussion, the children in the case study above worked in groups to prepare a performance. Corden (2000) suggests a range of strategies that can be used to support pupils during group work and try to instigate more extended conversations. He advises teachers to use questions that are thought-provoking rather than questions requiring factual recall as a starting point for discussion. This also encourages children to 'question, probe, and seek clarification and elaboration' (Corden, 2000).

Corden also believes that, in order for group work to be effective, children need to see the teacher in a non-evaluative role, leaving them free to explore their ideas without fear of judgment. If this is the case, however, how are we to ensure that all members of the group are involved and engaging in productive talk and we are addressing the diverse needs of the class?

One way to encourage interaction is to assign roles to the members of the groups. So, if there are six children in a group, one can ensure that the group does not stray too far from the topic, two can be listeners who will later feed back what is discussed to the class, while the other three can engage in the discussion and be prepared to offer their opinions and ask questions. These roles can be assigned by the teacher, thereby achieving differentiation according to the needs of the members of each group. As each new topic is introduced, the roles can be swapped around.

It is important to think about the mix in each of the groups so that they are effective. Too many strong characters in a group may result in disputes and disruption. Equally, too many placid children may mean a lacklustre session, with the children becoming disinterested in the task.

The careful placement of the teaching assistant (TA) is also crucial here. The TA needs to support a group, the members of which will benefit from targeted inputs. In relation to the case study above, where the activity was performance of poetry, this would not automatically mean supporting those who struggle with the mechanics of literacy, as written literacy was not required for that task. Indeed, allowing the child or children who are usually heavily supported by the TA or class teacher to have freedom away from them is a great way of boosting their confidence. Children with special educational needs or who have English as an additional language often thrive in these situations as they feel liberated from the constraints of writing and enjoy the fun of the collaborative work with their peers.

In the case study above, the children engaged with shared writing before writing their own poems independently. One way in which differentiated support can be offered when children are writing is to introduce writing frames. The next section explores this particular pedagogy and offers some examples.

# Writing frames

For many children, getting their ideas on to paper in the form of the written word is a considerable challenge. Others take great delight in completing all writing tasks and having something tangible to show for their efforts. Some children excel at writing stories and poems, yet struggle when it comes to non-fiction and vice versa. It is vital, therefore, to have a range of strategies available to support all these varying needs of our young writers. Thus, this section will focus on how writing frames can be used to scaffold children's non-fiction writing.

Writing frames offer children a structure for their non-fiction and/or their fiction writing and remove the often seemingly insurmountable barrier of the blank page. They usually include keywords or pictures or symbols to prompt the writer and indicate the sequence that is appropriate for the genre. It is very important that, before using writing frames, children have plenty of opportunities to engage with authentic non-fiction texts so they are able to absorb the features of the different genres. For example, if the genre under study is procedural/instruction texts, then the children could be asked to bring in examples from home, which might include recipes, instructions for putting furniture together, electronic game instructions, booklets relating to television remote controls, and so on. It is much more effective if the children collect these themselves as then they will be using texts that are real and relevant to them.

Once the authentic texts have been read, shared and discussed, the teacher needs to model how the children might produce a similar text themselves. Talking through the steps and allowing the children to observe how ideas are considered, written down, edited, removed, replaced, and so on gives them a true representation of the complexity of the writing process and the confidence to have a go themselves. For some, however, this will still be a daunting task and that is when writing frames can be very useful. Figures 6.1, 6.2 and 6.3 show three examples of writing frames for non-fiction that provide varying degrees of support.

Writing frame 1 (see Figure 6.1) provides a considerable amount of support for a child undertaking this task. It could be added to by including a word bank of the vocabulary that the children will need to complete their instructions for washing your hands. This writing frame provides an opportunity for very young children and emerging writers to draw or write the items that they will need in the boxes and then use the scaffolding of the 'dashes' to enable them to locate the appropriate vocabulary.

Although this may seem to offer a great deal of support, some children will make considerable gains in confidence from being able to finish the task and have their own set of instructions to publish in their books or on display. This will raise their self-esteem and hopefully also give them confidence with a later writing task (Wray and Lewis, 1997). The next time they tackle a similar task, the writing frame would need to offer a little less support to ensure that the child makes progress towards independence.

| Instructions for washing your hands |
|---|
| You will need: |
| |
| |
| |
| |
| First, turn on the  - - -. |
| Next, put both  - - - - -  under the tap and rub them together. |
| After this, put  - - - -  on your hands and rub them together again to make a lather. |
| Now rinse your  - - - - - , making sure all the soap has been removed. |
| Finally,  - - -  your hands using a towel. |

**Figure 6.1**  *Writing frame 1*

Writing frame 2 (see Figure 6.2) provides a structure and some initial ideas to get the children thinking about what a persuasive advertisement needs to contain. With any type of writing frame, it is important to emphasise to the children that it is only a guide to get them started and they should feel free to adapt and make changes to suit their own ideas.

With this writing task, the children may want to make it a multimodal text, using images and colour and, if the ICT resources are available, maybe even sound. They may still use the writing frame as a guide, but it is hoped that they will go far beyond the prescribed structure.

**An advertisement to persuade people to visit a theme park**

Listen up everybody! You need to come and visit ............................................................................

We have many fabulous rides, including ..............................................................................

The cost is ...............................................................................................................

You can find us easily by going .......................................................................................

Don't wait too long ......................................................................................................

**Figure 6.2**  *Writing frame 2*

Writing frame 3 (see Figure 6.3) provides minimal support for writing a recount of an event and would perhaps be used with more confident writers. Again, it gives children a structure and some keywords, but they will need to be made aware that they can still move away from these starting points for each paragraph because each of their experiences of the sports day will be different.

---

**Writing a recount of our school sports day**

Yesterday ...................................................................................................................................

The first race ...............................................................................................................................

By the end of the afternoon .......................................................................................................

Next year .....................................................................................................................................

---

**Figure 6.3**  *Writing frame 3*

From these three examples it can be seen that children can be provided with differentiated support for their writing of non-fiction by making use of writing frames. It must be remembered, however, that constant formative assessment is needed to ensure that the approach to the use of writing frames is flexible and responds to the individual needs of the pupils. The ultimate aim is to encourage the children to write without a frame and promote the creation of innovative and original texts. Before they can do this, though, they need to be confident with the structure, features and necessary vocabulary, and writing frames can help with this.

## Summary

It is hoped that we have been able to suggest useful ways in which the diverse needs of children might be met in early literacy. Here are summaries of the key messages that we wished to pass on.

Get to know all the children – understand what makes them tick. This cannot be done in a day, but, over the course of the first few weeks with a new class, you will begin to see them as individuals and this is vital to your thinking through what will

*(Continued)*

*(Continued)*

work for each child to help them with their literacy. It should also be the fun part of teaching and the most rewarding. Small group work is the ideal time to get to know them, as children are much more relaxed in this working situation. Also, breaktimes, 'Golden Time' or while they are waiting for parents at home time provide ideal opportunities to chat with them.

Make the children feel valued and show them that you are interested. A high-ability child in one of our classes went to pieces whenever she felt that she was under pressure. In passing, the teacher confessed to her her love of the *Great British Bake Off* programme and 'all things cake'. It turned out that the child also loved this programme and an immediate bond was formed. Literacy tasks could then be related to the programme and tests were no longer tests but technical challenges. Work in class then included home baking, and assemblies were real showstoppers! Such small things really can make a huge difference.

Familiarise yourself with the home backgrounds of the children so that you are able to link literacy topics with aspects of the children's lives – making it real for them. This might include an awareness of religious festivals, an understanding of the types of literacy 'events' the children might be engaging with at home and a recognition of the degrees of support the children might be receiving in their out-of-school lives.

Make sure that you and the TA 'share' yourselves among the children. Rotate the groups so that one day you are working with the more able, another day the less able, and so on. Every child deserves to work with a range of adults.

Finally, find that 'hook' – something to draw the children in so they are excited and motivated. Find something they can relate to their own lives and experiences or something they can do to create an end product that makes them feel proud and literacy lessons real events in their school lives.

## Further reading

Bower, V. (2011) *Creative Ways to Teach Literacy*. London: Sage.

This text examines the three central genres explored in primary schools – fiction, non-fiction and poetry – and provides a range of ideas to promote creative teaching and learning. If we can be more creative with our approaches, we are more likely to engage and motivate all our young literacy learners.

Grainger, T., Goouch, K. and Lambirth, A. (2004) *Creative Activities for Plot, Character and Setting*. Leamington Spa: Scholastic.

There are three texts in this series – for five- to seven-year-olds, seven- to nine-year-olds and nine- to eleven-year-olds. They are very practical books that provide excellent ideas for activities to support children's writing of fiction.

# References

Benton, M. and Fox, G. (1988) *Teaching Literature: Nine to fourteen*. Buckingham: Open University Press.

Bruce, T. and Spratt, J. (2011) *Essentials of Literacy from 0–7*. London: Sage.

Carrington, V. and Marsh, J. (2008) *Forms of Literacy* Futurelab and DCSF. Available online at: www.beyondcurrenthorizons.org.uk/forms-of-literacy (accessed 18 December 2013).

Corden, R. (2000) *Literacy and Learning Through Talk*. Buckingham: Open University Press.

Lee, J. and Eke, R. (2004) 'The NLS and pupils with special educational needs', *Journal of Research in Special Educational Needs*, 4 (1): 50–7.

Meek, M. (1988) *How Texts Teach What Readers Learn*. Stroud: Thimble Press.

Mercer, N. (2000) *Words and Minds*. Abingdon: Routledge.

Rosenblatt, L.M. (1995) *Literature as Exploration*. New York: The Modern Language Association of America.

Tancock, C. (2011) 'An exploration of traditional tales', in V. Bower (ed.), *Creative Ways to Teach Literacy*. London: Sage. pp. 12–22.

Whitehead, M. (2010) *Language and Literacy in the Early Years 0–7* (4th edn). London: Sage.

Wray, D. and Lewis, M. (1997) *Extending Literacy: Children reading and writing non-fiction*. London: Routledge.

# Children's literature referred to in the text

Andreae, Giles and Rees, Giles Parker (2001) *Giraffes Can't Dance*. London: Orchard Books.

Daly, Niki (2008) *Pretty Salma*. London: Frances Lincoln.

Gravett, Emily (2007) *Meerkat Mail*. London: Macmillan.

Speer Lyon, Tammie (2005) *Little Red Riding Hood/Caperucita Roja*. Greensboro, NC: School Specialty Publishing.

Stevens, Roger (2007) 'Teachers', in *The Truth about Teachers*. London: Macmillan.

Young, Ed (1989) *Lon Po Po*. New York: Philomel Books.

# Recommended authors of children's books

Jeannie Baker
Anthony Browne
John Burningham
Shaun Tan
David Wiesner

# Part 3
# Promoting language

# 7

# Diverse approaches to language development

Tracy Parvin

## Chapter Objectives

- to explore theory and pedagogy associated with language development
- to identify the importance of the home environment for language development
- to use case studies to demonstrate how pedagogy can differ from setting to setting.

## This chapter will cover:

- how children develop their communication and language skills
- the importance of early home experiences in relation to children's later development of literacy skills
- two case studies, in which the schools implement two very different approaches to language development.

It could be said that promoting language development is one of the key aspects of our role as practitioners working with children, whatever their age. Literacy and language are inextricably linked and early literacy needs to promote an awareness of the power of language as children learn in social contexts:

> Literacy has its beginnings in social relationships, movement and the senses, communication and language. (Bruce and Spratt, 2011: 18)

Being able to utilise language effectively in different contexts – whether through sign language, oral language or written communication – empowers children and adults and enables them to socialise, learn, reflect, develop rational opinions and arguments, discuss, improvise, negotiate and feel that they have interesting and useful things to say. Best practice in Early Years settings involves providing young children with safe and stimulating environments that promote interaction and communication; places where well-informed adults offer themselves as excellent role models who use language effectively and are aware of the importance of supporting children in their language development so they are able to take their rightful place in the world.

This chapter will look at different theories and pedagogies associated with language development and the importance of this process in ensuring that children acquire the ability to communicate their ideas in a range of forms. Two case studies of schools will be utilised to exemplify how two Early Years Foundation Stage settings approach language development, using very different strategies, to encourage speaking and listening skills. Where one school offers a highly structured programme that is delivered out of the classroom context, the other adopts a social constructivist approach, where the children's language explorations are encouraged through role-play and drama and are intrinsically embedded within classroom practice. Discussions will follow the case studies, exploring the implications of these two different approaches. Within these discussions, the themes of home and school literacy and language, the importance of parental involvement, embedded practices and knowledge of child development will be explored.

# The development of language and communication

Language development begins when babies are still in the womb. Research indicates that, during the later stages of pregnancy, a baby is able to distinguish its mother's voice and, once the baby is born, a communication system develops between mother and child and 'the internalisation of these early interactions provides a prototype for later relationships' (Hamer, 2012: 15). Hamer also describes the idea of 'contingency', whereby adults and young children interact 'back and forth' with gestures, babbling, facial expressions and repetition of words and phrases, all of which shape 'the architecture of the developing brain'. Contingency refers specifically to the degree that these communication exchanges are reciprocal and responsive.

Babies and young children also begin to learn the 'rules' of communication in such exchanges – turn taking, eye contact, the expectation of a response, and so on – and of course these are commonly explored and established through games, sharing rhymes and songs, asking questions and communicative exchanges during daily routines such as meal times and bath times.

Often, although not the case for all, young children will follow a pattern in their language development as follows:

- 0–3 months – 'cooing' and increasing responses to familiar carers
- from 3 months – 'babbling', when babies repeat sounds over and over
- 9–12 months – gestures such as waving, clapping, even 'high fives'
- 12 months – strings of babble and single words – these single words 'appear to have the import of full sentences, and linguists refer to them as holophrases' (Whitehead, 2010: 58), as well as more focused actions, such as pointing
- 2–4 years – children begin to develop their use of grammar, with typical 'errors of generalisation in plurals and tenses' (Whitehead, 2010: 61), and there is a rapid growth of vocabulary, with questions being a key aspect of this, as children use their newly acquired vocabulary – 'who', 'what', 'why' and 'when' – and experiment with word order and language that expresses cause and effect, chronology and sequencing.

By the age of four:

> most children can ask questions, give commands, report real events, and create stories about imaginary ones – using correct word order and grammatical markers most of the time. In fact, it is generally accepted that by age four, children have mastered the basic structures of the language or languages spoken to them in these early years. Three- and four-year-olds continue to learn vocabulary at the rate of several words a day. They begin to acquire less frequent and more complex linguistic structures such as passives and relative clauses. (Lightbown and Spada, 2006: 7–8)

So, what are the factors that contribute to this incredible ability of young children to develop language so they are able to communicate and interact, use language as a tool and comment on the world they inhabit? One of the key factors is children's interactions with the adults around them. Early language development relies very much on carers responding sensitively to their young children. This begins with 'motherese', which is 'characterised by a higher-pitched intonation, shortened or simplified vocabulary, shortened sentences and exaggerated vocalisations or expressions. As babies' communicative abilities develop, the complexity and amount of their mothers' speech increases, so extending the child's communication' (Hamer, 2012: 17). High-quality, frequent interactions between carers and young children are needed to promote language development. This is particularly successful if children are allowed to lead the way with the communication and carers respond and build on what has been said.

Language development also relies on children being able to use particular language in different settings with different people. As they socialise with their peers and adults, they begin to realise that different tones, registers and lexis are needed for particular situations and so they each start to find their own voice in these encounters. More and more, they realise the power of language and what it can do for them:

> Language supports children's cognitive development by providing them with a tool to make discoveries and make sense of new experiences and offering them a means of making connections between the new and what is already known. (Browne, 2009: 4)

Another key factor in language development is children's early experience of stories – being read to and gradually becoming confident readers themselves. The next section explores these links between reading and language development.

## Reading and language development

As well as conversational interaction, the sharing of books from a young age has been seen to have a positive impact on children's language development. Trivette et al. (2010) undertook a study to examine the characteristics of experiences of reading books (adults and children reading together), how these contribute to children's language development and how particular variables influence the level of effectiveness of these reading events. They identified 11 characteristics of these interactions – in relation to the contributions of adults – and these are useful to examine when we consider our own experiences of reading with children and how they can have a significant impact on their language development. The characteristics are:

- *attention getting* where adults might point out particular aspects of the story
- *labelling* actions, objects, settings, characters are identified
- *commenting* general discussion about the text
- *imitation* adults repeat what the children have said to reinforce, clarify or confirm
- *relating to the children's experience* making connections between an aspect of the book and things that the children might have experienced in their lives
- *correction* responding to children's misunderstandings – for example, a child might say, 'Look, a horse' and the adult would say, 'It's a unicorn'
- *positive feedback* reacting and responding to children's comments and questions positively
- *open-ended questions* ensuring that questions go beyond simply eliciting one-word answers from children
- *expansions* promoting exploratory talk in order to move the children's thinking forward and encourage the use of new vocabulary to articulate those thoughts

- *following up with questions* rather than leaving children's ideas 'hanging', the adults ask questions that encourage the children to expand on their original ideas
- *following the children's interests* the adults allow the children to lead the reading session, which might involve the book being read in a non-sequential way, pages being missed out, other pages being pored over and discussed.

The potential richness of this type of reading interaction between adults and children cannot be underestimated.

Within the early learning goals in the Statutory Framework for the Early Years Foundation Stage, one of the prime areas is, of course, 'communication and language'. The requirements in this area are:

**Listening and attention**: children listen attentively in a range of situations. They listen to stories, accurately anticipating key events and respond to what they hear with relevant comments, questions or actions. They give their attention to what others say and respond appropriately, while engaged in another activity.

**Understanding**: children follow instructions involving several ideas or actions. They answer 'how' and 'why' questions about their experiences and in response to stories or events.

**Speaking**: children express themselves effectively, showing awareness of listeners' needs. They use past, present and future forms accurately when talking about events that have happened or are to happen in the future. They develop their own narratives and explanations by connecting ideas or events. (DfE, 2012: 7–8)

If the 11 characteristics of high-quality interaction during reading events between adults and children highlighted above by Trivette et al. (2010) are recognised and promoted, children should be able to reach and then go far beyond the requirements of these listening, understanding and speaking goals.

Trivette et al.'s research also found that when children and adults engage actively together with texts, this promotes children's early expressive language – 'spontaneous verbalisations' and the use of expressive vocabulary – and children are more likely to participate actively when connections are made with their own lives. They also found that, if children received positive feedback relating to comments they made and were encouraged to follow their own thoughts and interests, it was more likely that there would be a positive impact on the children's language development.

So, as children move into educational settings, it is important to build on the existing experiences they may have had, but also be aware that some young children may not have had such opportunities to develop relationships where reciprocal communicative activities are part of the daily routine and may not have had books read to them or had the chance to discover the joys of flicking through picture books themselves.

The two case studies below describe how two schools support children with their language development using two very different approaches. Both settings are

Early Years classrooms. As you read the first case study, consider the practices and pedagogies being employed and think about how these relate to language development. The discussion following the case study will examine the approach taken in more depth.

## CASE STUDY 1

School X is larger than the average-sized primary school, with 374 children on roll. It nestles in the middle of a large mixed estate and serves pupils from the local community. The proportion of pupils who are known to be eligible for free school meals is higher than usual and there is an above average percentage of disabled pupils and those who have a wide range of special educational needs.

The EYFS classroom is filled with evidence of children's engagement with their learning, with child-made labels very evident on the displays. There is a book area with comfy seating and a wide range of books that have been chosen to appeal to the tastes of all readers. A puppet theatre sits in one corner, a listening station with many audio stories in another. There is a wooden box of clothing, hats and masks near the role-play area, which, at the time of the visit, represented a North American Native Indian tepee. In the outside area there is a beautiful living willow that has been woven into the shape of a tepee. It offers a serene and shady spot in which the children can 'play'.

Judith, the Deputy Headteacher and coordinator of teaching and learning in the EYFS, focuses her initial attentions on developing children's communication and oral literacy skills. Throughout her time at the school, Judith has noticed that the children come into school with very little knowledge of fairy and traditional tales or rhymes and ditties. As a result, the school day is punctuated with the regular reading and telling of stories and nursery rhymes. The children draw on these in their child-initiated time, using the puppet theatre and role-play area to re-enact what they have heard. As the children are also immersed in exploring North American Native Indian cultures and stories, these, too, have become a part of their repertoire.

The children's interest in the North American Native Indians' culture was fuelled by the reading of a storybook entitled *The Garden* by Dyan Sheldon. Following the reading, Judith was bombarded with questions from the children. Keen to respond to their curiosity and nurture and develop their understanding, she encouraged them to write down their questions. These were then displayed and became the starting point for their research.

# Developing the language-conscious environment

The practitioner in the case study above was clearly keen to develop and extend the children's literacy experiences via the environment she created for them. This is good practice as immersing children in stories and rhymes encourages them to not only pick up on the cadences of rhythm, rhymes and patterns of poems and story language, but also gives them the opportunity to engage in narrative structures and sequences. Indeed, Whitehead (2002, 2010) highlights the importance of storytelling and story reading activities, as narratives help children to gain a sense of the sequences of events, a sense of place and time and develops their knowledge of the words that hold all of these together. By listening to a wide range of stories, such as fairy tales, with distinct structures and patterns, the children are developing their ability to anticipate and predict (see Chapter 9, Tales and the oral tradition, for a more in-depth discussion of the importance of fairy tales for children's language development).

With the teacher then initiating focused conversations promoting an exploration of the sequences and characters in the stories, the potential for children to engage in active meaning making was enhanced (Riley, 2007). Rather than allowing the children to be passive listeners in relation to these narrative forms, they became involved in discussions and were then actively encouraged to participate in a co-construction of the stories via role-play and drama (Cremin, 2009). The dialogic nature of such discussions provides teachers with opportunities to support the children's language development, building on what they already know and what they bring from their home experiences:

> The focus is on students' growing understanding – growing knowing – as they bring their current experience-based knowing to bear on school-sanctioned contexts and ideas such as literature provides and engage in literate discourse practices. (Boyd and Markarian, 2011: 519)

The role-play area in Judith's class offers the children time to not only articulate their understanding of the action of the stories but also create their own versions of the characters, extending their understanding of how to use language in particular ways and for specific purposes. She encourages them to explore possibilities and potential:

> When we talk about the stories, I do sometimes ask the children what could happen if, for instance, Jack's mother had climbed the beanstalk instead. I do want them to play with possibilities. There are children who want to stick rigidly to the 'script' of the story, but one day I overheard Martha saying: 'My Cinderella is not going to do the cleaning'. It was fascinating to watch how the other children with her then reacted to this. At first, they didn't really like it; they couldn't see how the story would work. In the end, they decided that they would all do the cleaning together and talked about the dresses they would wear to the ball.

The offer of an alternative story made in the form of suggestions by the teacher and the role-play area becoming a space where these newly created stories might be explored open up all sorts of possibilities to the children. For Martha and her play-mates, the new version needed to be negotiated, considered and agreed on. In this and other ways, Judith has created an enabling environment that allows for such interactive explorations.

Shared reading clearly plays a central role in Judith's Early Years classroom. This is significant, as a key aspect of children's increasing metalinguistic awareness is related to learning to read:

> Seeing words represented by letters and other symbols on a page leads children to a new understanding that language has form as well as meaning. Reading reinforces the understanding that a 'word' is separate from the thing it represents. (Lightbown and Spada, 2006: 8)

Children begin to realise that words can have many meanings and can therefore be played with and manipulated to achieve certain ends. Children's rate of vocabulary acquisition accelerates as they enter the school setting. Inevitably, they will continue to encounter social language, but they will also have to negotiate the language of school. This will be in the form of oral language – questions and discussions with practitioners and peers – but also result from their access to texts. Research indicates that the increase in children's vocabulary is linked with the amount and types of reading they do. Different genres utilise particular types of language and children soon begin to recognise the styles, tones and registers to be found in different text types.

Referring back to the discussion earlier in this chapter, positive influences on children's language development include close interactions with texts, with adults and children reading, talking, questioning, exploring and making connections with their existing experiences and interests. As children explore a range of texts, they are developing both local and global coherence (Cain, 2010). Local coherence is where the reader gains meaning from a text by making connections between the words and sentences on the page. Global coherence is being able to see how the sentences fit into the bigger scheme of things, which might involve retrieving information from previous experiences and knowledge and understanding from other areas of our lives.

In the case study, we saw how Judith's classroom practices facilitate this by being designed to provide the children with opportunities to enrich their life experiences so that they are able to go beyond local coherence and be enabled to gain more than just a surface understanding of written language. She brings other countries, cultures and communities into the setting in physical forms – different outfits, puppets and masks, a tepee, relevant texts – and also in the pedagogies she employs – immersion in texts, drama and role-play and questioning and discussion. Sylva et al. (2004: 1) believe that 'Effective pedagogy includes … the provision of instructive learning environments and "sustained shared thinking" to extend children's learning'. Judith's classroom is designed to support such shared thinking and thereby promote early language and literacy development.

The next case study describes a very different approach to language development and offers another perspective to be analysed. Rather than focusing on one particular age group, the case study describes interventions that are part of day-to-day practice across the whole school as the interventions are for those children who it is considered need support with language and communication, whatever their age.

---

## CASE STUDY 2

School Y is a larger than average primary school. It opened in September 2007, following the amalgamation of separate infant and junior schools on adjacent sites. The school sits in the middle of a large estate that is a recognised area of social deprivation. As a result, the proportion of pupils who are eligible for free school meals is much higher than in most schools. The proportion of pupils supported at School Action Plus level or with a statement of special educational needs is also above average. Official inspection data suggests that the children have poor language and communication skills on entry and these are well below the expected average for their age.

This aspect of the children's development has been recognised by the school and, as a result, a cohesive language development support programme has been in place for a number of years. There is a team of dedicated language development staff who 'screen' the children on entry to the EYFS. The Language Link programme used by the team provides assessment tools to help staff determine whether the children experience receptive, expressive or articulation difficulties. The team, comprised of four higher-level teaching assistants (HLTA) under the guidance of a special educational needs coordinator, then group the children according to their identified language development needs. At the time of the visit, 60 per cent of the children in Key Stage 1 were receiving this particular intervention. This support is continued into Key Stage 2, if necessary, and at that time 28 per cent of the children in this age phase were receiving this continuing support.

Although each HLTA takes specific responsibility for the development of the children's differing needs, Susan acts as the team lead and has ensured cohesive support, identifying the areas for further development.

The children in EYFS and Key Stage 1 have timetabled sessions three times a week. There are also 12 children from Key Stage 2 who are receiving continued 'language enrichment' support, alongside what has been described as an 'alternative nurturing

*(Continued)*

*(Continued)*

curriculum'. All of these children regularly leave the main classroom to work in small groups in an area that is dedicated to language support. These rooms are bright and colourful, the walls filled with a range of artwork and children's displays that are used to stimulate conversations aimed at developing descriptive language. There are a number of persona dolls, all wearing the school uniform and sitting around tables. The cupboards are filled with a range of commercially available board games and large toys, such as forts and dolls' houses. There is a book corner with beanbags and large cushions, with a persona doll languishing there reading a Julia Donaldson picture book.

## Intervention groups: targeting specific aspects of language development

Targeted intervention groups, aimed at specific aspects of children's development, were identified as a useful approach for ensuring focused, personalised support in the school in the case study above. The children's language needs, as determined by the initial assessment, can be addressed either in small groups of two or three or, on occasions in one-to-one sessions. The members of the team feel very strongly that interspersing their support in a range of small group sessions alongside focused one-to-one times enables them to provide for the development of social communication skills and expressive language in conjunction with any difficulties associated with articulation. As highlighted in the case study, they use a wide range of resources to support the children's progress.

To support social communication skills, the children are encouraged to play board games with each other. They are first introduced to games such as 'Pairs' one-to-one or very small group sessions with a member of the team. This enables the rules of the game and the notion of taking turns to be explained. Playing such games allows the children to develop their understanding of words associated with both playing games and conversations, such as, 'It's your turn next', 'I think you should choose that one', and so on.

Working with individuals or small groups allows the practitioners to spend quality time with the children, focusing on specific needs. A conversation with Susan, revealed how this small group work allowed her to support the children with their language development:

> Because I work with four- to seven-year-olds, I use a lot of toys as resources. It is very hands-on and we can get good descriptive language. I start off with mirrors, though, and we begin by describing our faces.

Susan found that some of the children had difficulties with articulating sounds. This is not uncommon. Browne (2009) cites Wade and Moore (1987) when she observes that three quarters of speech disorders are to do with articulation, but most children will, as part of the developmental process, be able to articulate correctly by the age of six. If they do have problems, then intervention in conjunction with advice and support from a speech therapist can help them to recognise mispronunciations and practise in a safe and secure environment.

Susan found that using mirrors allowed the children to see the shape of their mouths as they were making certain sounds. This was then built on with the use of cued articulation. Cued articulation was devised by speech and language therapist Jane Passy and involves linking sounds with signs that indicate how the sound is made and which part of the mouth is used to articulate the sound. Susan found that, by raising awareness of mouth movements, the children were better able to use specific areas of their mouths to make the relevant sounds.

Susan was also able to identify specific linguistic features that the children needed support with and devised strategies to scaffold their learning in these areas. She used dolls to support the children's understanding of prepositions and general following of instructions – getting the children to 'put the blue socks *on* the feet', 'put their arms *through* the sleeves' or put the doll *under/on/alongside/between* particular objects (a chair, and so on), for example.

The environment in which these intervention activities took place was designed to promote an awareness of language – listening to others and using language appropriately – and support the children with articulation in a safe and secure atmosphere.

## Home and school literacies

As we saw, the practitioners in the two case studies were aware that some of the children in their schools did not receive support with literacy and language at home. In the first case study, Judith attempted to redress this balance by ensuring that the children were immersed in a language-rich environment at school, where discussion, role-play and reading were key pedagogies, consistently employed. During my discussions with Susan in the school in the second case study, it became clear that there was a concern there, too, about the degree of support the children received at home:

> It's actually a really needy area. I think that some of the problems are due to a lack of adult interaction: their parents don't seem to actually speak to them. They are left to watch television or play on their computer games, but they seem to lack the sort of experiences that help us to develop good receptive and expressive language skills. They can talk about programmes they have watched, but not about what they have done or books that have been read to them.

It could be said that a number of assumptions are being made here regarding what count as 'acceptable' literacy acts. That the children could talk about television programmes seems to have been viewed as inferior to being able to talk about reading books (Freire and Macedo, 1987: 52). That aside, the issue of adult and child interaction at home is recognised as being key to early literacy and language development. Weigel et al. found that:

> children's literacy skills are enhanced when parents engage them in direct literacy and language-enriching activities like joint book reading, playing rhyming games, singing songs, and drawing. (2010: 6)

Also, regular routines – eating dinner together and conversing at the table, reading aloud and completing homework activities – promotes early language and literacy skills.

The two practitioners in the case studies were aware of the importance of such home routines and practices, but accepted that many of the children would not have experienced these 'language-enriching activities'. Because of this, practices were developed in the schools to ensure that the children received the support they needed. As can be seen from the case studies, this was done in very different ways. Although the second school adopted a more explicit intervention programme, it could be said that interventions were put in place in both settings:

> At its broadest, an intervention is viewed as an action or technique or activity or procedure (or indeed combinations of these) that reflects a shared aim to bring about an improvement, or prevent a negative outcome. (Roulstone et al., 2012: 326–7)

An intervention, therefore, might involve modifying features of existing practice or, indeed, modifying the environment. In the first case study, Judith did just that – she recognised that some of the children may not have received appropriate support from home and so were likely to need specific support with language development, so she adjusted her classroom and practice accordingly. It is useful to make a link here with the 'waves of intervention' model devised as part of the Primary National Strategy in 2006 (DfES, 2006). This model describes Wave 1 as 'Inclusive quality first teaching for all', Wave 2 as 'Additional interventions to enable children to work at age-related expectations or above' and Wave 3 as 'Additional highly personalised interventions'. Judith's practice falls into the Wave 1 category as she devised activities and strategies to include all the children and implemented high-quality teaching and learning. The practice in Susan's school conjoined elements of Wave 1 and Wave 2, as the children were taken out of the classroom and taught in small groups or sometimes in one-to-one sessions, which is perhaps more 'typical' of what we imagine intervention to look like.

Roulstone et al. (2012), in their investigation into current practice with regard to interventions for children with speech, language and communication needs, found that, although there are many and varied interventions put in place in different settings, there is little evidence of their impact or whether the choice of intervention is based on research/hearsay/previous experience, and so on, or the view that because one intervention works for one child/group of children, it will work for others. It is important, therefore, to consider why we are adopting particular pedagogies and practices and how these might impact children's progress with early language and literacy.

Practitioners also need to be aware of how children use language in different contexts and with different people and, if it is felt that additional support is needed, then 'activities which enable children to use language in purposeful contexts and with real and supportive conversation partners' (Browne, 2009: 204) need to be planned and implemented. In the first case study, it is likely that these contexts would have been embedded in everyday classroom practice within the language-conscious environment. In the second case study, however, the children were taken out of the classroom and worked in smaller groups or individually with an adult. This gave the practitioner plenty of opportunities to assess the children and provide tailored support, but, arguably, conversational partners are often better if they are the children's peers as the language used will be more relevant (Toohey, 2003). In her research, Toohey focuses more specifically on children learning English as an additional language, but the issues for these children are very similar to those experienced by young learners coming to grips with their first language. They both need to practise in safe, supportive environments with adults and their peers so that they can experience the social language of children, while also receiving timely interventions from more able others.

For some children, however, listening and concentrating within whole-class contexts is a real challenge and, for them, the benefit of working in smaller groups may well outweigh the potential disadvantage of not conversing so much with their peers. Susan felt that the children who were removed from the classroom were able to focus more and concentrate on specific aspects of their language development as a result. She was concerned, however, that the specific work undertaken in these intervention groups outside the classroom was not followed up when the children re-joined their peers, which limited the value of those sessions. This is where discussions need to occur between those carrying out the interventions and the classroom teacher, so that aspects of the practices implemented in the small groups might perhaps be linked with everyday practice with the whole class. For example, all the children might benefit from and enjoy using mirrors to more fully understand how their mouths move and change shape in order to articulate particular sounds and the resources used within the small group interventions might be replicated in whole-class work, to enable those children within the small groups to orientate their learning in another context and ensure that good literacy practice is adopted by all the children in the class.

## Summary

It is clear that both schools in the case studies recognised the importance of language in early literacy and had a good knowledge and understanding of the levels of support the children received at home. Their approaches, however, were very different, and reflected the ethos and principles of the practitioners in the schools and the perceived impact of the approaches undertaken.

There is no *one* correct way to support children as they proceed along the path to becoming confident users of language who are able to adapt their linguistic style to different contexts and for different audiences. It is, however, vital that the ideas and practices adopted in schools are based on sound research and practitioners have an excellent knowledge and understanding of child development and, in this case, literacy and language development. Sylva et al. (2004: 6) found that the *most highly qualified staff* in preschool settings 'were most effective in their interactions with the children, using the most sustained shared thinking'. This sustained shared thinking is fundamental to early literacy and language development, as children are given opportunities to think and talk through their ideas, sharing, collaborating, discussing and exploring, using language as a tool for thinking:

> Language is a tool for carrying out joint intellectual activity, a distinctive human inheritance designed to serve the practical and social needs of individuals and communities and which each child has to learn to use effectively.
> (Mercer, 2000: 1)

An in-depth understanding of research, pedagogy and practice, combined with an excellent knowledge and understanding of the children's home backgrounds and level of support outside their educational settings, will make it more possible for us to be able to support children with their developing use of the vital tool that is language.

## Further reading

Browne, A. (2009) *Developing Language and Literacy 3–8* (3rd edn). London: Sage.
This text includes not only discussion of key aspects of early literacy, such as speaking and listening, reading and writing, but also chapters devoted to assessment, working with parents and bilingual learners, which make it an invaluable resource.

Whitehead, M. (2010) *Language and Literacy in the Early Years 0–7* (4th edn). London: Sage.
This excellent text combines theory and practice in a way that is interesting and accessible. Useful examples and summaries are provided throughout.

# References

Boyd, M.P. and Markarian, W.C. (2011) 'Dialogic teaching: Talk in service of a dialogic stance', *Language and Education*, 25 (6): 515–34.

Browne, A. (2009) *Developing Language and Literacy 3–8* (3rd edn). London: Sage.

Bruce, T. and Spratt, J. (2011) *Essentials of Literacy from 0–7* (2nd edn). London: Sage.

Cain, K. (2010) *Reading Development and Difficulties*. Chichester: BPS Blackwell, John Wiley & Sons.

Cremin, T. (2009) *Teaching English Creatively*. Abingdon: Routledge.

DfE (2012) *Statutory Framework for the Early Years Foundation Stage*. Runcorn: DfE.

DfES (2006) *Primary National Strategy*. Nottingham: DfES Publications.

Freire, P. and Macedo, D. (1987) *Literacy: Reading the word and the world*. London: Routledge.

Hamer, C. (2012) 'NCT research overview: Parent–child communication is important from birth', *Perspective*, March: 15–20. Available online at: www.literacytrust.org.uk/assets/0001/3375/Hamer_NCT_research_overview_Parent_child_communication_p15-20_Mar12.pdf (accessed 18 December 2013).

Lightbown, P.M. and Spada, N. (2006) *How Languages are Learned* (3rd edn). Oxford: Oxford University Press.

Mercer, N. (2000) *Words and Minds*. Abingdon: Routledge.

Riley, J. (2007) *Learning in the Early Years 3–7* (2nd edn). London: Sage.

Roulstone, S., Wren, Y., Bakopoulou, I. and Lindsay, G. (2012) 'Interventions for children with speech, language and communication needs: An exploration of current practice', *Child Language Teaching and Therapy*, 28 (3): 325–41.

Sylva, K., Melhuish, E., Sammons, P., Siraj-Blatchford, S. and Taggart, B. (2004) *The Effective Provision of Pre-school Education (EPPE) Project: Findings from pre-school to end of Key Stage 1*, DfES Research Report SSU/FR/2004/01. Nottingham: DfES Publications.

Toohey, K. (2003) *Learning English at School: Identity, social relations and classroom practice*. Clevedon: Multilingual Matters.

Trivette, C.M., Dunst, C.J. and Gorman, E. (2010) 'Effects of parent-mediated joint book reading on the early language development of toddlers and preschoolers', *Center for Early Literacy Learning Reviews*, 3 (2): 1–15.

Wade, B. and Moore, M. (1987) *Special children … Special Needs: Provision in the ordinary classroom*. London: Robert Royce.

Weigel, D.J., Martin, S.S. and Bennett, K.K. (2010) 'Pathways to literacy: Connections between family assets and preschool children's emergent literacy skills', *Journal of Early Childhood Research*, 8 (5): 5–22.

Whitehead, M. (2002) *Developing Language and Literacy with Young Children 0–8 Years* (2nd edn). London: Paul Chapman.

Whitehead, M. (2010) *Language and Literacy in the Early Years 0–7* (4th edn). London: Sage.

## Children's literature referred to in the text

Sheldon, Dyan (1995) *The Garden*. London: Red Fox.

# Rhythm, rhyme and repetition

## Virginia Bower and Susan Barrett

 **Chapter Objectives**

- to explore how rhythm, rhyme and repetition can play a significant role in early literacy development
- to introduce texts that help to promote an awareness and enjoyment of language.

## This chapter will cover:

- theories relating to the usefulness of rhythm, rhyme and repetition in early literacy
- case studies illustrating how rhythm, rhyme and repetition can support children with their early literacy development
- ideas for poems, poets, stories and authors to choose for early literacy work in connection with rhythm, rhyme and repetition.

It is widely accepted that children's oral language and their reading and writing can be supported by using rhythm, rhyme and repetition. From a very early age, children are able to clap along to a familiar rhythm, predict words in a nursery rhyme or poem, because of what comes before, and delight in repeating (often over and over!) favourite words and phrases from stories and conversations around them.

This chapter aims to highlight particular aspects of rhythm, rhyme and repetition and how they can be used effectively to support both teachers and learners with early literacy. The first section focuses on rhythm, in relation to both poetry and prose. Often, the idea of rhythm is connected more closely with poetry, as poems often have a distinct beat that children are very quick to hear and imitate. The rhythm in *prose*, however, can be equally powerful – particularly if the chosen author has a distinctive style and cadence to his or her writing in which readers can immerse themselves. An example of this is explored in the first case study.

The next section explores the idea of rhyme and how rhyming poems can support early literacy learners in a multitude of ways. We also identify particular issues and challenges that might occur when exploring rhyme and these are illustrated in the second case study.

Finally, repetition is examined using three separate lenses: reading and rereading stories, storytelling and the retelling of stories, and learning and playing with songs and rhymes. In this section, we return to the setting of the first case study to see how repeated readings of rhythmic prose supported a class of eight-year-old children with their narrative writing, then introduce a final case study that looks at the use of clapping songs with four- and five-year-olds.

In the first two sections, texts and/or poets and authors are recommended that we have found to be useful resources in relation to early literacy in general and rhythm, rhyme and repetition specifically.

# Rhythm

Responding to rhythm is a natural human reaction, since we each carry our own 'inner metronome' (Andrews, 1991: 130) – our heart – with us.

For native English speakers it is second nature, because our language is a stress-timed language with a 'tumpty-tumpty-tum beat', rather than the 'rat-a-tat beat' of syllable-timed languages such as French or Japanese (McArthur, in Beard, 1995: 27). Anyone who has watched a young baby in the early stages of language acquisition cannot fail to have noticed the evident physical pleasure the baby takes in making sounds (Whitehead, 2010), varying pitch and volume, and moving hands, arms and legs in time to vocalisations in sheer delight. Babies between 9 and 18 months can be heard developing their sounds, using a variety of rhythms, and they 'delight in words linked with rhythmic movement, bouncing and rocking' (Whitehead, 2010: 192). As they grow, children feel rhythm with their bodies and experience it in 'skipping, clapping, dance' (Lambirth, 2007: 2). Young children who *hear* nursery rhymes, for example, before they begin to read independently, are already attuned to 'a beating of rhythm, a fitting of word to pitch, a sense of structure' (Fenton, 2002: 22). In this process, they have acquired, quite naturally, a propensity to respond to one of the fundamental building blocks of both poetry and prose.

It is crucial, therefore, that children have opportunities to listen to poetry and prose being read aloud and to do so themselves. In this way, they absorb the cadences and rhythms of the language and this will raise their awareness of the power of language. According to Barrs and Cork (2001: 116), reading aloud to children allows them to 'take on the whole feeling and rhythm of a text'. This emphasis on the oral might also include the recounting of personal experiences and the telling, not just reading, of stories (this is explored in more depth later in this chapter). Fox (1993) found that, in their oral storytelling, children were using syntactic variations that they would ultimately require in writing. Prosodic features – repetition, rhythm and rhyme – may well have more influence over narrative structure than the plot (Fox, 1993) and participants in Fox's research were seen to be orally exploring these features.

The following case study looks at how the rhythms within prose supported a particular pupil with her narrative writing.

## CASE STUDY 1

The eight-year-old children in a Year 4 class were studying the work of a single author – Kevin Crossley-Holland. This particular writer has a very distinctive style and cadence to his writing (particularly his myths, legends and folk tales) and he was chosen because it was felt that his writing could be included in Meek's (1988) definition of 'texts that teach'. These kinds of texts provide a model of quality language and composition, while allowing readers opportunities to interpret the text in their own very personal ways.

It was hoped that one of the outcomes of implementing a single-author study would be that the children would enjoy being immersed in the literature and absorb the rhythms and cadences of the author's poetic prose.

During this unit of work, one of the children, Melanie, was asked how she felt about the stories:

VB:     So, did you enjoy any particular story by Kevin Crossley-Holland?

MW:     *Three Heads in the Well* is my best one. Because ... I like the heads and the princess – the nice one – gives the old man some food and the heads say, 'Wash me, comb me, lay me down softly.'

> VB: Wow! Fancy remembering the exact words. How did you do that?
>
> MW: Just because you read it. Even though it was ages ago, I remember every story you have read me. The storm story is my second best one.
>
> During this unit of work, Melanie produced three pieces of writing that far exceeded the quality of her usual attempts. All three compositions contained references to the original texts, whether they were direct 'liftings' from the story or connected closely in terms of style, language or content.

Melanie clearly enjoys being read to and has the ability to remember whole sections of text long after she has listened to them. Fox (1993) believes that prosodic features – for example, repetition and rhythm – have more influence over narrative structure than the plot and certainly the repetitive nature of this particular story and the rhythmic compositional style enabled Melanie to retain tracts word for word.

Despite her obvious enjoyment of literature, up to this point Melanie had always struggled when faced with a writing task and would often sit for long periods of time producing little or nothing on paper if she was not supported. When she did put pen to paper, it was often followed by copious amounts of erasing and starting all over again. It was clear that, from repeated readings of these stories, with their strong rhythms and powerful vocabulary, this child was able to develop her own confidence and writing voice.

Powerful texts that allow readers to hear and feel the rhythm, to the extent that they are able to transfer this to their own writing, are a vital component in the teaching of early literacy. Children need to hear the texts being read aloud and have the opportunity to reread them themselves to absorb the cadences and rhythms of the language.

It is, of course, important to have a range of texts at your disposal that have such strong rhythms, so here is a list of other authors who write rhythmic prose:

- Korky Paul
- Jeanne Willis
- Helen Ward
- Dyan Sheldon
- Shaun Tan.

And here are some examples of poems with a strong rhythm:

- 'Boneyard Rap' by Wes Magee
- 'I'm Watching You' by James Carter
- 'Father William' by Lewis Carroll
- 'Tarantella' by Hillaire Belloc
- poems by Ogden Nash, Roald Dahl and Charles Causley.

# Rhyme

Life experiences ensure that children arrive in classrooms with their heads already full of poetry:

> If it isn't nursery rhymes, it's jingles, adverts, raps, songs. (Harmer, 2000: 15)

As soon as they go out to the playground, children appear, spontaneously, to engage in rhyming – the result, perhaps, of exposure to idioms, proverbs, similes, tongue-twisters and adults' predilections for reduplicated words such as 'tittle-tattle', 'arty-farty', and so on. Their playground songs, chants, clapping and skipping games show evidence of complex rhythms and phonological patterning, as well as the use of alliteration and assonance (Grugeon, 1999). Their rhymes often show an exuberant use of language and strong metrical rhythm (Sedgwick, 2000), as well as a willingness to engage in language play, which is central to poetry. This social context is important because playing with language in this context 'is the open-ended process of trial and error, without worry of failure or derision, that enables us all to grow and learn' (Rosen, in Barrs and Rosen, 1997: 2).

So, what exactly do we mean by 'rhyme' and does it have any value for children beyond enjoyment? Definitions include the following:

- 'end-rhyme' as in:

  He went to *bed*
  And banged his *head*

- 'internal rhyme' as in:

  'In *bed*, visions swam in her *head*'

- 'half-rhyme' as in:

  ground/groaned

- 'eye' or 'vision' rhyme where spellings give the illusion of rhyme:

  slough, rough, through

- 'alliteration' of initial letters as in:

  sweet swallow

- 'assonance' in which vowel sounds are repeated:

  black hand

- 'consonance' as in:

  speck/flock

(adapted from McArther, 1995, in Beard, 1995)

It is important that we, as practitioners, are confident with the different types of rhyme occurring in poems and have examples of poetry to illustrate them clearly. Having this knowledge and the resources that go with it should enable us to provide effective support for children, and, as mentioned above familiarity and confidence with rhyme can aid children's reading skills. Bryant and Bradley's (1985) seminal longitudinal study of 400 children found that those with good initial rhyming skills tended to become better readers and speakers in later years.

Rhyme can also equate to syllables (one, two or three), such as 'dancer/chancer' or 'scattering/flattering', or even to phrases, such as 'Beanz meanz Heinz'. The 'primary phonological processing unit across the world's languages is actually the syllable' (Goswami, 2008: 68), so if children are able to recognise the syllabic structure of words and where the rhyming pattern occurs, this will support their reading. Goswami's work also showed that children able to use rhyme to make analogies made faster progress than did those children who had not grasped this:

> if the child recognises the similarity between 'light', 'fight' and 'night', then the child can use a rhyme analogy to predict that all these words will be pronounced in the same way. (Goswami, 2007: 23)

The 'rime' is the part of the word that contains the vowel and the end of the word. So 'br-*ing*' and 'st-*ood*' have the 'onsets' 'br' and 'st' and the rimes 'ing' and 'ood'. It is these rimes that allow for rhymes with other words. Adams et al. (1990) have noted that 500 simple words can be derived from a set of only 37 rimes.

Goswami (2007) found that those children with very poor rhyming skills appeared not to make rime analogies at all and advised that this should be taught explicitly to children in school. The work of Dr Seuss, she found, was particularly effective in supporting the reading development of dyslexic children. It is the predictability of text that is increased by rhythm and rhyme (Carter, 1998) and this is a vital aspect of learning how to read.

There is, however, an anomaly here when it comes to children writing poetry:

> From birth onwards, we give children lullabies, nursery rhymes, nonsense rhymes and rhymes in picture books. Then around the age of 7 children are told by a teacher that 'not all poetry rhymes'. We give children 7 years of rhyme … and then in KS2 we try and stop them writing it themselves. (Carter in Lockwood, 2011: 75)

This may be because children (and indeed adults) are not necessarily that skilled at writing rhymes. Any teacher will be able to recall instances of children having produced a random collection of rhymes, thinking they have produced a poem. By trying to find rhymes they have become 'imprisoned' by them, often because their vocabularies are not sufficiently extensive and they lack experience in what writing poetry is for.

Interestingly, two poets have warned about the pitfalls of rhyme: 'ban rhyme when we're writing for truth (for children under ten)' (Rosen, 1998: 44), comes from a poet committed to enabling children to write something *meaningful* from their own experience. The second is from Valerie Bloom (2000), who warns that rhyme is like fire; you need to control it rather than let it control you.

It might be helpful here to look at Carter's continuum:

Medium ———————————————————————————— Message

In nursery rhymes, the medium is paramount and so the message is absorbed. Carter explains:

> In most quality poems medium and message are integrated; the meanings of the words work through their textures, metaphors and patterns of sound. The words, the metaphors and the sounds point beyond the literal sense of the message, making poetry more intense and subtle than any other kinds of writing. (Carter, 1998: 30)

This is why it is vital that children hear their own written texts if they are to develop their ear for language (Barrs and Cork, 2001). Oral texts are enriched by pitch, volume and tone – qualities that are hard to replicate in a written text. Only by voicing texts and responding to them can children be enabled to give them that 'illocutionary force' (Olson, 1996). This needs to take place within an environment that celebrates the pleasure that words can provide (Sedgwick, 2000). It is only when a poem is lifted off the page, given voice and, thus, brought to life (Berry, in Barrs and Ellis, 1995) that children can assess the value of their work, their word choices and decisions to rhyme or not.

The case study below describes some of the experiences of a class of eight-year-olds exploring rhyme. Many of the key points mentioned above resonate with their experiences.

## CASE STUDY 2

The literacy unit of work started with the class of eight-year-olds being introduced to a range of rhyming poems by Christina Rossetti.

They were asked to identify which were the rhyming words and if they knew that they rhymed. The children were able to pick out words that rhymed if the words had the same spelling pattern, such as 'night' and 'sight'. When the teacher pointed out words that had a different spelling pattern, however, such as 'fruit' and 'shoot', the children predicted that these words would not rhyme.

The teacher encouraged the children to read these words aloud and listen to them carefully, then decide whether they rhymed or not. Many of the children then realised that the words *did* rhyme, although there were still some who found it hard to believe they could rhyme when they were not written in the same way on the page. As the week progressed, all the children began to appreciate that the same sound could often be represented in many different ways. The class teacher felt that, because many of the children were not secure with their grapheme phoneme correspondences (GPCs), this concept had taken longer to secure and she found the children with lower ability in particular found it very difficult to identify alternative graphemes.

Each morning, the children were given a chart to fill in. This chart had a list of words across the top and the children were encouraged to fill in other words that rhymed with the given words. The children thoroughly enjoyed this activity and took time to explore new vocabulary and discuss possibilities with their peers. Many of the children created non-words, as they sought to find examples of rhymes, and this provided an excellent opportunity to explore the meanings of words and new vocabulary. Interestingly, many of the children included words that fall into the category of 'half-rhymes'. For example, under the heading 'storm' one child wrote:

corn, torn, horn, born, warm, swarm

The charts were also useful because the children began to realise that they could collect more words if they were open to the idea of different spelling patterns. For example, one child included 'sigh', 'fly' and 'pie'.

The activity undertaken by the children, of them identifying words that rhymed with those provided by the teacher, demonstrated an awareness of the meaning of rhyme and an ability to distinguish different sounds. In the first example above, where the initial word was 'storm', as noted, the first three words selected by the child are half-rhymes – 'corn', 'torn' and 'horn'. Although, in this instance, the teacher did not follow up on this concept of half-rhymes, this activity would be an excellent way to promote an awareness of this aspect of rhyming poetry, particularly as it tends to occur naturally as children search for words.

The next two words recorded by the child were 'warm' and 'swarm', both of which rhyme with 'storm', but have a different spelling pattern. Again, this might have been a useful opportunity to explore the complexities of English spellings and raise children's awareness of alternative spellings for GPCs. Much of the teaching of phonics and spelling in primary classrooms is now taught 'discretely', as recommended by Rose (2006) in his review of reading. The example in the case study, however, demonstrates the usefulness of poems as contexts for the teaching of phonics and spelling. Poems provide rich contexts within which rhymes, spelling patterns, language anomalies and exciting vocabulary can be explored and children can begin to appreciate the complexities of written English.

The children in the case study above were given plenty of opportunities to read, explore and discuss poetry, which is vital if they are to understand the potential of both rhyming and non-rhyming poems. By reading other poets' work, alongside opportunities to 'engage with verse, feel its rhythms and connect to the content' (Cremin, 2009: 122), children are enabled to *experience* poetry fully.

The teacher in this example used a range of poems to engage and motivate the children, including a selection of poems by Christina Rossetti. Focusing on one poet can give children the chance to make connections and notice how particular poets use certain devices or rhyming schemes or lexical sets (groups of words focused on a topic). Subsequently moving on to explore different poets enables children to identify similarities and differences, hear a range of voices echoing through the poems and find poetic styles to their taste. It is important to remember that everybody's ideas about poems will differ and what engages and delights some may have very different effects on others! Because of this, having a range of quality rhyming texts to use in the classroom is vital. Here are some examples of rhyming stories that we have used and would recommend:

- *What the Ladybird Heard* by Julia Donaldson and Lydia Monks
- *Edward the Emu* by Sheena Knowles and Rod Clement
- *Jennifer Jones Won't Leave Me Alone* by Frieda Wishinsky and Neal Layton
- *Giraffes Can't Dance* by Giles Andreae and Guy Parker-Rees
- *Doing the Animal Bop* by Jan Ormerod and Lindsey Gardiner
- *Hairy Maclary's Bone* by Lynley Dodd
- *There's An Ouch in my Pouch!* by Jeanne Willis and Garry Parsons

Here is a selection of poets whose work includes rhyming poems:

- Tony Mitton
- Roald Dahl
- Valerie Bloom
- Grace Nichols
- Michael Rosen
- Spike Milligan
- Kit Wright
- Allan Ahlberg
- Andrew Fusek-Peters
- Brian Moses

You can find poems by all these poets at the Poetry Archive (www.poetryarchive.org/childrensarchive/home.do).

# Repetition

This section aims to suggest some ideas for how repetition might be used to pro-mote children's confidence and competence in early literacy. First, we will look at the reading and rereading of stories and what this offers young learners; then storytelling will be explored and the notion that telling and retelling stories can help children to find their own oral and written voice; and, finally, we will look at rhymes and clapping games and how these genres, particularly those with regular and repeated refrains, can support babies and young children with their early language skills.

Reading stories to children is seen as a crucial aspect of their formative experiences of literacy, but why might the repeated reading of particular stories be useful? Margaret Meek believes that:

> The reading of stories makes skilful, powerful readers who come to understand not only the meaning but also the force of texts. (1988: 40)

Repeated reading of stories provides more opportunities for children to be affected by this 'force' and begin to understand what stories can do for them. Stories can enable children to understand their place in the world. They can bring about a realisation that there are other worlds, cultures, languages, environments and experiences, which, though unfamiliar to them, can hold a fascination because of their 'strangeness'. Repeated exposure to texts that introduce unfamiliarity enables children to accept the world beyond their immediate knowledge and understanding and be more open to differences in people and places.

Through the repetition of particular stories, children can begin to develop a more extended vocabulary, which they can then utilise in their own oral and written com-munications. Many children arrive at school aged four or five with a well-established, rich vocabulary because their home environments have supported their language development via sustained conversations, books at bedtime, and so on. Some children will arrive, however, with what Moats (2001) calls 'word poverty'. Maryanne Wolf (2010: 102), in her delightful and informative text on language, *Proust and the Squid*, talks about this word poverty and how children from 'impoverished-language environ-ments' have, by the age of 5, 'heard 32 million fewer words spoken to them than the average middle-class child'. Somehow, for these children, we need to make every effort to fill this 'word gap' and the repeated reading of favourite stories is just one way to go about this.

The case study below returns to the setting of Case Study 1 and briefly describes the literacy experiences of an eight-year-old pupil – Satil – who has English as an additional language.

## CASE STUDY 3

The class were studying the work of Kevin Crossley-Holland in a three-week literacy unit. I read a wide range of Crossley-Holland's stories to the children and particular stories soon became favourites, which the children requested that we revisit on numerous occasions! The stories were also available to be accessed independently by the children. I spoke to Satil about the stories and his own narrative writing.

VB: Has reading all the stories by Kevin Crossley-Holland helped you with your writing?

ST: Very much.

VB: How?

ST: Well, you say good words and you speak the persons out and you describe the setting.

Later in the conversation Satil went on to quote specific examples from his own writing with which he was pleased:

ST: I like it where I wrote 'ghost flying by' and 'not moving a muscle'. Also 'eye of the storm'.

In the initial part of the conversation, Satil explained how the reading he had experienced impacted his writing. His focus is on the vocabulary, the characters and the setting – three aspects of literature that could conceivably be construed as key elements, crucial to one's enjoyment of a text. Rosenblatt states that:

> literature makes comprehensible the myriad ways in which human beings meet the infinite possibilities that life offers. (Rosenblatt, 1995: 6)

Satil's ability to articulate these key elements demonstrates his own use of the literature he has experienced to extend his comprehension of these 'infinite possibilities' and make use of this new knowledge in his own writing. It is unlikely that the impact would have been so considerable if he had heard just one story by Kevin Crossley-Holland, read once. The repeated readings have enabled him to absorb and utilise meaningful vocabulary.

By repeatedly using the word 'you' in his statement (by which he meant 'me', as the reader), Satil appears to associate his experience of Crossley-Holland's texts with having them read *to* him. According to Barrs and Cork (2001: 116), reading aloud to children allows them to 'take on the whole feeling and rhythm of a text'. Also, it is possible that the times 'you speak the persons out', as Satil calls it, he is hearing an echo of the words in his head as well because they have been read aloud to him previously and in this way he is reacting implicitly to immersion in these texts by a single author. He may also have been influenced by the drama activities, which played a significant role in the unit of work, and may have made him more aware of the 'persons' and their own unique voices than would have been the case if the books had only been read to him. Being able to 'hear these voices' like this is seen by some as having a significant impact on children's writing:

> Our written voices are intimately linked to the oral voices of others. (Grainger et al., 2005: 25)

It is interesting that Satil was able to identify specific linguistic aspects of his writing with which he was pleased. 'Eye of the storm' is taken directly from the text, but the other phrases are not. Satil has clearly drawn on a range of knowledge to extend his own vocabulary and produce what he considers to be effective writing. This would concur with Fox's belief that 'children take on new terminology if they meet it in meaningful contexts' (Fox, 1993: 39). Immersion in the texts of a single author may have not only provided Satil with explicit material for his own independent writing but also prompted further exploration of language, enabling him to make his writing unique to him.

In a similar way to repeated reading of favourite stories, repeated oral re*telling* is of great benefit to young literacy learners. *Telling* stories is very different from *reading* stories, however. If we are reading a story from a book, the story tends to stay the same every time it is read (indeed, this may well be one of the reasons children request the same story over and over – it is a 'safety net' of the known and inevitable). When we retell stories, however, the tendency is for the retelling to be a little different each time, affording the storyteller the freedom to embellish, reduce, exaggerate or, indeed, completely change the original. Repetition in this case therefore takes on a different meaning as, although the themes and perhaps the setting and the characters may stay the same, an exact replication of every word and phrase is unlikely. The retelling of stories enables children to understand the fundamental features of narrative and use them in their own writing:

> Through direct teaching and considerable experience of telling and retelling traditional tales with their clear structures, strong characters, repetitive and figurative language and archetypal issues, children come to make fuller use of these features in their own written narratives. (Cremin, 2002: 1)

Opportunities clearly need to be created within the early literacy classroom for children to tell and retell stories – stories that they have written, well-known fairy tales, folk tales, myths and legends and stories from other cultures. This should not be a tokenistic activity prior to writing; it needs to be a pedagogy that is embedded in classroom practice so that children are encouraged to find their own oral voice and develop their confidence and competence by the repeated exploration of narratives.

The final element within this section on repetition will look at the literacy benefits of repeated readings of rhymes and the benefits of clapping rhymes and games and the associated actions. Bruce and Spratt (2011) found that babies, in their first three months, have a fine sense of syllabic beat, phrasing, emphasis and intonation and the repeated sharing of rhymes, finger rhymes and songs laid the foundations for future literacy learning. When we read rhymes and poems with young children and babies, we often exaggerate the vowel sounds, 'and this helps the phonological awareness which will be crucial in learning to read' (Bruce and Spratt, 2011: 68). Bruce and Spratt also point out that finger rhymes raise an implicit awareness of syllables and 'chunks' of words that have the same rhyming patterns. Most children and adults find it easier to learn and remember rhymes and songs than straight prose because of the regular rhythm and predictable rhyme, not least because these particular literary forms are often repeated over and over at an early age.

The following case study describes the experiences of four- and five-year-old children in a Reception class as they explore a clapping rhyme.

## CASE STUDY 4

The children were introduced to the clapping rhyme, song and game 'A sailor went to sea, sea, sea', linking with their project 'Under the sea'. This is the song:

A sailor went to sea, sea, sea

To see what he could see, see, see

But all that he could see, see, see

Was the bottom of the deep blue sea, sea, sea.

The rhyme was sung to the class a number of times and the children gradually began joining in.

The class teacher then modelled the clapping actions that go with the rhyme and encouraged the children to practise them with a partner. The game was introduced at particular times each day and it could soon be seen that the children were learning to coordinate their movements with the song.

The teacher then introduced the idea of not saying the words 'sea' or 'see' and replacing each with a clap every time each word occurred. As the children grew accustomed to this, they were then asked to sing and clap the song with their eyes closed.

Ultimately, the children performed their clapping song in a class assembly in front of the school and parents.

The repetition of this clapping song and game enabled the children to make considerable progress in developing their literacy. Bruce and Spratt (2011: 102) point out that when children experiment with 'action songs', such as the clapping song and game above, 'they begin to understand that one thing can be made to stand for another'. In this example, the children became aware that they could clap in time with the words of the song, then that the specific rhyming words could be replaced by just claps.

Becoming a confident literacy learner involves effective communication as well as being able to recognise rhythms and beats in language in order to react appropriately to conversations and situations. The children in the case study were verbally and physically interacting, negotiating roles, supporting each other, discussing the issues and scaffolding each other's learning. The regular and repeated rhythm of the rhyme, which they soon adopted without having to explicitly think about it, allowed them to focus on remembering the words and the actions and putting these together.

Repeated attempts at such clapping games develop coordination and motor control, too, both of which are vital as children develop their writing, drawing and keyboard skills. Some of the children in the case study did struggle with this aspect of the game, but were able to practise and persevere in a safe and secure environment, having plenty of opportunities to hone their skills.

## Summary

Rhythm, rhyme and repetition are fundamental to children's pleasurable engagement with poetry. Teachers who are aware of their pupils' playground rhymes will have an insight into 'their genuine preferences and pleasures' (Mallett, 2010: 171), which can be exploited in class to their mutual benefit.

Reading, reciting, performing and experiencing poems together in a language-loving environment in which the shapes, sounds and rhythms of words can be savoured, will enable children to experience the 'dance in words' (Hughes, 1963) that is poetry. Children should experience, where possible, rhymes in other languages, too, to hone their ability to hear them and appreciate differences.

Learning English nursery rhymes is a valuable way for pupils with English as an additional language to become attuned to the rhythms and cadences of English, while at the same time learning something of British cultural heritage (Perkins, in Lockwood, 2011). In the same way, children from different countries and cultures whose first language is not English, can be encouraged to bring examples from their own homes and communities and parents can be invited in to read poems that are important to them. By sharing rhymes and hearing their peers and other members of the community reading and reciting, *all* children's literacy experiences

*(Continued)*

*(Continued)*

can be enriched. When teachers find a social place for poetry in their classrooms, then it will flourish (Lambirth et al., 2012).

Recognising the rhythms in some prose can enable children to find a rhythm of their own as they seek their own oral and written voice. Repeated reading of favourite texts immerses children in the language of stories, providing them with a rich textual background on which they can draw when needed. Stories and poems need to be read aloud, shared with friends, explored in a quiet cosy corner while lounging on cushions, talked about, written about, performed, revisited and cherished.

Holding the rhythm of a poem or story inside their bodies and minds, experiencing the feeling of rhymes as they trip off the tongue and being given the opportunity to repeat their encounters with favourite texts will all contribute to a successful start in literacy for young children and provide them with the motivation to continue forward on their literacy journey.

## Further reading

Bruce, T. and Spratt, J. (2011) *Essentials of Literacy from 0–7* (2nd edn). London: Sage.
This book has some excellent sections on finger rhymes, action songs and poetry cards.

Marsh, J. and Hallet, E. (2008) *Desirable Literacies: Approaches to language and literacy in the Early Years* (2nd edn). London: Sage.
This text includes chapters on a range of themes, including language development and early reading and writing. Theory and practical advice are interwoven to make this text useful and accessible.

## References

Adams, M.J., S.A. Stahl, J. Osborn and F.A. Lehr (eds) (1990) *Beginning to Read: The new phonics in context: A précis of the classic text*. Oxford: Heinemann.
Andrews, R. (1991) *The Problem with Poetry*. Buckingham: Open University Press.
Barrs, M. and Cork, V. (2001) *The Reader in the Writer*. London: CLPE.
Barrs, M. and Ellis, S. (eds) (1995) *Hands On Poetry: Using poetry in the classroom*. London: CLPE.
Barrs, M. and Rosen, M. (eds) (1997) *A Year with Poetry*. London: CLPE.
Beard, R. (ed.) (1995) *Rhyme, Reading and Writing*. London: Hodder & Stoughton.
Bloom, V. (2000) 'Rhyme like fire', interview with James Carter, *Literacy and Learning*. Birmingham: Questions Publishing.
Bruce, T. and Spratt, J. (2011) *Essentials of Literacy from 0–7* (2nd edn). London: Sage.

Bryant, P. and Bradley, L. (1985) *Children's Reading Problems*. Oxford: Blackwell.

Carter, D. (1998) *Teaching Poetry in the Primary School*. London: David Fulton.

Cremin, T. (2002) Storytelling: The missing link in story writing', in S. Ellis and C. Mills (eds), *Connecting, Creating: New ideas in teaching writing*. Leicester: UKLA.

Cremin, T. (2009) *Teaching English Creatively*. Abingdon: Routledge.

Fenton, J. (2002) *An Introduction to English Poetry*. London: Viking.

Fox, C. (1993) *At the Very Edge of the Forest: The influence of literature on storytelling by children*. London: Cassell.

Goswami, U. (2007) 'Analogical reasoning in children', in J. Campione, K. Metz and A.S. Palincsar (eds), *Children's Learning in Laboratory and Classroom Contexts*. Abingdon: Routledge.

Goswami, U. (2008) 'Reading, complexity and the brain', *Literacy*, 42 (2): 55–71.

Grainger, T., Goouch, K. and Lambirth, A. (2005) *Creativity and Writing: Developing voice and verve in the classroom*. Abingdon: Routledge.

Grugeon, E. (1999) 'The state of play: Children's oral culture, literacy and learning', *Literacy*, 33 (1): 13–16.

Harmer, D. (2000) 'Poetry in the primary school', *Education 3–13*, 28 (2): 15–18.

Hughes, T. (1963) *Here Today*. London: Hutchinson.

Lambirth, A. (2007) *Poetry Matters*. Leicester: UKLA.

Lambirth, A., Smith, S. and Steele, S. (2012) 'Poetry is happening but I don't exactly know how': Literacy subject leaders' perceptions of poetry in their primary schools', *Literacy*, 46 (2): 73–80.

Lockwood, M. (ed.) (2011) *Bringing Poetry Alive*. London: Sage.

Mallett, M. (2010) *Choosing and Using Fiction and Non-fiction 3–11*. Abingdon: Routledge.

Meek, M. (1988) *How Texts Teach What Readers Learn*. Stroud: Thimble Press.

Moats, L. (2001) 'Overcoming the language gap', *American Educator*, 25 (5): 8–9.

Olson, D.R. (1996) 'Literate mentalities: Literacy, consciousness of language, and modes of thought', in D.R. Olson and N. Torrance (eds), *Modes of Thought: Explorations in culture and cognition*. Cambridge: Cambridge University Press. pp.141–152.

Rose, J. (2006) *Independent Review of the Teaching of Early Reading*. Nottingham: DfES Publications.

Rosen, M. (1998) *Did I Hear You Write?* (2nd edn). Nottingham: Five Leaves Publications.

Rosenblatt, L. (1995) *Literature as Exploration*. New York: Modern Language Association of America.

Sedgwick, F. (2000) *Writing to Learn: Poetry and literacy across the primary curriculum*. London: RoutledgeFalmer.

Whitehead, M. (2010) *Language and Literacy in the Early Years 0–7* (4th edn). London: Sage.

Wolf, M. (2010) *Proust and the Squid: The story and science of the reading brain*. Cambridge: Icon Books.

## Children's literature referred to in the text

### Some poems and poets you might find useful

'Tarantella' by Hillaire Belloc
'Father William' by Lewis Carroll
'I'm Watching You' by James Carter
'Boneyard Rap' by Wes Magee
Poems by Ogden Nash, Roald Dahl, Christina Rossetti and Charles Causley.

## Authors of rhythmic prose

Kevin Crossley-Holland
Korky Paul
Dyan Sheldon
Dr Suess
Helen Ward
Jeanne Willis

## Examples of rhyming stories that we have used and would recommend

Andreae, Giles and Parker-Rees, Guy (2001) *Giraffes Can't Dance*. London: Orchard Books.
Dodd, Lynley (1986) *Hairy Maclary's Bone*. London: Puffin.
Donaldson, Julia and Monks, Lydia (2012) *What the Ladybird Heard*. London: Macmillan.
Knowles, Sheena, and Clement, Rod (1999) *Edward the Emu*. St Louis, MO: Turtleback Books.
Ormerod, Jan and Gardiner, Lindsey (2005) *Doing the Animal Bop*. Oxford: Oxford University Press.
Wishinsky, Frieda and Layton, Neal (2004) *Jennifer Jones Won't Leave Me Alone*. London: Picture Corgi.
Willis, Jeanne and Parsons, Garry (2008) *There's An Ouch in my Pouch!* London: Puffin.

## Poets whose work includes rhyming poems

Allan Ahlberg
Valerie Bloom
Roald Dahl
Andrew Fusek-Peters
Spike Milligan
Tony Mitton
Brian Moses
Grace Nichols
Michael Rosen
Kit Wright
You can find poems by all these poets at the Poetry Archive at: www.poetryarchive.org/childrens archive/home.do

# Tales and the oral tradition

## Caroline Tancock

### Chapter Objectives

- to raise awareness of the power of traditional tales
- to identify how traditional tales can have a positive impact on children's language and reading development
- to explore the notion that the oral nature of traditional tales can support children with their early literacy development.

---

### This chapter will cover:

- an introduction to the typical characteristics of traditional tales
- how this particular genre might support children with their language and reading development
- how oral storytelling can support young literacy learners
- two case studies to illustrate how tales have been used to motivate and involve children in their use of language and their reading skills.

## Traditional tales

Traditional tales originate from oral storytelling traditions and include a range of narratives, such as myths, legends, fables and fairy tales. These are tales that have been told by one generation to the next across decades and centuries, countries and cultures. Many are also described as folk tales because they were originally told by 'ordinary' people to explore their lives, share their experiences and justify their beliefs. Such folk tales offered comforts such as second chances, good luck and stories of love in contrast to their harsh ways of living. Favourite stories, such as *Cinderella*, *Sleeping Beauty* and *The Three Little Pigs* can all be classified as folk tales. The oral telling of these tales relied on key features, such as a predictable story structure, repetition and patterned language to make them memorable.

Originally, traditional tales had an important social purpose, in the sense that they were a means of establishing cultural links between one community and another. These stories enabled a sharing and passing on of wisdom and experience. They contained important knowledge of life and came to represent cultural traditions and spiritual beliefs. They gave examples of how to behave in different situations and often included humour and suspense:

> In these narratives, now fixed in print, we can still sense the active creation of cultural meanings as patterns of values and beliefs were thrashed out. (Whitehead, 2004: 115)

The themes of traditional tales often tackle key issues in life, such as who we are and where we come from, how we should behave and how to deal with life's problems. Universal concepts, such as rich and poor (*The Little Match Girl*), good and evil (*Cinderella*), beautiful and ugly (*Beauty and the Beast*) are often explored. Other common themes include a journey (not just a physical journey but also a journey as a symbol of self-discovery), some type of quest (often a metaphor for the search for truth or the self), trials, the origins of the people and animals on earth and relationships between peoples.

Characterisation within traditional tales is often simplistic, with archetypal characters, predictable actions and clear 'goodies and baddies'. Many of the principle characters are male, which is a reflection of the male-dominated social, political and cultural world that existed when these tales originated, but has led to some criticism of such tales. Gamble and Yeats (2008: 108) argue, however, that the archetypal nature of the characters in traditional tales is deliberate as they are 'representing ideas rather than attempts at realistic characterisation' and the gender of the characters is often irrelevant and could be 'transposed without affecting the moral purpose of the story'. Even so, more modern 'traditional' tales, such as *The Paper Bag Princess* by Robert Munsch and *Princess Smartypants* by Babette Cole, are making an effort to redress what might be perceived by some as a gender imbalance.

At the heart of all traditional tales is a cultural belief, value, message or moral demonstrated in the actions of the characters. The nature of traditional tales enables us to adapt their themes to our own individual needs. The powerful opposites so common within these narratives can provide young children with one of their earliest experiences of values and morals and give them an insight into lives far removed from their own:

> Well-written stories invite the readers to recreate and examine familiar and unfamiliar worlds and experiences and offer readers the opportunity to know themselves, others and the world more fully. (Browne, 2009: 58)

Bettelheim (1991) argues that traditional tales make a significant contribution to children's psychological and emotional development as they enable them to deal with the difficult issues associated with growing up. Indeed, traditional tales have stood the test of time not just because they are entertaining and enjoyable but also because 'they offer alternative worlds which embody imaginative, emotional and spiritual truths about the universe' (Grainger, 1997: 23). The way traditional tales deal with archetypal issues enables them to give children an insight into the patterns and motives of human behaviour. Complex issues that challenge us can be accessed by children through these tales (Grainger, 1997).

How is all this relevant to early literacy? Wells (1987) found that children's early knowledge of stories was the most influential indicator of later educational achievement. A more recent piece of research – *The Effective Provision of Pre-school Education (EPPE) Project: Findings from pre-school to end of Key Stage 1* (Sylva et al., 2004) – identified one of the most significant factors in relation to children's social and academic progress as being the reading of stories with an adult.

The following sections will explore why tales and oral tradition might be considered such powerful tools as children develop as language users and readers. This will begin with a discussion relating to children's oral language development, before moving on to exploring reading. This chapter does not discuss the nature of very early language development, as this is examined in Chapter 1, Baby rooms, and Chapter 7, Diverse approaches to language development.

## Language development

Theories of how children acquire and develop language have evolved and been built upon over the years. These theories are significant if we are to realise the benefits of using tales and storytelling with young children.

In the 1950s, behaviourists argued that adults provided a model of language that was imitated by children and then encouraged by positive reinforcement (Skinner, 1957). This was later challenged, however, by those who contended that humans have an innate ability and children's natural ability to learn language results in them learning new and more complex patterns in language as they mature (Chomsky, 1965;

Lenneberg, 1967; McNeil, 1970). More recent theories propose that learning language is an active and social process, often involving interaction with more able others (Halliday, 1975; Vygotsky, 1978; Hart and Risley, 1999).

Thinking about these theories in relation to reading and retelling traditional tales, it would seem that there is something useful to be gained from all of these concepts. By reading, rereading, telling and retelling tales, adults are providing a particular body of language that children are then able to adopt and adapt to suit their needs. Because this particular genre contains structures that are often repetitive, organised sequentially in a recognisable way and contain patterns in their plots, children can imitate, both in an oral and written form, the familiar story structures as scaffolds for their own development as literacy learners. Children also need to understand, however, that 'story language' is not 'normal' language:

> The fact is that stories, by their very nature, use language in a different way than it is used in everyday transactions. (Wray and Medwell, 1993: 49)

Children have an innate ability to recognise different language forms and this can be exploited in a positive way by practitioners as it promotes discussions relating to formal and informal, concrete and abstract through the medium of stories.

Regarding the third theory described above, tales and oral tradition lend themselves to reading aloud, sharing, discussing, oral retelling and re-enacting and form the basis of many rhymes and games. All of these activities are active and social, with children and adults working together and using language to gain a better understanding of what they are experiencing as they enter the story world:

> The relation of thought to word is not a thing but a process, a continual movement back and forth from thought to word and from word to thought. In that process the relation of thought to word undergoes changes which themselves may be regarded as development in the functional sense. Thought is not merely expressed in words; it comes into existence through them. (Vygotsky, 1978: 125)

It would seem, then, that in their encounters with tales, children are developing language through a combination of imitation, their innate ability to use language to suit particular purposes and social interaction. So, it is important, as practitioners, to identify the specific language support this genre might offer so that we are able to realise its potential.

As they were originally oral stories, traditional tales usually have a distinctive but basic plot and structure, to aid both the teller and listener in remembering and enjoying the tale. Children soon recognise this predictability and it helps them to absorb and memorise the words and phrases used, expanding their vocabularies. Traditional tales use rich, evocative and memorable language, such as rhyme and alliteration ('fee, fi, fo, fum ...', for example). There can be a deliberate overuse of adjectives, such as, the 'great big enormous turnip', and use of rhythm, repetition and refrains, such as, 'Run,

run as fast as you can. You can't catch me, I'm the gingerbread man'. Again, the repetition of such refrains not only encourages listeners to join in and become more engaged with the story but also begins to imprint on their memories particular words and phrases that they can then 'borrow' for their own purposes, whether this be during play or in the more formal setting of a classroom. It is very common to see children running and chasing others in the playground reciting rhymes such as 'Run, run as fast as you can'. Indeed, linking the language of traditional tales with the playground rhymes enjoyed by so many children encourages young learners to experiment, linguistically and semantically, in safe, informal environments (Grainger, 1997). Simile, metaphor and symbolism are also key features of traditional tales, as are formulaic openings and endings ('Once upon a time …', '… and that's how the … got its …'). The combination of this typical traditional tale language and more atypical lexis that children would not encounter in everyday exchanges – in certain versions of *Cinderella*, for example, words such as 'widow', 'cinders', 'rags', 'pumpkin' and 'coachman' – provide children with a rich diet of language.

The following case study describes a Reception class of four- and five-year-olds who are engaged with a topic based on the traditional tale *The Gingerbread Man*. As you read this study, think about how the development of oral language might be promoted by using this text and consider why traditional tales appear to offer such a wealth of ideas and support for both practitioners and young children as they learn to be effective users of language.

## CASE STUDY 1

The children in a Reception class had just started a topic centred on *The Gingerbread Man*.

First, they enjoyed hearing the story read to them by the class teacher from a Big Book and being given the opportunity to discuss the illustrations with their talk partners, then feed back their ideas to the rest of the class. They then went on to access a different version of the story (on the BBC CBeebies website at: www.bbc.co.uk/cbeebies/stories) and discussed any differences they noticed. By this time, the children were joining in with the repeated refrain, 'Run, run as fast as you can. You can't catch me I'm the Gingerbread Man' whenever it appeared in the story.

The children then engaged in elements of process drama, whereby, as the story was read, they devised freeze frames to depict certain events and actions, the teacher 'thought tracked' the children as they stepped into the shoes of different characters and several children volunteered to be in the 'hot seat' as the gingerbread man and

*(Continued)*

*(Continued)*

the fox. As well as some children taking a more prominent role at times, all the children were involved throughout the activities as they joined in the refrain at the relevant points, asked questions, discussed their ideas and offered opinions. By this time, they knew the story very well!

Another of the story-based activities involved creating a display depicting some of the scenes from the story and, within this display, particular vocabulary was highlighted. This specifically focused on sets of nouns, such as 'fox', 'cow', 'horse', 'nose', 'tail' and 'river', and prepositions, such as 'in', 'on', 'under' and 'across'.

During the rest of the week, the children engaged in storytelling, retelling the story using puppets and props, they made their own gingerbread men and decorated them with sweets and they wrote their own alternative version of the story as a shared writing activity using different animals and settings.

Interestingly, the following week, the class teacher shared the story *Rosie's Walk* with the class and some of the children gleefully pointed out the fox in this story, referring back to the fox in *The Gingerbread Man*.

One notable feature of this case study is the way the children were actively involved throughout. Children need to be active participants in their learning of language:

> Children who are constantly exposed to an environment rich in language and who interact with adults using language in a social context develop more facility with oral language than children lacking these opportunities. (Morrow, 2009: 98)

It could be said that other pedagogies utilised in the case study above are relevant to any stories used in the classroom to promote early literacy – shared reading, dialogic talk, process drama, storytelling, story writing from a model, and so on. It is useful, therefore, to identify specifically what traditional tales bring to this mix and how they enhance the teaching and learning of early literacy. I have therefore decided to focus on oral storytelling next as this was a significant element within the planning and teaching in the case study above and because of the natural and necessary link between traditional tales and the spoken word.

# Oral storytelling

Narrative is central to early learning and thinking and young children live in a world of stories. Narrative plays a significant role in helping children to shape experience and make meaning and, when children engage in storytelling, they develop multiple language and literacy competencies. If children are given the opportunity to 'play' with tales, by manipulating and reconstructing them to suit their own requirements, and then have the chance to retell them, they will learn about the structure of stories and the language patterns within them and how they can make language 'work' for them. The power of traditional tales combined with storytelling 'can liberate children's imaginations, release their creativity and enable them to weave dreams together, as they journey along this road of never-ending stories' (Grainger 1997: 10).

In retelling traditional stories, children are able to develop confidence in their spoken language. They see that they have power over language as they organise the structure of the tale to suit their needs and make choices about vocabulary, characters, settings and events. The oral nature means that each telling is unique and children have the freedom to embellish. The patterned, memorable and rhythmic nature of the language in traditional tales is easy for children to replicate. As we saw above, the children in the case study soon picked up the repeated refrain that is a central element of the story and this still tended to be repeated in their retellings even if other aspects of the story were changed.

The practice of narrating stories, either invented or retold, helps young children to come to know what it is to think through problems, argue cases, see both sides of questions, find supporting evidence and make hypotheses, comparisons, definitions, and generalisations (Fox, 1990). All of these facilities are integral to early literacy development, as children begin to use language in empowering ways.

Very young children's first experiences of telling stories might take the form of short conversations about people, objects and activities in their immediate environment. These are characterised by frequent turntaking. As children develop further, they are able to convey a narrative about events that happened in the not too distant past. It is these discussions that lay the foundations for the development of narrative skills and the ability to tell coherent stories (Brooks and Kempe, 2012).

First stories are autobiographical in nature. For example, children might tell a tale based on their birthday party or a holiday experience. Gradually, however, children learn to recount third person accounts, albeit not coherently to begin with. To tell a story coherently requires a command of plot, themes, use of grammatical devices, use of time-related language and cohesive markers and an understanding of different points of view. It is these skills that need to be developed as a child develops early competence in literacy by the means of storytelling and the use of the powerful examples of traditional tales.

In the case study, the children had ample opportunity to listen to, tell and retell the story of the gingerbread man. Because of this they were able to discuss their ideas with some authority, utilising and experimenting with the vocabulary they had learnt. They worked collaboratively to produce an alternative version (which is only possible if the original is very well known and understood) and they were able to make links between characters in this tale and those in a very different story at a later date. All of these achievements are vital aspects of becoming confident, competent users of language, both oral and written.

The use of traditional tales and oral storytelling can also support children whose first language is not English. The sharing of stories from different cultures demonstrates a respect for a child's background, culture and language and the children then realise that the stories they bring with them are valued. I shall never forget a moment in the classroom when I was reading *Cinderella* to the children. Before I began reading, I asked if any of the children knew the story already. Many did, but one of the children who had English as an additional language shook her head. Halfway through the story, though, the same child suddenly leapt up and said, 'I know this – we call it …' and she gave the name of the story in her own language. This was a great moment and we were able to follow it up by inviting her mother in to read the story in their home language.

In such ways, children for whom English is not their first language can develop confidence through oral storytelling, whether in their first or second language (see Chapter 5, Supporting learners with English as an additional language, for more discussion about this). The use of gestures, facial expressions and body language support children in their learning of English, as they offer layers of meaning and facilitate understanding. The repetitive nature and clear plots of traditional stories can also help by introducing them to the vocabulary, grammatical structure and tunes of the stories enabling them to remember these features.

As well as supporting children with their oral language development, traditional tales can play a significant role in children's progress in reading. The next section explores this in some depth.

# Reading and making meaning

This section will consider how the reading and retelling of traditional tales can support early and developing readers. First, I shall consider decoding and the strategies that children can deploy within the context of reading traditional tales. I shall then go on to consider how this genre can support reading comprehension. Decoding and comprehension need to go hand in hand and assuredly both can be practised within the context of traditional tales.

Language processes and language learning are an important part of learning to read. The printed word represents the oral sequences of language and, when attempting to read, we look and listen for patterns and recognisable grammatical sequences. Using what we already know about language structure, we try to make sense of what we are reading and familiarity with both semantics and syntax enables children to reconstruct the meaning of the written word. Young literacy learners need to become resilient readers who recognise that, at times, reading will pose particular problems, but who are determined to overcome these because they are aware of the joy and excitement reading can bring. Resilience can be promoted by providing children with a range of strategies to support them as they explore different texts. These strategies include:

- being able to employ their phonic knowledge
- recognising whole words
- using their understanding of grammatical constructions
- using the context
- making predictions based on all of the above.

All of these strategies can be utilised as children engage with traditional tales. Let us consider the opening of a typical traditional tale and explore how these reading strategies might be promoted as children encounter the text. Here is the beginning of *Cinderella*, taken from the Ladybird version by Vera Southgate (no date):

> ONCE UPON A TIME there was a little girl called Cinderella. Her mother was dead and she lived with her father and two stepsisters.
>
> Cinderella's stepsisters were fair of face but, because they were bad-tempered and unkind, their faces grew to look ugly. They were jealous of Cinderella because she was a lovely child, and so they were often unkind to her.
>
> The stepsisters made Cinderella do all the work in the house. She worked from morning till night without stopping.

This is the first page of this particular version of the tale and it contains many elements typical of a traditional tale with regard to language and themes.

The text contains some phonically regular words – 'but', 'grew', 'look', and 'night' – and, depending on the stage of development regarding linking letters and sounds, children might well employ this strategy for some of these words. This might be by 'sounding out' one phoneme at a time (synthetic phonics) or looking for the bigger patterns in words and using onset and rime (analytic phonics). This short section of text, however, contains many words that might prove difficult to 'sound out' and, indeed, traditional tales will not offer a diet of formulaic, decodable words. Children might, instead, rely more on the familiarity of the text – perhaps if they have heard this story many times before – and recognise particular words. 'Once upon a time' is in capital letters in this version, which emphasises the key role played by this phrase in traditional tales and may well trigger children's memories of having seen this typical story starter before. Other words that they might recognise are 'mother', 'father', 'two', 'because' and 'morning', as these are words they may have encountered at home or in an educational setting and are very common.

Children might also recognise the typical grammatical constructions of the sentences, beginning with 'Once upon a time', which is often followed by – as in this case – 'there lived'. Sentences that begin 'She worked from morning …' are likely to end in a certain way because of the syntactic arrangement and this provides children with invaluable clues and cues to support them with their reading. The context is also key to unlocking the words on the page. Children will know that the story is called *Cinderella* and many will already be aware of the story. They will have an understanding of the characters and the setting and this may well support them with decoding words such as 'stepsister', 'ugly', 'jealous' and 'work'. All of these strategies can be combined with developing the skill of prediction. From the way a word is structured, children might predict phonically plausible possibilities; from their knowledge of common words found regularly in traditional tales they can predict language that might occur; from typical grammatical constructions it is possible to accurately predict the order of words in a sentence; and from the context and their existing knowledge of the story, they can predict words, phrases and, indeed, whole sentences.

All of the above rely very much on children's exposure to this genre in repeated readings, sharing ideas about the text and engaging in discussions about the story. For children whose home lives do not include these aspects of engagement with stories, their time in Early Years and primary settings may be the only opportunities they have to develop their reading skills within meaningful contexts. Therefore, time spent immersing children in traditional tales is a crucial aspect of early literacy. This is recognised in both the early learning goals (DfE, 2012: 7):

> **Early Years Foundation Stage**
>
> They listen to stories, accurately anticipating key events and respond to what they hear with relevant comments, questions or actions.

And the 'Draft national curriculum programmes of study' (DfE, 2013: 7, 12, 16):

> *Year 1*
>
> becoming very familiar with key stories, fairy stories and traditional tales
>
> recognising and joining in with predictable phrases
>
> *Year 2*
>
> becoming increasingly familiar with a wider range of stories, fairy stories and traditional tales
>
> recognising simple recurring literary language in stories and poetry
>
> *Years 3 and 4*
>
> increasing their familiarity with a wide range of books, including fairy stories, myths and legends
>
> identifying recurring themes and elements in different stories and poetry (e.g. good triumphing over evil, magical devices).

Traditional tales and the oral retelling of them can also support fluency in reading. The rhythms, lyrical nature and language patterns enable children to play with the words and sounds and develop verbal patterns and voices of their own. This can support both expression in their reading out aloud and also their understanding of meaning when reading to themselves.

Children's developing ability to decode text goes hand in hand with their natural curiosity and desire to make meaning from the printed word. From an early age, children need to discover the power of language and the excitement, illumination and comfort that can be derived from both new stories and familiar tales. As children's ability to comprehend improves, they are able to gain more from a text. Ann Browne (2009: 34) cites Guppy and Hughes (1999) when she talks about three levels of comprehension – reading the lines, reading between the lines and reading beyond the lines. Think about the passage from *Cinderella*. If the children are reading the lines, they will understand that Cinderella lives with her father and stepsisters, she is treated unkindly by the jealous stepsisters and is made to do all the work. As far as reading between the lines, however, there is little work left for the reader to do. Traditional tales have very few uncertainties and contain 'unambiguously one-dimensional characters' (Waugh et al., 2013: 104). There is very little subtlety and rarely any need for children to work hard to interpret the meaning:

> Quick-wittedness and native cunning are character assets which will win rewards; lying and deception are acceptable when they are for a good end; princesses are good and beautiful, and marriage is the desirable conclusion for any princess. (Waugh et al., 2013: 104)

Although it is true that a reader of traditional tales does not need necessarily to read between the lines in the same way they might with a text written by authors such as Anthony Browne and John Burningham, they do still need to read *beyond* the lines, bringing *themselves* to the text and understanding the implications of what they have read:

> the meaning of a text is not something static that lies within it: meaning is created by the real reader's engagement with the text. (Gamble and Yeats, 2008: 20)

Going beyond the lines in relation to the extract above might involve exploring the thoughts and feelings of the characters in more depth via process drama. The children might relate this version to their own experiences of this particular tale – Disney, alternative versions, pantomime – and discuss similarities and differences and they might go on to produce their own adaptation, using alternative characters or settings or actions. The language of traditional tales encourages rich visualisation, but children also need the opportunity to discuss how they 'see' the story and bring their own ideas to the table:

> Some readers might 'rewrite' the text in their heads, selecting alternative endings or expressing a preference for a different ending to the one that the author has written. (Gamble and Yeats, 2008: 16)

Hopefully this section has successfully argued the case for the usefulness of traditional tales in supporting children's reading development. As you move on to the second case study, identify some of the ways in which the activities and pedagogies employed, using a range of traditional tales, might enhance children's enjoyment of reading and thereby promote further reading development.

In this case study, the children (aged five and six) studied many traditional tales over a period of five weeks, leading to the creation of their own book of fairy tales.

## CASE STUDY 2

A student teacher was working with a Year 1 class on a five-week unit entitled 'Fairytales'. This unit not only focused on literacy but also science, art, ICT and RE.

First, the children were introduced to many different traditional tales to familiarise them with the plot, characters and sequencing of narrative stories. They engaged in the retelling of the fairy tales, focusing on the use of story language and the typical story layout of traditional tales.

Throughout the five weeks, the children were given the opportunity to act out the fairy tales in the role-play area and retell stories using story boxes. They engaged in guided reading using a selection of different fairy tales and listened to story tapes.

One week was devoted to looking at the characters' behaviours and appearance in some depth. Links to art were made by focusing on portraits and there was a visit to the local art gallery where the children were posed the question, 'Why do we have portraits?' This was followed up in class with the production of portraits and character profiles. Many traditional tales end with the marriage of the central characters, so, in RE, the children explored the topic of weddings in different cultures.

Another week was devoted to the performance of fairy tales, with links being made with an exploration of sound (in science and ICT). After learning about how we make sounds, different types of sounds, identifying noises, listening to examples and electronic sound exploration, the children used instruments and their own voices to bring the fairy tale to life. In particular, they explored how certain sounds could create different effects within the tales.

The unit culminated in the children writing their own fairy tale book using everything they had learnt over the course of the unit of work. The final day was a fairy tales day, with all the children dressing as their favourite fairytale character and lots of wedding celebrations!

In this example, the children were immersed in the genre of fairy tales. This immersion is a vital part of becoming a confident reader. Not only that but it is also well known that children love to hear their favourite stories over and over and they thoroughly enjoyed the opportunities during the five weeks for this to occur. The retelling of the stories supported their early reading development, as they revisited vocabulary typical of traditional tales. This was reinforced by listening to audio versions of the tales, giving the children a chance to hear the rhythms and tunes of the stories (see Chapter 10, Picture books, for more discussion of the musicality of stories) and via drama and role-play, where a deeper understanding of character and setting was promoted.

Links were made throughout the unit with other curriculum areas and this is significant in relation to children's acquisition of global coherence in relation to texts (Cain, 2010). Global coherence enables children to draw from existing knowledge, understanding and experience in order to gain a deeper meaning from what they read. Very young children will have a limited range of experiences to draw on, but, by including visits to places outside the classroom and exploring fairy tales in curriculum areas other than just literacy, the practitioner is building on these experiences, making it more likely that young literacy learners will make useful links and deepen their understanding of different words and worlds.

During the unit of work, the children were also encouraged to explore sound and use the production of sound to bring the fairy tales to life. Any activities that raise children's awareness of sounds will support them with their reading as they make links between the letters they see and the sounds they hear and this also makes them memorable. These children were developing this awareness within the joyful activity of creating music to match the stories.

Every opportunity was taken during this extended unit of work to support children with their early literacy development – by speaking and listening, reading and writing. Traditional tales were central to this, with their strong rhythms, predictable vocabulary and recognisable characters and settings. Not only were the children making progress but they were also having a great deal of fun in a social, productive and collaborative environment.

## Summary

Traditional tales are a significant part of our lives and fundamental to literacy development. As human beings, we constantly tell stories about events, people and our feelings. Young children also have this urge to talk about their lives, recall actions, repeat stories and wonder about feelings and values. It is this that provides a sound basis for literacy learning (Whitehead, 2004). Early literacy is all about instilling into children a love of and a curiosity about language, laying the foundations for literary appreciation and the ability to communicate with different people in a range of settings. Traditional tales have the ability to ignite this passion, encapsulated so well in the following quotation:

*(Continued)*

*(Continued)*

> Traditional tales have been refined and reshaped from powerful ingredients and still retain their imaginative essence, their ability to move, excite, fascinate and enthral the reader or listener. They also build on children's oral language experience of rhythm, rhyme and story. (Grainger 1997: 48)

It is hoped that you have the opportunity to use these 'powerful ingredients' as you share with children the excitement of other worlds through the medium of traditional tales.

## Further reading

Gamble, N. and Yeats, S. (2008) *Exploring Children's Literature* (2nd edn). London: Sage.
The authors of this book believe that a deep subject knowledge of language and literature enables practitioners to support children's literacy development. The text includes discussion relating to many different types of literature, including traditional tales.

Waugh, D., Neaum, S. and Waugh, R. (2013) *Children's Literature in Primary Schools*. London: Sage.
This text explores a range of genres and includes case studies that model good practice with suggestions for practical activities using literature.

## References

Bettleheim, B. (1991) *The Uses of Enchantment: The meaning and importance of fairy tales*. London: Penguin.

Brooks, P.J. and Kempe, V. (2012) *Language Development*. Chichester: BPS Blackwell, John Wiley & Sons.

Browne, A. (2009) *Developing Language and Literacy 3–8* (3rd edn). London: Sage.

Cain, K. (2010) *Reading Development and Difficulties*. Chichester: BPS Blackwell, John Wiley & Sons.

Chomsky, N. (1965) *Aspects of the Theory of Syntax*. Cambridge, MA: MIT Press.

DfE (2012) *Statutory Framework for the Early Years Foundation Stage*. Runcorn: DfE.

DfE (2013) *The Draft National Curriculum*. London: DfE.

Fox, C. (1990) 'The genesis of argument in narrative discourse', *English in Education*, 24 (1): 23–31.

Gamble, N. and Yeats, S. (2008) *Exploring Children's Literature* (2nd edn) London: Sage.

Grainger, T. (1997) *Traditional Storytelling in the Primary Classroom*. Leamington Spa: Scholastic.

Guppy, P. and Hughes, M. (1999) *The Development of Independent Reading: Reading support explained*. Buckingham: Open University Press.

Halliday, M.A.K. (1975) *Learning How to Mean: Explorations in the development of language*. London: Arnold.

Hart, B. and Risley, T.R. (1999) *The Social World of Children Learning to Talk*. Baltimore, MD: Paul H. Brookes Publishing.

Lenneberg, E.H. (1967) *Biological Foundations of Language*. New York: John Wiley & Sons.

McNeil, D. (1970) *The Acquisition of Language: The study of developmental psycholinguistics*. New York: Harper & Row.

Morrow, L.M. (2009) *Literacy Development in the Early Years: Helping children to read and write* (6th edn). Boston, MA: Pearson.

Skinner, B.F. (1957) *Verbal Behaviour*. Boston, MA: Appleton-Century-Crofts.

Sylva, K., Melhuish, E., Sammons, P., Siraj-Blatchford, S. and Taggart, B. (2004) *The Effective Provision of Pre-school Education (EPPE) Project: Findings from pre-school to end of Key Stage 1*, DfES Research Report SSU/FR/2004/01. Nottingham: DfES Publications.

Vygotsky, L.S. (1978) *Mind in Society: The development of higher psychological processes*. Cambridge, MA: Harvard University Press.

Waugh, D., Neaum, S. and Waugh, R. (2013) *Children's Literature in Primary Schools*. London: Sage.

Wells, G. (1987) *The Meaning Makers: Children learning language and using language to learn*. London: Hodder & Stoughton.

Whitehead, M. (2004) *Language and Literacy in the Early Years* (3rd edn). London: Sage.

Wray, D. and Medwell, J. (1993) *Literacy and Language in the Primary Years*. London: Routledge.

## Children's literature referred to in the text

Cole, Babette (1986) *Princess Smartypants*. London: Hamish Hamilton Children's Books.

Hutchins, Pat (2003) *Rosie's Walk*. London: Red Fox.

Munsch, Robert (1980) *The Paper Bag Princess*. Toronto: Annick Press.

Southgate, Vera (no date) *Cinderella*. London: Ladybird Books.

# Part 4

# Inspiring readers and writers

# Picture books

## Roger McDonald

---

 **Chapter Objectives**

- to develop an understanding of the complex nature of picture books
- to identify the importance of choosing suitable picture books
- to know the relationship between the words in a text and the pictures
- to identify how the musicality of picture books can enhance language development and the reading experience.

---

## This chapter will cover:

- the history of picture books
- the complexity of picture books
- choosing suitable books
- how wordless picture books might support early literacy
- the musicality of picture books and the link between this and early literacy.

It would be easy to take picture books for granted. We find them in nurseries, class-rooms, playgroups, newsagents, doctors' surgeries and even free with certain news-papers. They arguably form part of our lives, to varying degrees, from birth and continue, in some form, into adulthood:

> Picture books are invariably the first books that children in the developed world encounter. They shape aesthetic tastes, they introduce principles and conventions of narrative. They are part of artistic and literary culture but they are also entertaining, moving, thought-provoking and witty. (Graham, 2004: 106)

We all have unique experiences and memories of our own personal interactions with picture books – those we hold dear because they were gifts from loved ones, some signifying an important time in our lives, others we can remember being read to us at home or in school and particular examples that have connected with us in some way. These experiences and interactions can enhance or detract from the way we, as pro-fessionals, use picture books with the children in our classrooms.

This chapter will explore the history of picture books to provide a context with regard to their place in our history and culture. The complex nature of picture books will also be explored before assessing the relationship between the pictures and the words. Case studies are also included to illustrate particular ways in which picture books might be used to promote early literacy. Finally, the chapter will look at the musical nature of some picture books and how this can be used to enhance language and literacy with young children. Throughout the chapter, a wide range of picture books and authors will be suggested and discussed, which, hopefully, will provide useful starting points for your own decisions as to the books you will share and enjoy with the children in your class.

# A brief history of picture books

Picture books have a relatively short history, dating back just some 130 years when the role of the image and the narrative were first evaluated (Salisbury and Styles, 2012). Illustrated books and pictorial stories, however, have a longer history, originating with the paintings found on walls and in caves from possibly up to 60,000 years ago.

It is important here to clarify the distinction between a picture book and an illus-trated story. A picture book is a story told in words and pictures. Each makes an important contribution to the way the story is told and meaning is created. This is not the same as an illustrated story, where:

> the words alone could tell the story and the illustrations simply break up the words or decorate the text … In the best picture books, the illustrations are absolutely neces-sary. They carry parts of the story or narrative and in some cases the language is dropped and the pictures alone are all that is needed. (Gleeson, 2003: 2)

The oldest illustrated book is believed to be from 1980BC, in the form of an Egyptian papyrus roll. There is, of course, some debate over this fact as it was not until the facilities to publish things were invented that there were more reliable records. Indeed, the first major development was the invention of printing and then the ability to produce multiple copies of the same text.

The first children's picture book, 'in the sense that it was a book of pictures designed for children to read' (Salisbury and Styles, 2012: 12), was published in Nuremberg in 1658. Developments continued, among them the introduction of colour printing, leading to the start of the modern picture book era in the late nineteenth century.

Born in Chester on 22 March 1846, Randolph Caldecott is heralded as the transformer of children's literature, publishing books in which the text and the pictures were *both* valued as elements in storytelling. Indeed, the Caldecott Medal is named after this pioneering illustrator and is awarded annually by the Association for Library Service to Children to the artist who has illustrated the most distinguished American picture book for children.

From this point on, the picture book industry grew as changes took place, such as revolutionary technical improvements, a shift in the perception of childhood as the Victorian age passed, as well as a range of new artists coming on to the scene, poised to exhibit their talents. World War II meant that there was a greater focus on the *cost* of publishing books, but this did not hinder them being published, albeit on reduced-quality paper during this period of austerity.

The 1960s brought to us some of the excellent picture books that are still used regularly in classrooms across the country, including *Granpa* and *Oi! Get Off Our Train* by John Burningham, as well as *The Tiger Who Came to Tea* and the *Mog* books by Judith Kerr. Having a considerable influence was *Where the Wild Things Are* by Maurice Sendak, published in 1963 and since having sold over 19 million copies worldwide (Nettell, 2012). Characterised by a robust portrayal of children's fears and aggression, *Where the Wild Things Are* has been made into a film and is still read and talked about in many primary schools.

Much attention has rightly been given to Anthony Browne, who was first published in the 1970s, his debut book being *Through the Magic Mirror* ([1976] 2000). His picture books brought a unique feature to the genre, which was to promote the continual rereading of his pictures. Other prolific picture book authors in this era were David McKee, who wrote *Elmer*, and Janet and Allan Ahlberg, writing together in the 1970s and then Allan writing alone after the untimely death of his wife.

Currently, there is a wealth of picture books to excite teachers and learners and, increasingly, some authors are producing titles in this genre specifically for children in Key Stage 2 and beyond. Some of these are wordless picture books – authors such as David Wiesner and Jeannie Baker excel in this genre – and these books create deep and intense connections with readers as they aim to make sense of the messages within the pictures.

Many authors focus on producing picture books that are multimodal and exploit features such as the use of different fonts and text sizes (Lauren Child's *Charlie and Lola* series, for example), opportunities for readers to interact and physically involve themselves with the book (the Ahlberg's *The Jolly Postman* and *Meerkat Mail* by Emily Gravett are two great examples) and use of colours, textures and sound.

Over the years, then, the picture book genre has become increasingly complex. This is explored in more depth in the next section, in relation to how this might support the teaching and learning of early literacy.

## The complexity of picture books

As we have seen, picture books can be complex and may present stories, poems and information in a number of ways, all of which can be used to support children with their early literacy development.

Studies of picture books tend to focus predominantly on the illustrations in specific texts (Styles and Arizpe, 2001; Unsworth and Wheeler, 2002; Lysaker, 2006). It is also important, however, to recognise the intrinsic relationship between the pictures and the text:

> the picture book is a unique literacy experience, where meaning is generated simultaneously from written text, visual images and the overall design. (Serafini, 2009: 10)

It could be argued, therefore, that it is too simplistic to analyse just one element and not look at it together with the other. Indeed, by focusing just on the pictures, we are in danger of losing the whole meaning and full power of the text. Nodelman (1988: 223) makes this exact point, stating that the text and pictures 'take on a meaning that neither possesses without the other'. The relationship, therefore, is not one of two separate elements that simply complement each other, but, instead, an interwoven relationship, with the text and pictures transcending and transforming each other. Indeed, Sipe (1998) calls this 'synergy' – the combination of the two sign systems having a greater impact than either the written or visual text taken alone.

This relationship between the words and pictures can lead to tensions, exemplified in the way we read picture books – often going backwards and forwards, comparing pictures, relating pictures to each other and also to the text. This tension is caused by the different ways in which the words and pictures affect us.

When looking at the pictures, we have an inherent drive to form what Sipe (1998: 101) calls 'unified atemporal structures'. This means that we aim instinctively to understand and make meaning from the pictures, but, in order to do this, we need to give ourselves time to explore the images and make connections before succumbing to the power of the written text, which often tempts us to keep on reading, to find out more – to get to the end! Rushing through a picture book may mean that we do not do ourselves or the text justice as the power of the text and illustrations are not given a chance to weave their magic.

Lewis (2001) delineates a range of levels that highlight the sophistication of picture books. He notes that, on the first level, there is the interaction between (for the majority of books) the words and the pictures. For early readers, if the words and pictures are aligned closely, this can support children with their comprehension as they look for clues in both the words and images.

On the second level, there is the consideration that pictures can be manipulated to affect interpretation and the words, too, can be presented in a number of ways to affect how the text is read. As mentioned in the previous section, an example of this technique is Lauren Child's work, in which she uses font type and size, orientation on the page and multimedia to create her popular effects. Children born into the twenty-first century will have an understanding – via television, the Internet and computer games – of how text, images and sound can be manipulated in a range of media and books such as those by Lauren Child may appeal to them as they encounter what appears to be familiar territory in book form.

The third order of sophistication Lewis (2001: xiii) describes is when the pictures and words begin 'to drift apart from one another'. An excellent example of this can be seen in the seminal text *Rosie's Walk* by Pat Hutchins. In the book, the *pictures* need to be read for the full story to be understood; simply reading the words will not allow readers to grasp the full implication of the possible dangers that threaten Rosie the hen.

At some point during the reading of a picture book, readers need to explore where the author and illustrator are taking them. This can be an uncomfortable experience if preconceptions are challenged and we begin to explore a range of possibilities until, in some cases, the author allows the words and pictures to join in meaning again. With these more sophisticated texts, readers have to read beyond the words and pictures, bringing to the text their own knowledge and understanding of the world in order to gain a deeper and more affective understanding.

The fourth level is when the unexpected happens, such as characters stepping out of one story into another, and, once again, readers' expectations are challenged. This is superbly illustrated by the text *The Three Pigs* by David Wiesner. This Caldecott Medal-winning picture book begins placidly (and familiarly) enough, with three pigs collecting materials and going off to build houses of straw, sticks and bricks. However, the wolf's huffing and puffing blows the first pig right out of the story … and into the realm of pure imagination.

Texts at this fourth level challenge readers as they quickly try to make sense of what is happening. There have been more and more texts bringing the characters out of the texts and, in effect, developing the story in the space around readers as well as actually in the book. This has the effect of unsettling readers, as their preconceived ideas about how the narrative will develop are challenged.

These levels of interaction have implications for the developing language and literacy of young children. The Early Years Foundation Stage Framework includes, as part of one of the early learning goals relating to the 'prime area' of Communication and Language, the requirement that children 'listen to stories, accurately anticipating key events and respond to what they hear with relevant comments, questions or actions' (DfE, 2012: 7). Interacting with picture books, even at the very first level, provides young children with the opportunities to respond and question what they see and hear. In the draft national curriculum programmes of study for Year 1, the reading requirements include (DfE, 2013: 10):

- discussing the significance of the title and events
- making inferences on the basis of what is being said and done
- predicting what might happen on the basis of what has been read so far

and, for Year 2, children need to be seen to be (DfE, 2013: 18):

- making inferences on the basis of what is being said and done
- answering and asking questions
- predicting what might happen on the basis of what has been read so far.

Just from this small sample of statutory requirements, it can be seen that picture books, with their differing levels of complexity, have the potential to support children in their development of reading skills. For this to be truly effective, however, practitioners need an extensive knowledge of picture books in order to be able to recognise which texts are suitable for all ages, abilities and interests – texts that will inspire and excite young readers.

## Motivating readers: making choices

If young readers are to be motivated to read in a world that contains many other distractions and attractions, they need to be exposed to texts which are 'right' for them. The aim is to look for a book they can immerse themselves in; a book that makes some sort of connection with their lives or their imaginative fantasies; a book which opens up possibilities of thinking. That does not necessarily mean we can define what a 'good' book is, however.

Different texts lead to different responses in readers. A text that can evoke the emotions of laughter, intrigue and excitement in one reader can leave another totally unmoved (Martin and Leather, 1994). In part, this is due to the fact that all of us and the children we teach, of whatever age, have our own reading lives, our reading identities. These are continually being shaped by our experiences and interactions and it is important that we understand this is true of ourselves and the children we teach.

We can explore these reading identities – and thereby 'tap into' the interests of our young readers – in a number of ways. One useful activity to undertake with a group of children is a 'reading river'. This promotes memories of favourite books and special situations, as well as times when the experience of reading may not have been an enjoyable one. The following case study describes how the reading river was introduced to a class of five- and six-year-olds.

## CASE STUDY 1

The children in a Year 2 class were exploring their own reading experiences, sharing with one another their favourite books and reading habits. Surveys were undertaken with the class relating to where children enjoyed reading and the range of reading experiences they encountered on a daily basis. Children brought photographs from home showing them reading in their favourite places. These were accompanied by teachers' own photographs, which they shared with the children to the delight of the young learners!

There was a real reading 'buzz' in the classroom as talk centred on a love of and interest in books at a variety of levels. It was interesting that all the children appeared absorbed and inspired and were able to access the activities. The teacher was able to cater expertly for all preferences, ensuring that the children had a choice of texts and learning activities to immerse themselves in and no children felt alienated. It was important that all the children felt included in the activities and all their responses were valued. This was modelled by the teacher and, in turn, replicated by the children.

One activity that took place at the end of the first week involved the children exploring their own personal reading histories in the form of a 'reading river'. The preceding activities meant the children had a bank of memories and experiences that had been brought to the surface and they were eager to record them pictorially.

The activity involved the children first, drawing their river outline. It was explained that this depicted their reading journey from their earliest memory until the present day. The children could indicate times of enjoyment with sunshine and fast-flowing elements to their river and periods of dissatisfaction with clouds and boulders in the river, causing it to slow down.

The children set to work in groups, busily discussing and drawing their rivers. Conversations started as the children remembered books read to them in class and stories shared at home. At times, disagreements were apparent as views about shared texts differed from one child to another, but this was a healthy and productive discussion that allowed the children to rekindle their memories of texts and associate them with personal feelings.

Immersing ourselves and the children in picture fiction is a starting point for evaluating and choosing relevant books to explore with them. Gathering a range of picture books and spreading them over a number of tables in the classroom will invite the children to gravitate towards them. As they pore over them, model the excitement of picking up a text, looking, pondering, discarding and choosing another. It is important that the children see adults engaging in such a way with texts and not only asking 'teacherly' questions but also responding, as readers, with them.

There have been a number of studies focusing on teacher identities, most notably the 'teachers as readers' project from 2006–2007 led by Teresa Cremin. These studies emphasise the importance and power of the teacher in a class being seen as 'a reader who teaches' rather than 'a teacher who reads'. Teachers who were motivated themselves, successfully developed children's eagerness and enthusiasm to read (Cremin et al., 2009). The activity described above in the case study, provides an ideal opportunity for a teacher and children to enjoy picture books together and share their ideas and opinions.

When we are thinking about choice and motivating young readers, it is useful to have a treasure chest of books that you can dip into. As mentioned at the start of this section, different books appeal to different audiences. There are several elements, however, that you might take into consideration when choosing your books and these are outlined below. This list is not exhaustive and there should be a caveat of 'it is not necessarily the case that the more elements the book includes, the better the book'.

- The front cover – is it eye-catching? Does it set your mind wondering about the setting, characters or themes of the book? Does the title match the picture or does it raise questions in your mind?
- Can you identify gaps in the text, areas that need to be filled and explored, possibly in drama?
- Does the text lend itself to 'possibility thinking'?
- Does the text connect with you in some way, reminding you of experiences, other texts, imagined places?

One of the key elements in choosing a text is the emotional connection a book makes with readers. This is intrinsically understood by adults, who can choose what they read and have the 'right' to discard a book after looking at the cover or reading the first few pages if they so wish. How disheartening and demoralising it would be to be told that we *had* to read a range of texts with which we were unable to make a connection. In some schools, however, that is the daily experience of some younger children who are given no choice in what they read and their individual interests are not considered as they move through staged/levelled or 'banded' books.

It is obvious that children, just as we do, need guidance on suitable texts and also teachers need to develop each child's reading ability and confidence, but relying solely on prescribed routes or schemes takes away the individual rights of each child as a reader (Pennac, 2006). It is our responsibility to ensure that we know every child and his or her reading identity and preferences. In this way, we can utilise the power of picture books in the most effective ways.

Some of the most powerful picture books are those without words. The next section explores how these texts might support early and developing literacy learners.

## Wordless picture books

To understand a visual image without words is crucial in our day-to-day lives. While driving, for example, we are constantly making meaning from the images on the road signs; colourful, often dramatic advertisements assault our eyes at every turn and we engage constantly with images on electronic devices. An understanding of and competency with the visual image is becoming more important as the modern world increasingly depends on their effects (Lewis, 2001).

From the 1970s onwards, words disappeared altogether from some texts and now wordless picture books are a unique genre in their own right. There are many excellent wordless books available, appealing to all ages, backgrounds and experiences. Some titles that you might want to explore are:

*Belonging* by Jeannie Baker
*Window* by Jeannie Baker
*Zoom* by Istvan Banyai
*Clown* by Quentin Blake
*Invisible Visible* by Katja Kamm
*Archie* by Domenica More Gordon
*The Chicken Thief* by Béatrice Rodriguez
*Midsummer Knight* by Gregory Rogers
*Slam!* by Adam Stower
*Flotsam* by David Wiesner
*Magpie Magic* by April Wilson.

When reading a wordless book, readers comes to it with their background experiences and own personal histories, which will affect their interpretation of the visual images encountered (Arif, 2008). Arif believes that the power of wordless books lies in the potential for divergent types of reading and meaning that can evolve from the texts and the range of possible interpretations because of the lack of words to explain or tell. In Years 3 and 4 of the draft national curriculum programme of study, children need to be seen to be:

> drawing inferences such as inferring characters' feelings, thoughts and motives from their actions, and justifying inferences with evidence predicting what might happen from details stated and implied. (DfE, 2013: 26)

Wordless picture books really challenge children and adults to infer and deduce. A justification of these inferences can occur via high-quality discussion and exploratory talk.

In the following case study, Chelsea, a Year 1 child and David, a Year 2 child, respond to a range of wordless books and the teacher records their responses.

## CASE STUDY 2

Chelsea is a Year 1 child who enjoys reading, has positive support from home, regularly visits the library and talks about books in school. David, who is in Year 2, sees himself as a non-reader and has low self-confidence. At home, David receives little help, due to the family's own difficulties and experiences with reading.

The reason for choosing these two children was to investigate their initial responses to wordless books and how they reacted to the visual images.

From six texts, Chelsea and David could choose one to read. In separate sessions, Chelsea chose *The Chicken Thief* and David chose *Zoom*. Each child then read their books while observations were made of any changes in tone, facial expressions and physical movements.

Before the session, both David and Chelsea looked at the range of books. They demonstrated eagerness and excitement – possibly because they had individual attention as well as the fact that we were exploring a range of texts. Chelsea showed the characteristics of a child who was used to the process of browsing, discarding and choosing books, whereas David picked up the first book he saw. Of course, this could have been due to the fact that he saw the red cover and the title *Zoom* and so did not need to consider any further texts.

Once Chelsea and David had made their decisions as to which books they wanted, they were given time to read and reread the books. They had the opportunity to take the books back to class, share them at home and have them as their current reading books.

While observing David, it was clear that, to begin with, he raced through the pages taking cursory glances at them before turning to the next. After four pages, however, David suddenly stopped and retraced his reading, flipping forwards and backwards through the pages. People familiar with the text will understand why this might have happened – the pictures zoom out from an image and the reader slowly starts to understand the full scene. In order to make sense of the text, the reader is, in effect, forced to look back at previous pages.

In contrast, Chelsea read her book page by page, mainly in sequence, studying the pictures carefully. Her facial expressions indicated interest and curiosity. It could be argued that her knowledge of the narratives of stories helped her understanding of the way the text would develop and instinctively she could predict that the chicken would, in fact, be safe.

The wordless picture books chosen by the children in the case study above challenged them in different ways. Chelsea was able to make an informed choice, based on her previous experience of picture books and her own interests. She tended, however, to read the book in the way that she would read a picture book with words. In this instance, this procedure worked for her and she was able to make predictions, stay focused and enjoy the text. It would have been interesting to see how Chelsea would have read a book such as *Zoom*, which requires a different approach.

For David, *Zoom* had the effect of slowing him down, 'forcing' him to backtrack and re-examine the images in order to make sense of the storyline. These are characteristics that we should promote as they signify readers are becoming more sophisticated in their understanding of authorial intent and the potential for ambiguity. You might want to set up similar opportunities for children to engage with wordless picture books in your classroom. This is the time when you can assess the children with regards to their motivation, interests and level of understanding – all crucial to their reading development.

The final aspect of picture books to be explored is the musicality that can be found in some examples of this genre and the link between this and children's language development.

## The musicality of picture books and the link between this and early literacy

The musical nature of some picture books – the rhythm and tune of the text – makes them an invaluable resource for all readers. Through repeated readings, the tune of the text is embedded within the child and the musicality can be evidenced by 'seeing rhythm travel through a child's arms and legs and hearing words from a story sung' (Heald, 2007: 228). Children are reassured by the predictability of the rhythm, building their confidence as early readers and meaning makers. Infants as young as six months old remember particular tempos and timbres for music and, as Trehub observes:

> it is clear that infants do not begin life with a blank musical slate. Instead they are predisposed to attend to the melodic contour and rhythmic patterning of sound sequences, whether music or speech. (2003: 14)

So, what are the links between music and early literacy and language and how is this transposed to picture books? Philpott (2001: 32) defines language as 'a symbolic medium through which knowledge is held, understood and articulated'. On the one hand, therefore, music does resemble a language because it has both a symbolising and expressive function (Deveson and O'Sullivan, 1995). On the other hand, music differs from a language because it does not convey precise meaning. The difficulty in aligning music and language is recognised by Philpott (2001), who notes that arts as a whole are not regarded as languages, in part due to the tribulation of evidencing the forms of knowledge disseminating from them. This argument is furthered by Bernstein (1967), who suggests that music does not have any equivalence in the written language form. He concludes words can make the metaphorical leap that makes them art, but music is only able to operate on a level of meaning that is metaphorical. Therefore, music is able to express, but not assert, meaning. Discussing this point, Cross (2005) notes that language has specific meaning, but for music this is rarely the case because it appears to be a malleable and flexible phenomenon and the meaning of a piece of music 'can rarely be pinned down unambiguously; music appears to be inherently ambiguous' (Cross, 2005: 30).

This ambiguity can be addressed by considering whether spoken or written language itself can also be ambiguous in nature. Indeed, Cross goes on to note:

> accepting that a degree of ambiguity seems to be inherent in all acts of human communication, the music's apparent ambiguity does not debar it from being considered to be a communicative medium. (Cross, 2005: 32)

It is further argued that music is linked to language because some aspects of language are musical and some aspects of music are linguistic. Slobada (1985) noted the salient similarities between music and language:

- both are particular to humans
- both contain the potential for infinite combinations of possibilities
- both can be learned listening to models
- their natural medium is vocal and auditory sound processes
- both involve the use of notational systems
- the necessary skills must be received and absorbed before they can be used
- there is some universality of form across cultures
- they can be examined in terms of their phonetic, syntactical and semantic structures.

This, however, does not address the point made previously that music cannot be a media within which knowledge can be held and expressed (Philpott, 2001) and so cannot be classed as a language. Cooke (1959) addresses this point by stating that we can understand the composer once we understand the vocabulary or the language of the music. This shows a link between the sounds and the object of meaning. This point is exemplified by Budd (1992), who notes that the force with which music can give meaning, especially of the emotions, moods and feeling, means it uses a language. So, how does all this relate to picture books?

It is interesting to turn to the early development of music and language, even before birth. Deveson and O'Sullivan (1995) suggest that children each experience the beat of their mother's heart and the rhythm of her breathing. Once born, they experience the tunes of people's words and the sounds that surround their world; indeed, children's early attempts at language often sound quite musical.

Parents and schools then incorporate music and language together when playing with songs and rhymes, often via picture books. Bradley and Bryant (1987) found that young children knew a great deal about the common sounds in words as a result of their knowledge of rhymes and spontaneous word play. Indeed, as children's early development in reading progresses, they use their ears as well as their eyes and 'taste the word tunes on their tongues, feel the text's rhythm and beat in their bodies' (Grainger et al., 2005: 30). Therefore, if music is bound up in human development and is an intrinsic part of our lives, the power of picture books in child development cannot be underestimated.

The final case study describes how a class of four- and five-year-olds explored the musicality of picture books.

## CASE STUDY 3

A Foundation Stage class decided to explore the musical nature of the picture books they were sharing as a whole class and in groups. The children were asked to choose a book from a wide selection, but ones that had already been used in class. The three books that were finally chosen were:

- *Owl Babies* by Martin Waddell and Patrick Benson
- *Farmer Duck* by Elaine Hampton and Karen Leigh
- *Commotion in the Ocean* by Giles Andreae and David Wojtowycz.

The children were then grouped depending on their own preferences. The aim of this was for the children to bring to the groups their own previous experience of the text with the hope that the 'tune' of the text had been embedded within them. The groups had a range of musical instruments to use, as well as body percussion, and set about selecting sounds to depict each main character. This then developed into making the main music for the theme of the text. The group working on *Commotion in the Ocean*, for example, used their choice of instruments to depict the ocean in different states. They showed an expert understanding of pitch, tone and volume in their compositions.

Group compositions resulted, reflecting the narrative of the text. The books were then read to the class while the compositions were played. The teacher used effective questioning to elicit information about the narratives, such as the mood of the character, the setting, the time of day and the pace of the story.

This exploration of the musicality of picture books, extending into compositions, includes many of the ingredients that are a crucial part of early literacy learning and teaching. Children need to recognise sounds in order to develop both their oral language and their early reading:

> An important aspect of learning to talk is the development of the ability to break the sound stream into separate units and this requires that children can tune into sound. (Neaum, 2012: 101)

Neaum (2012: 102) writes that children need to develop 'steady beat competence', wherein they come to have a sense of timing and are able to recognise patterns in what they hear – all vital for their language and reading development. Many picture books have a recognisable, steady beat – a musicality into which the children can be absorbed, giving them the opportunity to hear the 'prosodic units' (Neaum, 2012: 101) and move on to use them in their expressive language and their reading aloud.

## Summary

Picture books are often the first books children encounter, so form an important part of their early reading experiences. Indeed, the exploration of these texts can foster excitement, engagement and a passion for reading. This is evidenced by fond memories older children or adults have when browsing in a library or along bookshelves and coming across texts such as *The Very Hungry Caterpillar*. Memories are rekindled and connections made across life experiences.

Picture books should surround children as they grow up and never leave them. The skill of teachers lies in adjusting the types of books given to them, based on the children's needs and interests. Indeed, as noted above, there are now many picture books aimed specifically at older readers, such as texts by Gary Crew. By ensuring immersion in a range of texts, discussions about them, hearing the tune of the text and, most importantly, enthusing about the texts, children will gain the interest and excitement about reading that will help them as they develop into literate users of language who are able to make informed choices about the texts they choose to read.

## Further reading

Arizpe, E. and Styles, M. (2005) *Children Reading Pictures: Interpreting visual texts*. Abingdon: Routledge.
This book describes the results of a longitudinal study into the responses of primary age children to picture books. The text explores the importance of visual literacy.

Neaum, S. (2012) *Language and Literacy for the Early Years*. London: Sage.
This text explores many different aspects of language and literacy. However, the section on rhymes, poems, songs, music and stories links very well with the ideas expressed in this chapter.

# References

Arif, M. (2008) 'Reading from the wordless: A case study on the use of wordless picture books', *English Language Teaching*, 1 (1): 121–6.

Bernstein, N.A. (1967) *The Co-ordination and Regulation of Movements*. Oxford: Pergamon.

Bradley, L. and Bryant, P.E. (1987) *Rhyme and Reason in Reading and Spelling*. Ann Arbor, MI: University of Michigan Press.

Budd, M. (1992) *Music and the Emotions: The philisophical theories*. Abingdon: Routledge.

Cooke, D. (1959) *The Language of Music*. Oxford: Oxford University Press.

Cremin, T., Mottram, M., Collins, F., Powell, S. and Safford, K. (2009) 'Teachers as readers: Building communities of readers', *Literacy*, 43 (1): 11–19.

Cross, I. (2005) 'Music and meaning, ambiguity and evolution', in D. Miell, R. Macdonald and D. Hargreaves (eds), *Musical Communication*. Oxford: Oxford University Press. pp. 27–44.

Deveson, T. and O'Sullivan, O. (1995) 'Language and music', *Language Matters*, 2 (2): 95–6.

DfE (2012) *Statutory Framework for the Early Years Foundation Stage*. Runcorn: DfE.

DfE (2013) *The Draft National Curriculum Programmes of Study*. London: DfE.

Gleeson, L. (2003) *Making Picture Books*. Lindfield, New South Wales: Scholastic.

Graham, J. (2004) 'Picture books: Looking closely', in P. Goodwin (ed.), *Understanding Children's Books: A guide for education professionals*. London: Sage. pp.95–109.

Grainger, T., Goouch, K. and Lambirth, A. (2005) *Creativity and Writing: Developing voice and verve in the classroom*. Abingdon: Routledge.

Heald, R. (2007) 'Musicality in the language of picture books', *Children's Literature in Education*, 39 (3): 227–35.

Lewis, D. (2001) *Reading Contemporary Picturebooks: Picturing text*. London: RoutledgeFalmer.

Lysaker, J. (2006) 'Young children's reading of wordless picture books: What's self got to do with it?', *Journal of Early Childhood Literacy*, 6 (1): 33–55.

Martin, T. and Leather, B. (1994) *Readers and Texts in the Primary Years*. Buckingham: Open University Press.

Neaum, S. (2012) *Language and Literacy for the Early Years*. London: Sage.

Nettell, S. (2012) 'Maurice Sendak obituary', *The Guardian*, 8 May. Available online at: www.guardian.co.uk/books/2012/may/08/maurice-sendak (accessed 18 December 2013).

Nodelman, P. (1988) *Words About Pictures: The narrative art of children's picture books*. Athens: University of Georgia Press.

Pennac, D. (2006) *The Rights of the Reader*. London: Walker Books.

Philpott, C. (2001) 'Is music a language?', in C. Philpott and C. Plummeridge (eds), *Issues in Music Teaching*. Abingdon: Routledge. pp. 32–46.

Salisbury, M. and Styles, M. (2012) *The Art of Visual Storytelling*. London: Laurence King Publishing.

Serafini, F. (2009) 'Understanding visual images in picturebooks', in J. Evans (ed.), *Talking Beyond the Page*. Abingdon: Routledge. pp. 10–25.

Sipe, L. (1998) 'How picture books work: A semiotically framed theory of text–picture relationships', *Children's Literature in Education*, 29 (2): 97–108.

Sloboda, J. (1985) *The Musical Mind: The cognitive psychology of music*. Oxford: Clarendon Press.

Styles, M. and Arizpe, E. (2001) 'A gorilla with "Grandpa's eyes": How children interpret visual texts – a case study of Anthony Browne's Zoo', *Children's Literature in Education*, 32 (4): 261–281.

Trehub, E. (2003) 'Musical predispositions in infancy: An update', in I. Peretz and R. Zattore (eds), *The Cognitive Neuroscience of Music*. Oxford: Oxford University Press. pp. 3–14.

Unsworth, L. and Wheeler, J. (2002) 'Re-valuing the role of images in reviewing picture books', *Reading, Literacy and Language*, 36 (2): 68–74.

## Children's literature referred to in the text

Andreae, Giles and Wojtowycz, David (2010) *Commotion in the Ocean*. London: Orchard Books.
Ahlberg, Janet and Alan (1999) *The Jolly Postman*. London: Puffin.
Baker, Jeannie (2002) *Window*. London: Walker Books.
Baker, Jeannie (2008) *Belonging*. London: Walker Books.
Banyai, Istvan (1995) *Zoom*. London: Viking.
Blake, Quentin (1998) *Clown*. London: Red Fox.
Browne, Anthony ([1976] 2000) *Through the Magic Mirror* London: Walker Books.
Burningham, John (1991) *Oi! Get off our Train*. London: Red Fox.
Burningham, John (2003) *Granpa*. London: Red Fox.
Child, Lauren *Charlie and Lola* series.
Gravett, Emily (2007) *Meerkat Mail*. London: Macmillan.
Hampton, Elaine and Leigh, Karen (2008) *Farmer Duck: KS1: Read & Respond: Activities based on* Farmer Duck *by Martin Waddell & Helen Oxenbury*. London: Scholastic.
Hutchins, Pat (2003) *Rosie's Walk*. London: Red Fox.
Kamm, Katja (2006) *Invisible Visible*. Zürich: North-South Books.
Kerr, Judith (2007) *The Tiger Who Came to Tea*. London: HarperCollins.
Kerr, Judith *Mog* series.
McKee, David (2007) *Elmer*. London: Andersen.
More Gordon, Domenica (2012) *Archie*. London: Bloomsbury.
Rodriguez, Béatrice (2009) *The Chicken Thief*. Wellington, New Zealand: Gecko Press.
Rogers, Gregory (2009) *Midsummer Knight*. London: Allen & Unwin.
Sendak, Maurice (2000) *Where the Wild Things Are*. London: Red Fox.
Stower, Adam (2005) *Slam!* Dorking: Templar.
Waddell, Martin and Benson, Patrick (1996) *Owl Babies*. London: Walker Books.
Wiesner, David (2001) *The Three Pigs*. New York: Clarion Books.
Wiesner, David (2006) *Flotsam*. New York: Clarion Books.
Wilson, April (1999) *Magpie Magic*. New York: Dial Books.

# 'This is how we teach reading in our school'

Tracy Parvin

 **Chapter Objectives**

- to raise awareness of how systematic synthetic phonics has become a key aspect of the teaching of early reading
- to explore different perspectives on the teaching of early reading.

## This chapter will cover:

- the government initiatives that have led to the introduction of systematic synthetic phonics as the prime approach to developing early reading
- the difference between decoding and reading
- reading for meaning
- early reading approaches
- using case study material as the basis for discussion about the teaching of early reading.

# The 'Independent review of the teaching of early reading'

In 2006, the *Independent Review of the Teaching of Early Reading* (Rose, 2006) was published. The review was undertaken by Sir Jim Rose and came as a response to the belief that the first nine years of the National Curriculum (1989–1998) had had very little impact on raising national reading standards.

Rose (2006) made a number of key recommendations for how early reading should be taught – the main emphasis being on using synthetic phonics as the prime method of teaching early reading. Since the report's publication, schools have been required to ensure that children receive discrete systematic synthetic phonics instruction on a daily basis. This, for some, has meant completely reorganising their teaching approaches and, in some instances where schools buy in to published schemes, costly staff training being seen as necessary. Thus, since its publication, the Rose Review has had a profound impact on the teaching of reading in primary schools.

Let us look at the background to this review. When New Labour came into power in 1997, the government's overall aim was to focus even more on raising standards, especially in the basics – namely, literacy and numeracy. That education was to be the party's number one priority was highlighted in the 1997 manifesto, with an increased focus on raising standards and a zero tolerance approach to underperformance.

The 1996 end of Key Stage 2 statutory assessments had yielded what were perceived to be disappointing results, with 57 per cent of 11-year-olds achieving the expected level of attainment (Level 4) – 'a level originally set as an average' (Alexander, 2010: 35). Thus, literacy, especially reading, became the initial primary focus.

In May 1997, David Blunkett, the then Secretary of State for Education, announced a target had been set, that, by 2002, 80 per cent of children would achieve Level 4. This might appear to have been a confident goal, but Blunkett had, in 1996, established a Literacy Task Force, chaired by Professor Michael Barber, the remit of which was to develop:

> an education system which ensures that all children are taught to read well by the age of eleven. (Literacy Task Force, 1997: paragraph 3)

The Literacy Task Force perceived that there was evidence of entrenched views, with teachers supporting either 'real books' approaches, as advocated by theorists such as Frank Smith and Ken Goodman, or the teaching of reading by using 'phonics'. The Task Force felt that a return to basics was necessary and all teachers should recognise the 'critical importance of phonics in the early years' (Literacy Task Force, 1997: paragraph 43).

Moreover, it was felt the National Literacy Project (NLP) – a detailed and prescriptive framework for the daily teaching of literacy initiated by Ofsted but run by the DfEE that, in 1996, had been piloted in 15 local authorities – was, at the time, proving to be successful (Stannard and Huxford, 2007). With a speed rarely seen in education (Earl et al., 2003), this project was rolled out nationally in September 1998. The aims of the project, the National Literacy Strategy (NLS), were to raise standards, initially in reading but also, in the long term, in writing.

The NLS approach to reading was determined by the 'searchlights model'. This model was intended as a graphic representation of the four types of information that readers use to gain an understanding of what they are reading (Brooks, 2003):

- contextual information
- grammatical information
- word recognition and graphic knowledge
- phonics.

In order for teachers to develop an understanding of the teaching of phonics, the NLS provided schools with teaching materials – initially 'Progression in phonics' and then, later, 'Playing with sounds'.

A House of Commons Education and Skills Committee (HCESC) inquiry (2005: paragraph 1) further explored how 'all children should get the best teaching possible in this crucial area'. The main recommendation of the inquiry was for a government review of the methodology for the teaching of reading as presented by the NLS. Despite Brooks' (2003: 14) assertion that 'a major redirection of the phonics element of the NLS was neither necessary nor appropriate', it was argued the review was required to establish the effectiveness of different approaches, such as analytic and synthetic phonics, the use of mixed strategies for teaching reading and the effect of using texts with children matching their decoding abilities.

At the time of the inquiry, the reading debate had entered new levels of discussion with regard to specific phonics approaches. On the one hand, the NLS appeared to be favouring the analytic phonics method, which involves children being encouraged to analyse whole words by means of the letters they see and the context in which they are being used. On the other hand, elsewhere synthetic phonics approaches were being advocated, which encourage children to hear and synthesise the smallest units of sounds (individual phonemes) in words and align what they hear with the graphic representations they see. The inquiry recommended that full-scale comparative research be undertaken into the different approaches. Thus, Jim Rose was invited by the government to carry out an independent review of the teaching of early reading.

The following section aims to explore the recommendations of his review – the Rose Review (2006), as it has become known – investigating the decision to recommend the implementation of systematic synthetic phonic teaching approaches, as opposed to other forms of systematic phonics instruction, alongside the remodelling of the 'searchlights model' as the 'simple view of reading'.

## Why synthetic phonics?

While Rose does acknowledge the importance of a rich curriculum to support engaging prereading activities, such as being introduced to stories and nursery rhymes, an assumption is made that these activities are introduced to children prior to them commencing full-time education. The onus at this stage, therefore, is on parents and carers.

The main thrust of Rose's review focused on the supposition that the essential component in developing reading is the systematic teaching of phonics: 'children should have a secure grasp of phonics which should be sufficient for them to be fluent readers' (Rose, 2006: 7). Rose does not explore the notion of reading fluency and what it might mean. Rather, he infers that fluency is determined by acquiring the ability to rapidly decode the written word and so decoding should be sufficient.

To support this position, Rose (2006: 10) focused only on the aspect of the National Curriculum (DfEE, 1999: 46) programme of study for English that concentrates on what he perceives to be 'early reading' – namely, the development of 'phonemic awareness and phonic knowledge' – neglecting other areas, such as grammatical awareness, contextual understanding and literature.

In order to determine which approaches might best aid children's reading development, the DfES also commissioned academics from York and Sheffield universities to 'conduct a systematic review of experimental research on the use of phonics instruction in the teaching of reading and spelling' (Torgerson et al., 2006: 1). Their review highlights that systematic phonics teaching does aid the development of accuracy in reading, although there was no evidence to suggest that one approach was more favourable than another. That is to say, synthetic and analytic phonics were found to be on a par in terms of their effectiveness. Thus, Torgerson et al. (2006) emphasise that what is important is the *systematic* concept – that is, there is a focus on a clearly defined teaching sequence concerning the relationships between letters and sounds in order to decode words, as opposed to an ad hoc or non-systematic approach – a view held by many others (Stahl et al., 1998; Cain, 2010).

Despite the underwhelming evidence and lack of robust research to support the decision (Hynds, 2007; Wyse and Styles, 2007; Wyse and Goswami, 2008), something Rose (2006: paragraph 47) does acknowledge, his review determined that the best way forward would be for all schools to adopt the *synthetic* phonics approach. One of the main reasons for this decision was that:

> While robust research findings must not be ignored, developers of national strategies, much less, schools and settings, cannot always wait for the results of long-term research studies. They must take decisions, based on as much firm evidence as is available. (Rose, 2006: paragraph 31)

The underlying message here is that the decision had been made and all parties concerned needed to accept it, without question, regardless of the absence of the comparative research requested by the HCESC (2005: 36).

The reason for this volte-face can only be supposed. Perhaps it was the 'particularly strong response from supporters of synthetic phonics' (HCSEC, 2005: 13). Maybe it was the results from the longitudinal study undertaken by Johnston and Watson (2005) in Clackmannanshire, which appeared to provide evidence that synthetic phonics is a superior method. Indeed, the Clackmannanshire research did seem to identify that children's ability to decode words was improved by the synthetic phonic approach, but it was not the comparative study it purported to be as the children were taught the different approaches – synthetic and analytic phonics – at different rates (Torgerson et al., 2005; Wyse and Goswami, 2008). Also, the results yielded suggest that the children's ability to understand what they had read was not in line with their ability to decode.

## The simple view of reading

The recommendations of the Rose Review also heralded a reconstruction of the 'searchlights model', as it was guilty of 'paying too little attention to securing word recognition skills' (Rose, 2006: 4), and the model now recommended is the 'simple view of reading' (SVoR). Unlike the searchlights model, which highlights the complex processes that are used to gain an understanding of written texts, the SVoR represents two dimensions of reading – word recognition processes (decoding) and language comprehension processes (understanding).

While acknowledging the complexity of reading as an activity, Rose (2006) nevertheless adopts the two-dimensional model originally proposed by Gough and Tunmer in 1986 and remodelled by Stuart for the review. This model seems to neglect the complexities involved in the act of reading (Harrison, 2010). In addition, Rose suggests that 'reading equals the product of decoding and comprehension' and 'decoding' is 'the ability to recognise words presented singly out of context, with the ability to apply phonic rules a crucial contributory factor of this context-free word recognition ability' (Rose, 2006: 76).

This cognitive psychological approach could pose a problem for those who believe that reading should be developed within a context. In many respects, advocating this model contradicts the premise originally asserted by Rose that beginning readers should be stimulated by a language-rich literacy curriculum. Identifying reading as these two distinct dimensions also appears to lend support to the synthetic phonic view that decontextualised decoding should be secured before children are expected to engage with books. The approach advocated also restricts the texts to those that are completely and independently decodable by the children, thus further diminishing the possibility of having a language-rich literacy curriculum.

Thus, it appears that reading has been redefined and before children can be allowed to engage and enjoy a rich diet of literature, they must first 'become fluent and automatic readers of words' (Rose, 2006: 78) – that is to say, proficient decoders. It seems, then, that this situates decoding and comprehension as linear processes – children reading to decode first and, when that has become an accomplished skill, develop comprehension (Hall, 2003). This, of course, has implications for those children for whom decoding is a difficult to acquire skill, with the possibility of encounters with meaningful texts being delayed even more.

The past 20 years have provided teachers with many opportunities to question not only their professional standing but also their pedagogical principles and beliefs. While the National Curriculum specifications for English gave teachers a broad framework within which to develop children's literacy skills, the NLS made prescriptive recommendations as to how that framework should be taught. Now, with the Rose Review (2006) recommending that the teaching of reading is to be undertaken within discrete daily synthetic phonics instruction, it is possible, while some teachers might welcome the recommendation, others might feel their core principles as to what reading actually is and how it could be taught are being challenged and compromised.

## The difference between decoding and reading

Despite the plethora of literature devoted to the subject, there appears to be no one simple, single definition of reading.

At a very basic level, reading could be described as the act of decoding words, leading to an understanding of what those words might be communicating. This approach, known as the cognitive–psychological view of reading (Hall, 2003; Cain, 2010), is generally held by psychologists with an interest in determining how the process of reading begins and the subset of skills required in order to translate written words into spoken form (Cain, 2010).

The research in this area includes scientific studies aimed at exploring children's ability to hear the individual sounds in words (phonemic awareness), 'decompose a syllable into its constituent phonemes' (phoneme segmentation; Adams, 1994: 67), manipulate and delete phonemes from given words in order to determine phonological awareness and blend individual phonemes in order to derive the word. These studies, however, represent a scientific or psychological approach and present the given units of sound in decontextualised forms. While they provide educators and researchers with a wealth of information regarding the acquisition of phonemic awareness and decoding skills, they reveal very little about the complexity of skills and interactions involved when reading for meaning, so could, in fact, lull teachers into believing that reading is limited to the ability to differentiate, segment and blend sounds in order to decode.

Deriving meaning from texts is, however, a complex process that involves a wide range of skills, such as inference, prediction and hypothesising (Holdaway, 1980; Meek, 1988; Cain, 2010). If, as suggested by psycholinguists such as Goodman (1973) and Smith (1988), reading is an active process and not simply a 'linear process of letter by letter deciphering, sounding out, word recognition and finally text comprehension' (Hall, 2003: 42), then, it could be argued that, alongside developing phonic skills, teachers could also engage in a repertoire of approaches aimed at reading for both meaning and, equally importantly, enjoyment.

The following case study describes a particular school and the approach to reading taken by Monica – the deputy head and EYFS class teacher and coordinator. As you read it, think about the theories that have been discussed so far and how these link with the reality of the classroom.

## CASE STUDY 1

Sea View School is a two-form entry primary school, catering for children aged from 4 to 11 years old. It is situated in the middle of a large housing estate near a small coastal town. While the socio-economic intake is varied, the imbalance at this school is marked in that the majority of the parents are in the lower income bracket. Of the 357 children on the school roll, 23 per cent have been identified as requiring additional educational support, 13 per cent of whom have a statement of special educational needs. In comparison to national levels, these percentages indicate an above average level of additional educational support. Also, 28 per cent of the pupils are entitled to free school meals.

The Ofsted report (2009) indicates that the outstanding pastoral care and support enables the children to feel safe and secure. It is evident on entering the Early Years Foundation Stage classrooms (where the children are four to five years old) that this is a language-rich environment. The walls are filled with evidence of the children's writing on posters and displays, while the bookshelves display a wide range of 'real' books (there is no evidence of any reading scheme books).

Monica is the school's deputy headteacher. In addition to this role, Monica is the Early Years coordinator and teaches in one of the EYFS classes, so she agreed to share her views on developing readers. Monica has been working as a qualified teacher for 20 years and has focused on Early Years children and literacy development for the past 10 years. When asked for her thoughts on reading, this was her response:

> Reading is the most valuable tool that we have. Personally, it gives me so much pleasure that I can't imagine not being a reader. It's about the written word and the pictures that help to make sense of the word; it is gaining and sharing knowledge. It is the one thing that I want to do for my children. I know

*(Continued)*

*(Continued)*

that not every adult gains as much enjoyment as me, but I want to give the children the opportunity to be in a position to make that choice ...

I will encourage the children to engage in a book walk and we talk about it first. We discuss the relevance of the pictures and how they help us to understand the story ... They might act out sections of a story in the role-play area or use the puppet theatre. I have always taught phonics – it is part of my role as a Foundation Stage teacher. However, I don't think that we should ever put the cart before the horse – children will not learn to read by learning phonics; children will learn to read with phonics being part of the jigsaw ... and I think that visual literacy is so important, so reading pictures and developing their inference and deduction skills orally through questioning is vitally important for both reading and language development. We could get so hooked up on phonics that this development might be lost ... and *then* we would have a generation of 'non-readers'.

Monica clearly feels strongly that children should be reading for pleasure and meaning and understanding, so she provides a 'book-rich' setting for the children to promote this. Although the school follow a phonics scheme, the emphasis appears to be more on ensuring that children have a choice of reading materials that appeal to them and are given the opportunity to talk about books, make predictions and inferences and use a range of strategies to enable them to make sense of the written word.

Monica's philosophy regarding early reading could be seen to link with the psycho-linguistic approach, where reading is seen as a 'problem solving activity' (Hall, 2003), focused on the reader's ability to construct meaning by looking at words and sequences of words, the grammatical structures of the sentences and utilising the reader's prior knowledge or experience of what is being read (Hall, 2003). The children in the case study above are given plenty of opportunities to gain understanding by learning to read words in a contextual way rather than learning dislocated sounds and their representative symbols. Book walks, role-play, puppet theatre and guided reading are just a few examples of how these children are provided with contexts for their reading experience.

Context is vital. A child might learn that the letters 'b', 'a', 'n' and 'k' can, when blended together, produce the word 'bank'. In the English language, however, 'bank' can have many meanings. It could be a river bank or a bank where money is deposited, it could even be part of an idiomatic expression. It is only by being given the context that its meaning emerges (Cain, 2010). It is important for developing understanding that children are able to contextualise what they are learning and for phonics teaching to be embedded in real texts (Stahl, 1992; Wyse, 2010). This appears to be what Monica means when she talks about not putting 'the cart before the horse'.

The development of comprehension and reading for meaning is an area that Cain considers at length, highlighting that:

> good comprehension involves going beyond the literal meaning of the text, making links between ideas within the text and between the text and general knowledge, in order to construct a coherent representation of a text's meaning. (Cain, 2010: 96)

Cain (2010) also suggests that, while knowledge of vocabulary and decoding are important aspects of developing reading skills, an important factor is the ability to comprehend the meaning of not only the decontextualised word or even in a single sentence but across a range of successive sentences (global cohesion) and this skill can be developed before formal literacy instruction begins.

Before further discussion relating to the first case study above, I would like to introduce a second case study to serve as a comparison. Again, as you read it, consider the implications of the reading practices evident in this setting.

## CASE STUDY 2

Town View School is situated on the outskirts of a large town. It is a small, one-form entry primary school, but the EYFS children are taught in two small classes. The pupils are predominantly white British and there is a higher proportion of girls than boys. Of the 208 children, 25 per cent have been identified as requiring additional educational support, with 15 per cent having statements of special educational needs. Like Sea View School, the percentage of children entitled to free school meals is, at 28 per cent, higher than average (Ofsted, 2009).

The school has a well-stocked library for general use and, during the visit, a number of parents were observed working as librarians. There were photos of children reading in strange and wonderful places on display throughout the library.

The past year had seen a number of changes in terms of how the support staff are deployed throughout the school. In an effort to boost the reading results at Key Stage 1, the role of the special educational needs coordinator (SENCO) had been expanded to include the development of strategies aimed at ensuring higher levels of attainment in reading. To this end, the SENCO had reorganised the roles of the teaching assistants so that they now all work throughout the school, providing specific support for the teaching of systematic synthetic phonics. The phonics programme used is organised by the SENCO, who has been trained to deliver the Read

*(Continued)*

*(Continued)*

Write Inc (Miskin, no date) systematic synthetic phonics scheme. In addition to this, the same team undertakes guided reading activities in each class three times a week for half an hour each time, using a variety of books from published reading schemes to support this particular activity.

June, the SENCO, agreed to discuss her views on the teaching of reading. June has been teaching for 30 years and has a wide range of experience, having worked across all the primary phases. She has been at Town View School for 20 years and, prior to her new role, has worked as a SENCO for 10 years. Here are June's views on learning to read:

> I taught him [my son] to read, in the same way that my mum taught me, by making him do 'Toe by Toe' ten minutes a day. I know that he is not dyslexic, but he couldn't read. I said to him, 'Son, if you can read what it says in this book – if you can read those words – then I shan't worry about you, but you have to learn to read otherwise you won't have access to anything' ... he was five then ... they have to learn to decode ... They love being read to, but they need to see that to read words like that is going to take some effort and a lot of them haven't got the determination or perseverance.

From the case study above, it would appear that June's focus is on the need for children to learn to 'decode' the words: 'they *have* to learn to decode ... They love being read to, but they need to see that to read *words* ... is going to take some effort'. This suggests that children need to understand that it is a difficult process and they need dogged determination and perseverance in order to master the skill of decoding. Later in the interview June says:

> All children get intensive input related to ... phonic work ... even if you have children who are really, really keen, there is a process that they have to go through, they have to learn to decode.

Here there is no sense of reading being a pleasurable activity; rather it becomes a mechanical process of decoding achieved by hard work. By concentrating on her belief in the importance of literal word reading, June appears to align herself with the cognitive–psychological approach.

June believes that the teaching of decoding skills is the primary route to developing readers and children have got to put in a bit of effort to learn to read. It could be argued that June's unilateral approach to reading is perpetuating the children's belief that reading is hard. Rather than encouraging the children's language development via a range of book experiences, they are being limited to the decontextualised decoding of words, which, possibly, make no sense to them. June's statement 'they have to learn to decode' signifies her support of this approach. It is a belief she appears to have long held, having been taught to read herself by means of decontextualised phonic approaches and, indeed, used the same methods to teach her own son. It is also worth considering if her role as a SENCO and her use of highly structured phonics schemes, such as 'Toe by Toe', to support struggling readers, might have further reinforced her conviction that this is the best approach to teaching reading. In her practice, it is evident that June maintains a steadfast grip on her own beliefs as to how reading should be developed within the school.

## Two different perspectives

Although both Monica and June recognise the importance of reading, they take what can only be described as polarised stances to the teaching of early reading. These diverse beliefs appear to be based, to a certain extent, on their own reading autobiographies and experiences.

Although Monica began talking from a somewhat utilitarian perspective – 'reading is the most valuable tool' – suggesting a possibly perfunctory approach, this was completely dispelled by the words that followed. Fuelled by her own passion for reading, Monica wants to empower the children, equip them with the appropriate 'tools' that will allow them to make an autonomous lifelong choice – whether or not to join the 'reading club' (Smith, 1988).

Thus, looking at what Monica said, it could be suggested that, for her, reading is all about the book and the personal pleasures gained from being immersed in books, that these are the important factors: 'personally, it gives me so much pleasure'. Interestingly, this is an area that was not explored at all in the Rose Review (2006). Monica believes that children should be encouraged to search for the meaning by reading the pictures, which might give a clue to what the words might be telling them and what the author intended to communicate. This is in direct contrast to the recommendations in the 'Letters and sounds' synthetic phonics materials guidance notes, which state that 'attention should be focused on decoding rather than on the use of unreliable strategies such as looking at the illustrations' (DfES, 2007: 12).

The quest for meaning appears to be the most important aspect of reading for Monica:

> I will encourage the children to engage in a book walk and we talk about it first. We discuss the relevance of the pictures and how they help us to understand the story.

By engaging in social acts, such as story times and shared reading experiences, the children are actively encouraged to make meaning. The reading of the pictures and ensuing discussions enable the children to make sense of the book. Cain (2010) suggests that successful reading comprehension is gained, in part, by an understanding of the text as a whole; global coherence. In her practice, Monica is not only immersing her class in the texts but is also helping to develop the children's understanding of the structure of the story and, via drama activities, an understanding of and empathy for the characters. She is encouraging the children's deeper explorations of the text, which, in turn, promote the higher-order reading skills of inference and deduction. It could be argued that it is the refining of these sophisticated skills that ensures enjoyment of and proficiency in reading, rather than simply engaging in phonics instruction.

The development of higher-order reading skills is an aspect that Monica believes needs to be developed with the children in her class:

> I do get the children to read pictures and paintings and we ask questions ... 'Why is he looking like that?', 'What do you think this means?'

These forms of speaking and listening activities are, to some extent, supported by Rose's (2006: paragraph 35) recommendation, which states that 'phonic work [is] to be securely embedded within a broad and language-rich curriculum'. In his review, however, they are suggested as good practice for *prereading* activities rather than viewed as essential methods for encouraging a deeper understanding of the texts being read or studied or as methods that could be used throughout the primary phase. Indeed, there is an assumption made in the review that children's early interests in reading will have been stimulated by 'play, stories, songs and rhymes' from the 'earliest stage' by 'carers and parents' who 'should be strongly encouraged in these pursuits' (Rose, 2006: 4). This does imply that all children will have had very similar preschool experiences and will come in to school armed with this prerequisite knowledge. Both June and Monica, however, work with children who they believe have *not* had these preschool reading experiences. As Monica noted, 'We do have a lot of children who do not read at home.'

With regard to teachers' practice in school, the review's prevailing message is that early reading is secured by systematic, discrete, synthetic phonic teaching and children 'must learn to process *all the letters in words* and read words in and out of text' (Rose, 2006: paragraph 45, my emphasis). This suggests that the children should be taught to pay total attention to every letter in a word in order to be able to 'read' that word and they should be able to 'read' a word without the contextual cues of a story or a book. As discussed earlier, however, the meaning of a word is derived from its context (Cain, 2010) and this suggested decontextualised approach could be difficult for children who have not yet encountered a wide range of children's books or developed the broad and rich vocabulary associated with children's literature (Cain, 2010). This is something Monica is acutely aware of:

> I do teach phonics, but it is in the context of a shared or guided reading activity, I then feed it into my literacy teaching ...

Children's lack of book experiences is a significant issue for June and Monica, both of whom work in schools set in areas where the children's parents have low socio-economic backgrounds. While Monica attempts to overcome this issue by giving the children 'a real and rich diet of books and literature', June's focus is on decoding and the systems set up within the school – with teaching assistants trained to deliver a synthetic phonics scheme using decodable books – are part of this.

Thus, it appears that these teachers' practices are firmly entwined with their beliefs. Monica appears to have developed practices that involve the children searching for meaning, while June has focused her attentions on the decoding of words. It is interesting to note, while these teachers have both been subject to the same governmental recommendations and statutory requirements, they have managed to mediate and interpret these recommendations to develop reading approaches that appear to enable them to hold on to their diverse professional principles.

## Summary

It would be fair to say that the teaching of early reading has always been of prime importance to those practitioners working with young children. Of late, however, it has become something of a 'political football', thereby raising its status even higher. From an optimistic perspective, this might be regarded as potentially constructive in that a higher profile can lead to funding initiatives, creative thinking and a wealth of resources emerging. In reality, funding has gone towards a phonics check for six-year-olds which a survey by the United Kingdom Literacy Association (UKLA) found to be 'costly, time-consuming and unnecessary' (UKLA press release, 2012); and match funding for government-endorsed phonics schemes, such as Read Write Inc, whereby schools are encouraged to buy into particular phonic schemes. These shemes prescribe what and how to teach systematic synthetic phonics, with little room for innovative and exciting teaching and no appreciation of children's existing skills and experiences.

How early reading is taught in schools can be down to a number of factors, including funding and resources, management within schools, top-down pressure with regard to results and league tables and fear of reprisals if government recommendations are not followed, as well as the personal beliefs and reading histories of practitioners. Notably, these factors do *not* include the importance of children reading for pleasure, what children have already achieved before they step into a classroom, teachers being allowed the autonomy that enables them to respond to the needs of the children in their classes and acknowledging that our young readers have been born into the twenty-first century, so their exposure to multimodal

*(Continued)*

*(Continued)*

texts from a very young age will influence their attitudes and abilities in relation to reading.

Those of us at the 'chalk face' need to heed the myriad research into early reading and use this to inform our principles and practice. Most of all, though, we need to respond to the needs of our young readers, instilling a desire to read as they discover the power and the pleasure to be derived from reading.

## Further reading

Cain, K. (2010) *Reading Development and Difficulties*. Chichester: BPS Blackwell, John Wiley & Sons.

This is an excellent text that, among other things, explores reading comprehension in some depth, providing examples demonstrating why particular aspects of comprehension might cause early readers difficulties.

Hall, K. (2003) *Listening to Stephen Read: Multiple perspectives on literacy*. Maidenhead: Open University Press.

This seminal text provides a real-life context from which a range of perspectives relating to the learning and teaching of reading are explored. A very useful and accessible book.

## References

Adams, M.J. (1994) *Beginning to Read: Thinking and learning about print*. Cambridge, MA: MIT Press.

Alexander, R. (2010) *Children, their World, their Education: Final report and recommendations of the Cambridge primary review*. Abingdon: Routledge.

Brooks, G. (2003) *Sound Sense: The phonics element of the National Literacy Strategy: A report to the Department for Education and Skills*. DfES' former website. Available only online at: http://core.roehampton.ac.uk/digital/general/soundsense.pdf

Cain, K. (2010) *Reading Development and Difficulties*. Chichester: BPS Blackwell, John Wiley & Sons.

DfEE (1999) *The National Curriculum: Handbook for primary teachers in England*. London: DfEE and QCA.

DfES (2007) *Letters and sounds: Notes of guidance for practitioners and teachers*. Nottingham: DfES Publications.

Earl, L., Watson, N., Levin, B., Leithwood, K., Fullan, M. and Torrance, N., with Jantzi, D., Mascall, B. and Volante, L. (2003) *Watching & Learning: Final report of the external evaluation of england's national literacy and numeracy strategies*. Ontario: Ontario Institute for Studies in Education, University of Toronto.

Goodman, K. (ed.) (1973) *Miscue Analysis: Applications to reading instruction*. Urbana, IL: National Council of Teachers of English.

Gough, P.B. and Tunmer, W.E. (1986) 'Decoding, reading, and reading disability', *Remedial and Special Education*, 79 (1): 6–10.

Hall, K. (2003) *Listening to Stephen Read: Multiple perspectives on literacy*. Maidenhead: Open University Press.

Harrison, C. (2010) 'The simple view of reading: A moral debate?', in K. Hall, U. Goswami, C. Harrison, S. Ellis and J. Soler (eds), *Interdisciplinary Perspectives on Learning to Read: Culture, cognition and pedagogy*. Abingdon: Routledge. pp.207–219.

Holdaway, D. (1980) *Independence in Reading* (2nd edn). Sydney: Ashton Scholastic.

House of Commons Education and Skills Committee (HCESC) (2005) *Teaching Children to Read: Eighth report of Session 2004–05*. London: Stationery Office.

Hynds, J. (2007) 'Putting a spin on reading: The language of the Rose Review', *Journal of Early Childhood Literacy*, 7 (3): 267–79.

Johnston, R. and Watson, J. (2005) *A Seven Year Study of the Effects of Synthetic Phonics Teaching on Reading and Spelling Attainment*, Insight 17, Information Analysis and Communication Division, Scottish Executive, Education Department, Edinburgh. Available online at: www.scotland.gov.uk/Publications/2005/02/20682/52383 (accessed 18 December 2013).

Literacy Task Force (1997) *A Reading Revolution: How we can teach every child to read well: Interim report of the Literacy Task Force*. London: Literacy Task Force. Available online at: www.leeds.ac.uk/educol/documents/000000153.htm (accessed 18 December 2013).

Meek, M. (1988) *How Texts Teach What Readers Learn*. Stroud: Thimble Press.

Miskin, R. (no date) Read Write Inc Programmes. Available at: www.ruthmiskintraining.com/home/index.html (accessed 8 October 2013).

Neuman, S.B. and Dickinson, D.K. (eds) (2002) *Handbook of Early Literacy Research* (Volume 1). New York: Guilford Press.

Rose, J. (2006) *Independent Review of the Teaching of Early Reading*. Nottingham: DfES Publications.

Smith, F. (1988) *Understanding Reading: A psycholinguistic analysis of reading and learning to read*. Mahwah, NJ: Lawrence Erlbaum.

Stahl, S. (1992) 'Saying the "p" word: Nine guidelines for exemplary phonics instruction', *The Reading Teacher*, 45 (8): 618–625. Available online at: www.jstor.org/stable/20200939 (accessed 18 December 2013).

Stahl, S.A., Duffy-Hester, A.M. and Dougherty Stahl, K.A. (1998) 'Everything you wanted to know about phonics (but were afraid to ask)', *Reading Research Quarterly*, 33 (3): 338–55. Available online at: www.jstor.org/stable/748309 (accessed 18 December 2013).

Stannard, J. and Huxford, L. (2007) *The Literacy Game: The story of the National Literacy Strategy*. Abingdon: Routledge.

Torgerson, C.J., Brooks, G. and Hall, G. (2006) *A Systematic Review of the Research Literature on the Use of Phonics in the Teaching of Reading and Spelling*. Nottingham: DfES Publications.

UKLA (2012) *UKLA Analysis of Schools' Response to the Year 1 Phonics Screening Check*. Available at: www.teachers.org.uk/files/y1psc-survey-october-2012.pdf (accessed 8 October 2013).

Waterland, E. (1998) *Read with Me*. Stroud: Thimble Press.

Wyse, D. (2010) 'Contextualised phonics teaching' in K. Hall, U. Goswami, C. Harrison, S. Ellis and J. Soler (eds), *Interdisciplinary Perspectives on Learning to Read: Culture, cognition and pedagogy*. Abingdon: Routledge. pp.130–149.

Wyse, D. and Goswami, U. (2008) 'Synthetic phonics and the teaching of reading', *British Educational Research Journal*, 34 (6): 691–710.

Wyse, D. and Styles, M. (2007) 'Synthetic phonics and the teaching of reading', *Literacy*, 41 (1): 35–42.

# 12

# Empowering young writers

## Susan Barrett

 **Chapter Objectives**

- to discuss the theories relating to the writing process
- to understand, via two case studies, how children's writing can be affected by particular pedagogies and assessment strategies
- to consider ways in which we can empower young writers.

---

### This chapter will cover:

- a discussion of the writing process
- what is meant by 'school' writing and the implications of a particular approach to this
- particular issues relating to writing, leading to suggestions of how we might empower young writers.

---

## The writing process

Writing is a hard (Stainthorp, 2002), complex process (Yarrow and Topping, 2001; Medwell et al., 2009) and full of paradoxes (Sharples, 1999). Scholars have long attempted to analyse and describe its unique properties, recognising that, although its signs represent speech (Olson, 2009), it is more than mere translation of speech, it is a 'transformative act' (Myhill, 2009). Thoughts and ideas need to be generated and then encoded in graphical representations by means of a hand-held implement or keyboard (Latham, 2002). While this might suggest a linear process, the reality is more hesitant, recursive (Hayes and Flower, 1980) and subject to bursts of activity following periods of reflection, even daydreaming (Sedgwick, 2011). Many find it is 'bound up in personal identity' (Chamberlain, 2011) and there is the ever-present danger that 'the more you think about how you do it, the more difficult it becomes' (Sharples, 1999: 3).

There are three paradigms or models of writing: genre, skills and process (Grainger et al., 2003). The first specifies the range of fiction and non-fiction genres that should be taught, along with their organisational and linguistic features, while the second focuses on the transcriptional skills of spelling and handwriting – arguably in order to free up the mental resources needed to generate the ideas for composition. This has tended to create a focus in schools, often for both teachers and children, on the writing *product*, which can be easily assessed, rather than on the *process* itself. Yet learning to write includes learning both the mental and practical processes involved in composing text (Ivanic, 2004).

The process approach constructs children primarily as authors, with a focus on meaningmaking, rather than as 'secretaries' (Latham, 2002). Here, children are involved in gathering ideas, writing, revising, editing and 'publishing' in a recursive process in which they move seamlessly between being both producers and readers of their own text to ensure it meets the needs of their chosen purpose and audience. That is not to say technical aspects are unimportant or devalued, merely that they should not dominate the central purpose of communication, but be more of an aid to empower young writers (King, 2000).

If children are engaged in making choices about structure, tone and language, increasing competence in this helps 'the young writer develop a voice and gradually control the written word to make meaning' (Collins in Graham and Kelly, 2010: 52). Graves' memorable phrase, 'Voice is the imprint of ourselves on our writing' (1983: 227), is perhaps a salutary reminder for classrooms, where writing is sometimes reduced to the 'toolkit approach' at increasing levels of competence. Is there a danger that children develop knowledge but not control (Packwood and Messenheimer, 2003)?

# 'School' writing

Heavily enshrined in the English National Curriculum (NC) (DfEE, 1989) and its later offshoots the National Literacy Strategy (NLS) (DfEE, 1998) and Primary National Strategy (PNS) (DfES, 2006), is the influence of Australian genre theory, which has radically altered the range of forms taught specifically to primary-age children. Add to the mix greater prescription in teaching the curriculum, coupled with high stakes testing regimes, and the focus in the later twentieth and into the twenty-first century has been on skills or 'testable features' (Grainger et al., 2005). This has also led to a boom in the 'industry' of literacy, spawning a host of programmes or experts who can supposedly help both pupils and practitioners in this area (Lankshear and Knobel, 2003).

Among these experts is Ros Wilson (2002), whose work has been appropriated by many schools in the South East of England in an attempt to combat low scores in writing tests at the end of Key Stage 2. Wilson has identified four generic aspects of writing that need to be taught specifically and discretely to pupils: vocabulary, connectives, openers to sentences and punctuation (VCOP). Extending pupils' range in these four areas, she claims, along with supporting evidence, will enable progress to be made linearly through the National Curriculum levels. Pupils are meant to be given the opportunities to use these regularly in independent, controlled writing in a weekly 'Big Write' session. This is when, often, a whole school will set children a piece of independent writing from a common stimulus that is then assessed and levelled against Wilson's Criterion Scale of statements within each National Curriculum level.

One of the tenets of Wilson's work is that improving pupils' skills in reading will not sufficiently improve their skills in writing:

> It has become evident that around 60% of the population will never read widely enough, regularly enough, at a high enough challenge or with enough pleasure to subconsciously absorb higher-order structures and consciously apply them in writing. (Wilson, 2002: 4)

This is part of the rationale for teaching these four generic areas (VCOP) explicitly. One might argue that this writing formula is successful because it develops, for example, the skill of complex sentence writing (evident in the case study below). This is a requirement for achieving the appropriate government-imposed level at the end of Key Stage 2, so is part of 'playing the game', and may, to an extent, help to develop more mature, stylish expression. The danger is that children apply VCOP uncritically so effects can appear contrived. Most research points to writing to a formula being counterproductive:

> Direct teaching of particular language features of prose … is less likely to produce good writing than is a close focus on the meanings that children want to express … or … the regular reading and discussion of literature of quality. (Barrs and Cork, 2001: 203)

Instead, it could be argued that children need more exposure to 'texts that teach' (Meek, 1988) to read in their entirety, thereby being given a chance to write like readers.

The following case study describes the experiences of one child, Jenny, in relation to writing. When her teacher identified her to me, she said:

You may be interested in Jenny. She's done really well in everything this year. She came to me as a 2C and now she's a 3B!

As I had expressed an interest in looking in detail at a child as a writer, I was immediately intrigued by this introduction. Would this link with National Curriculum levels be a key part of Jenny's perception of herself as a writer? After observation, interviews with the child and the teacher and the collection of documents, I was able to begin to form a picture of Jenny as a writer. The case study contains some pertinent data that will then be discussed.

## CASE STUDY 1

Jenny is a happy, confident seven-year-old girl with plenty of friends in school, but confidence has not always been evident in her school life and she has received out of class support two to three times a week for the past two years because of under-achievement in reading. Much of this work has been reinforced at home.

I observed the teacher input session prior to the 'Big Write' session and the session itself as a part of my observation schedule. In Jenny's classroom, by far the largest and most prominent display is the VCOP board with examples of all four generic targets displayed. Jenny often referred to this when asking questions orally and during her writing. She, like her peers, was confident in providing answers to quick-fire questions: 'What's a connective?' and 'Which of these sentences is at a higher level?' The children were asked to write a sentence in pairs on their whiteboards using an 'opener card' from their desks. Jenny and her partner were chosen to read out their example: 'Spookily I walked into the old castle', with Jenny suddenly adding, unprompted, 'and walked up the creaky broken stairs', which she had just made up.

The children were then engaged in highlighting descriptive words in an extract taken from *The Firework Maker's Daughter* by Philip Pullman. Although her partner monopolised this task, when the teacher came to her table and asked what a simile was, Jenny responded immediately with, 'It was like walking on apple crumble ... or ... as beautiful as a rainbow.'

The final activity was for the children to write adjectives, similes and metaphors for the firework pictures on their tables. Jenny wrote, 'It looks like a thunderous storm of colourful clouds', but as soon as she heard the teacher tell them not to begin with, 'It looks like ...', she rubbed it out immediately, replacing it with 'a giant hoola-hoop of all colours. It shot up all beautiful colours, as beautiful as a rainbow.'

*(Continued)*

*(Continued)*

In the 'Big Write' session that followed, the children were required to write a letter to a friend recounting their experience of a firework display. Jenny settled to write, often making reference to display boards of vocabulary to inform her work. Counting the number of lines she had written, she announced 'Eighteen!' triumphantly to her neighbour. While children were peer reviewing each other's work, Jenny added two further lines and turned her work over, shielding it from prying eyes. In it she used some adverb openers such as 'Amazingly' and some complex sentence construction: 'Later on I met my companion at the food bar and we had a bite and chatted while watching the amazing and beautiful fireworks.' She also included the similes she had practised in the lesson beforehand.

Within the description of the fireworks, Jenny wrote 'bang' and used a different font to emphasise the sound effect. Elsewhere in her work the word 'suddenly' was surrounded by a halo of lines like the rays of the sun to create emphasis.

Jenny's 'Big Writing' book begins with an assessed piece of writing. Despite the lack of punctuation and transitional spelling, there are real echoes of grammatical constructions and vocabulary from her reading. For instance, she wrote, 'Who in this castle is making you work?' In much of her writing, there are examples of vocabulary or sentence constructions that are unlikely to come from her everyday speech and so are the product of her reading. For example, her ending of a class story describes climbing the 'twisting staircase' rather than the more normal 'stairs'. Later in the piece, she comments, before going into the room, 'I told myself to be brave', followed later by, 'now I was scared, too scared to even go any further'. This demonstrates a deft handling of narrative voice and an effective use of repetition.

In her other literacy work, there is a poem:

In bed one night … listening to the

howling wind.

What could it be?

Suddenly I can hear a little

bash on my window.

It is the whirling and howling.

Oh whistling wind why do

you never rest?

When Jenny had completed the poem, the teacher asked her to add a simile to describe how it moves, along with 'keep going Jenny, more adverbs'. This was her response:

The wind is like a snow storm

when it's crashing violently and curling.

In bed one night ... listening

to the howling thunderously wind.

Sometimes the wind howls like a lonely wolf.

The wind wanders wildly around the woods.

Oh whistling wind why do

you never rest?

Throughout her books the written feedback is in relation to Jenny's use of VCOP and usually includes a 'wish' or her next steps. These she generally complies with.

When she was asked in my interview how she liked people to respond to her writing, she replied, 'I like it when they write little messages like "please put some more punctuation in" or "put more -ly or -ing" and that.' When I asked if she wanted people to say they had enjoyed it, she laughed ruefully and answered, 'Yeah – but they don't really do that.' She also tried to explain to me what goes on in her head as she writes, providing a revealing reply:

When I'm writing, I say the words through my head and then I start typing them and then more great words come up while I'm writing the others. When I, like, want to put er VCOP in, I'm like, 'Wait there brain, I need to put some VCOP in so that Miss can mark it'.

When I asked her why she includes VCOP she replied, 'To make her proud of me.'

This case study raises some very interesting issues relating to empowering young writers. The following discussion will address some of these issues.

## The influence of home and school

Activities such as the one in the observed lesson, where the children were to highlight descriptive words in a written passage, have, undoubtedly, contributed to Jenny's understanding of how linguistic features are used by real writers. Indeed, the teacher's suggestion to 'see what ideas you can borrow' is an effective way to encourage children to become scavengers, taking and using ideas from wherever they can find them. For this to have had more impact, however, it might have been better to have used a whole text as a model as decontextualised extracts do not necessarily enable children to attune themselves to the rhythms and cadences of language used in quality whole texts (Barrs and Cork, 2001).

A closer look at the opportunities afforded to Jenny to develop her writing reveal an interesting selection of genres. Out of the 16 pieces of work in total in her books, 4 are letters, 3 appear to be sections of narrative that are unrelated and unfinished, 2 are the same narrative continued, 1 is a draft narrative chapter, 1 is a poem, 1 is the ending to a class story and 3 are preparatory activities for writing a story that remains unwritten. There is only one example of non-fiction writing – a newspaper report – and all have been teacher-directed, with the children having no opportunity to select the subject, form or audience. They appear to be very clearly 'rehearsal activities' (Rosen, 1998) rather than embodying any purpose in their own right. With so many pieces unfinished, Jenny has had little opportunity to develop her skills of composition and is in danger of understanding that completing writing is unimportant.

On the one hand, it is possible that the emphasis on this heavily teacher-directed skills approach could be seen as a form of 'scaffolding' in Bruner's (1966) terms, in anticipation that Jenny will develop eventual competence in using these for her own purposes. On the other hand, it might be deemed to be merely a toolkit (Wells cited in Mercer, 2000), associated in Jenny's own mind with the cultural practices of school. So, when she was seen to add more adjectives orally to the paired sentence she and her partner had prepared, it became clear that Jenny was aware of school expectations and was quick to adopt certain words or phrases 'that appeal to or appease the current social scene' (Dyson, 2001: 16). She has clearly come to equate writing with wanting to please the teacher. She has grasped the idea that using adjectives elicits praise and is able to 'turn it on' at will. She thus uses VCOP to create a specific teacher response rather than as a result of any sense of ownership or authorship.

This leads me to ask, why exactly are children writing? It would seem that very often it is not to preserve things, reflect on experience or ideas or change the relationship between the writer and the experience (Rosen, 1998). In much literacy and 'Big Write' work that I have seen, it does not appear to be related to Vygotsky's (1986) idea of a psychological tool for organising children's thoughts or for reasoning. It appears to be far more the blending of ingredients within a given form.

Teacher modelling and shared writing are often undertaken, giving the children the opportunity to see skills and processes demonstrated by an expert writer (Corden, 2003), but this is not the same as seeing the teacher and other adults in the classroom writing alongside the children in a community of practice where risktaking is encouraged and the emphasis is on meaningmaking within meaningful contexts rather than simply employing a 'recipe' (Medwell et al., 1998).

If, as Grainger et al. (2005) assert, there are three paradigms of writing – genre, skills and process – then the focus for many children is clearly on skills. The process approach as advocated by Graves (1983), with the opportunities for individual writing conferences and children being able to track their own development as a writer in ways other than assessed levels, is missing. While there is evidence in many schools that children are encouraged to edit and redraft their writing, it seems that often they are not given control of their linguistic choices. Graves believes that 'the energy for revision is rooted in the child's voice, the urge to express' (Graves, 1983: 160). Frequently, redrafting is adult managed and, although the children oblige, they often succeed in merely producing a set of disparate sentences that have lost the flow of the original and lack the cohesion of the first draft. This is particularly evident in the second draft of Jenny's poem in the case study above. Her line, 'Oh whistling wind, why do you never rest?' is surely an example of poeticised speech and a child who is developing a real 'ear' for language so should be encouraged to take ownership of her revisions.

Constant adult-managed redrafting would seem to indicate that children become trapped at Bereiter and Scardemalia's (1987) 'knowledge-telling' stage, where idea follows idea and they never get to the 'knowledge-transforming' stage, usually demonstrated by the process of textual change, which can take place between the first and last drafts. Changes driven by *context* and *purpose* help develop children's writing skills and thus enable them to develop their knowledge (Wyse, 1998). Sufficient time needs to be provided for these stages and prescriptive, formulaic suggestions need to be avoided. Instead, it is important to allow the children to make their own choices, perhaps just guiding them towards the writing of a particular author whose work illustrates distinct linguistic devices that might be useful to them (see Chapter 8, Rhythm, rhyme and repetition, for a case study that exemplifies using the work of a particular author to support children's writing).

We need to provide writing opportunities that serve a purpose for our young learners. They need to parallel oral language or encourage children 'to inform, to communicate, to interact with others' (Hall, 2003: 40) rather than focus on reproducing adult forms of writing by using a number of formulaic techniques.

One might ask, whose interests are being served by being able to write like this? Supporters of this methodology would argue that no knowledge is neutral. Rather, it is based on some group's perspective on what it is important to know. If we consider the requirement in the National Curriculum for children to be taught standard English (which Ros Wilson tackles by getting children to write in 'their posh voice'), this could be seen as 'culturally arbitrary', the imposition of ruling-class knowledge over working-class varieties (Hill, 2001). If the testing regime only validates this kind of writing, then this might be deemed to be an act of 'symbolic violence' (Hill, 2001), ensuring the social reproduction of certain linguistic forms at the expense of others.

In her interview, Jenny described and recounted the content of a range of screen texts with which she was familiar, videos such as *Mary Poppins* and TV programmes such as *Hounded*. These recounts included dramatic renditions of snippets of dialogue and revealed an understanding of character and which were the important scenes – the underlying 'grammar of film' (Marsh and Millard, 2003). This 'cultural capital' (Bourdieu, 1986) possessed by Jenny was not drawn on in her independent writing. Yet, 'if children are allowed to mine the caverns of media material, their written compositions could be richer and more meaningful to them' (Marsh and Millard, 2006: 159).

'Fortunately' for Jenny, the language from her primary discourse – home – closely mimics what is required at school. 'Overnight a robber had dug …' begins with a prepositional phrase that would be unusual in a seven-year-old's everyday speech. In the piece of writing I observed, however, she wrote a complex sentence with an adverb 'opener': 'Later on I met my companion at the food bar and we had a bite and chatted while watching the amazing and beautiful fireworks.' This appears to be rooted firmly in Jenny's personal experience (food bar) and the inclusion of the adult-sounding expression 'we had a bite and chatted' would seem to be an example of the 'cultural capital' garnered from her home experience. The end of the sentence contains two adjectives, somewhat unnecessarily. They are there because of the emphasis on VCOP rather than Jenny's considered choice of what would fit the sentence best. Nevertheless, it suggests Jenny comes from a family where 'favoured' grammatical structures are used naturally.

## The impact of assessment on Jenny's writing

Unfortunately, in many classrooms, due to the pressures of test results and league tables, writing has been reduced to a series of testable features. This is not intended to be a pejorative statement, merely an observation. It is all too easy to criticise from outside, but I well remember, as a class teacher, the pressure there was to raise standards in writing and just how beguiling the VCOP approach appeared to be. Often, though, when we discuss children's writing in terms of assessment, very little mention is made of the 'engagement of the reader, content or meaning of their writing, the writer's style, their ability to take risks, their authorial voice or commitment to the writing' (Grainger et al., 2005: 6).

Sensitive to her teacher's comments, there is plenty of evidence in Jenny's work that shows how she has responded to requests for adverbs, connectives and similes. She understands this and can apply it, but 'Does the text meet the purpose it is intended for?' (Bearne, 2002: 48) is a concept with which she is less secure. When writing letters for instance, Jenny predominantly uses the narrative mode regardless of the audience and she adheres to the VCOP formula of descriptive vocabulary and adverbial openers no matter what. In one of the letters she wrote, she included a sentence demonstrating how adept she is at '-ly' openers, adjectives and simile: 'Normally, the firework looks like a rainbow in the sky. The firework dazzled in the water like a shooting star.' This is clearly her key focus, so the audience remains firmly her teacher, who will assess her.

Indeed, assessment is so much at the forefront of Jenny's mind that she commented, 'When it's in tests I do as much as I can to get so many points'. She did not, however, want anyone but her teacher to read her work because 'that's called cheating, looking at mine'. Being asked to read her work aloud was equated with achievement on a linear scale: 'I know that I've completed a level that I haven't completed yet'. She is as yet unable to see that progress is *not* linear, but dynamic, recursive and cumulative (Bearne, 1998). Not once, during our conversations, did she speak about herself as a writer.

Frank Smith (1988: 15) warned that, once children form the impression that activities are worth doing only for assessment, 'they learn that the activity is intrinsically worthless'. Writing only to score points must, in the end, militate against developing fluency in purposeful communication (Merchant et al., 2006).

Jenny has, undoubtedly acquired a metalanguage (adverbs, similes, even VCOP), but it needs to be more than just a 'naming of parts' that have to be used – it needs to be part of a dialogue, perhaps within a collaborative writing 'conference', where she is encouraged to consider how she might achieve a particular effect and adapt her language to suit a purpose (Graves, 1983; McCormick Calkins, 1986; Bearne, 2002). Inclusion of these features – or not – should be driven by the requirements of purpose and audience and a young writer needs to be empowered to make those choices.

Interestingly, although Jenny reads widely (according to her reading record), makes mention of adult books during the interview, describes herself as a 'free reader' and is successful in terms of her writing levels, she does not admit to finding anything about *writing* easy – perhaps because of the demands of having to think of VCOP. She does not see her success with meaningmaking and style as being significant and writing is seen as something that is assessed (by a significant 'other' in the culture of school), which moves up a linear scale if the right ingredients are included. Writing does not appear to her to be an opportunity for making her own choices about form, structure or linguistic features, because these are largely prescribed. Adult suggestions and adult judgements are accepted unquestioningly (Hall, 2003). She is being given *some* knowledge about language and writing, 'but we need to ensure that children are able to make good use of this knowledge in critical applications for their own purposes' (Grainger, in Hall, 2003: 35).

Lucy McCormick Calkins (1986) noted that eight-year-olds show 'concern for correctness and convention' and no longer want to take risks. Jenny falls into this category – her spelling concerns, her urge to create a clean copy to replace what she describes as 'the dirty one where our ideas are muddled up' all attest to this. This explains, perhaps, why she keeps producing the same things that have worked and gained her praise – ellipses, similes, '-ly' openers, and so on

> Writing that is imposed upon children in a mechanistic way and tested formally against set criteria may ... prompt them to focus on passing the tests and pleasing the teacher. (Grainger et al., 2005: 20)

Jenny undoubtedly conforms to this and is learning to play the game called writing.

# Empowering young writers

So how do we empower our young writers? This section suggests some ways in which this can be achieved, including a case study that describes how the foundations might be laid with very young children to enable them to be empowered as writers from an early age.

Children need opportunities to experience writing that is relevant and has a real purpose (Frater, 2001), rather than as a rehearsal activity (see Chapter 3, Getting outside, for ideas about how this might be achieved outside of the formal classroom setting). One way to promote this is by using writing journals. These journals allow children to select subjects of their choice to write about that, combined with opportunities to discuss their composing processes with peers and experts alike, can enable them to transform their knowledge by redrafting and revising. This needs to take place in a culture of working together, so that the children can be part of a community of writers, interacting with peers and adults around the shared interest in writing, all being encouraged to take risks. To this end, note that the United Kingdom Literacy Association publishes an excellent 'mini-book' entitled *Children's Writing Journals* by Lynda Graham and Annette Johnson (2012), which provides plenty of ideas as to how to take writing journals forward into the classroom and promote their use across the school.

Children also need to experience whole texts in class within a print-rich environment, giving them a greater understanding of text structure than is possible when they are only presented with decontextualised extracts. Whole texts that have 'real' characters to engage with enable children to add to the range of 'literary' voices in their repertoire. In this way, when they come to write their own whole texts for a range of audiences and purposes, they have this experience to draw on.

Even more powerfully, children should have their work read for its meaning. Teachers' responses should prioritise how successfully a piece has communicated to the reader and engage children in a dialogue about the choices they have made and alternatives. Only then can they begin to see themselves as *real* writers with something to say that is valued by others and has an impact on them (Cremin, 2009). For this, the audience needs to vary and be authentic, rather than always be just the teacher as, even though this might be in many guises, he or she is constantly the assessor. Meaningful contexts that appeal to the children's interests will spark writing in which their writer's voice 'rings with authenticity and conviction' (Grainger et al., 2005: 83).

Perhaps one of the most powerful ways in which we can empower children is through the use of drama and role-play. By these I am referring not so much to performance drama in the form of end of term or year productions or nativity plays, but drama-based on texts and drama as part of the ongoing formative activities that constitute excellent literacy practise.

The following case study describes an Early Years Foundation Stage classroom where the children have been empowered to be writers by means of a range of pedagogies and practices including drama. Rather than describe the writing that emerged from these practices, the case study aims to exemplify the types of activities which need to occur prior to and during writing in order to provide children with the ideas, vocabulary and innovations required to help them to do so.

## CASE STUDY 2

The class of four- and five-year-olds were involved in a project all about the sea and underwater creatures. They had engaged in shared reading activities with books such as *The Snail and the Whale* and *Tiddler* by Julia Donaldson and *Commotion in the Ocean* by Giles Andreae and David Wojtowycz and had accessed websites showing submarines, underwater filming, and so on. A story box had been introduced that had been designed with a 'porthole' lid so the children could use this for the shadow puppets of various sea creatures. The story box also included knitted sea creatures and the children had the opportunity to act out the various scenes from *Commotion in the Ocean* using these props.

Later the same week, a drama specialist came to work with the children. He had been informed in advance about their topic and arrived armed with the book *Smiley Shark* by Ruth Galloway. For an hour, he got the children involved in process drama based on this text – there was a great deal of movement around the room, taking on roles, listening to the story and watching this very talented actor bring the story alive. The session was lively, fun and memorable and, alongside the activities the children had already been engaged in, provided the perfect foundations for future writing.

This case study describes some of the ways in which drama might be used with young children. The benefits of drama in relation to empowering children as writers are many and varied. First, children have the opportunity to become deeply involved with narratives and situations:

> Drama enables young learners to actively interrogate texts, exploring and making meaning as they take on roles and reach into the heart of the narrative. (Grainger, 2005: 26)

The children in the case study were given opportunities to do just this – to reach into the heart of the topic by means of their engagement with texts and role-play.

Second, in the process of this immersion, the children are exposed to a wide range of language that they might then utilise in their own writing. Shared reading and the ensuing discussions provided the children in the case study with access to relevant and useful vocabulary. When they used the shadow puppets and other props, they could be heard experimenting with this new lexicon.

Third, and for me perhaps most importantly, is that drama and role-play are about active learning. The children can engage at their level of understanding and, either through explicit participation or by observing and responding, gain a better understanding of character, setting, real-life and fictional scenarios and how life and society work. All this provides a rich and powerful foundation on which writing skills can be built. By the time these very young children came to record their experiences in written form, they were very well equipped with ideas and vocabulary, leaving them free to focus on the more technical aspects of putting pencil to paper.

## Summary

Children have an ear for language and a range of often sophisticated grammatical constructions from their reading or conversations with the large number of adults with whom they come into contact daily. They are social beings (Bearne, 2002) who usually have something to say about their own experiences, so opportunities to empower them to express these both orally and in written form need to be seized. Unless this happens, their very sense of self is at risk. The Cox report expressed a core principle each teacher should hold dear:

> Because language is a fundamental part of being human, it is an important aspect of a person's sense of self; because it is a fundamental feature of any community, it is an important aspect of a person's sense of social identity. (Cox, 1989: section 6: 18)

Children's 'voices' need to be nurtured because of this link with the development of identity and the sense of who they are. To subsume that by insisting on artificial formulaic writing is to risk stripping them of their power as writers and silencing these voices forever.

Daniel Pennac (1994) once produced a challenging list of the 'Rights of a reader'. This chapter has prompted me to consider the need for a corresponding list for the writer. It might include the right to choose what to write and who to write for; the right to finish a piece of writing; the right to write for one's own pleasure and to have one's writing read for its meaning. It is to be hoped that there are classrooms where this list is honoured.

## Further reading

Myhill, D. and Cremin, T. (2011) *Writing Voices: Creating communities of writers*. Abingdon: Routledge.
This draws on research projects to explore the nature of composing and the experience of being a writer, unusually incorporating the perspectives of children, teachers

and professional writers. It offers both insight and practical suggestions to inform your pedagogy.

Chamberlain, L. (2011) 'Writing', in R. Cox (ed.), *Primary English Teaching*. London: Sage. This very readable chapter looks at the teaching of writing, models of writing and how to teach and inspire writers by means of creative approaches. The interactive task boxes engage readers in the process and challenge thinking!

## References

Barrs, M. and Cork, V. (2001) *The Reader in the Writer*. London: CLPE.

Bearne, E. (1998) *Making Progress in English*. London: Routledge.

Bearne, E. (2002) *Making Progress in Writing*. London: RoutledgeFalmer.

Bereiter, C. and Scardemalia, M. (1987) *The Psychology of Written Composition*. Hillsdale, NJ: Lawrence Erlbaum.

Bourdieu, P. (1986) 'The forms of capital', in J. Richardson (ed.), *Handbook of Theory and Research for the Sociology of Education*. Westport, CT: Greenwood.

Bruner, J.S. (1966) *Toward a Theory of Instruction*. Cambridge, MA: Belknap Press.

Chamberlain, L. (2011) 'Writing', in R. Cox (ed.), *Primary English Teaching*. London: Sage. pp.37–51.

Corden, R. (2003) 'Writing is more than "exciting": Equipping primary children to become reflective writers, *Literacy*, 37 (1): 18–26.

Cox (1989) *English for Ages 5–16* (the Cox report). London: HMSO.

Cremin, T. (2009) *Teaching English Creatively*. Abingdon: Routledge.

DfEE (1989) *National Curriculum*. London: DfEE.

DfEE (1998) *The National Literacy Strategy: Framework for teaching*. Sudbury: DfEE Publications.

DfES (2006) *Primary National Strategy: Primary Framework for literacy and mathematics*. Nottingham: DfES Publications.

Dyson, A.H. (2001) 'Where are the childhoods in childhood literacy?: An exploration in outer (school) space', *Journal of Early Childhood Literacy*, 1 (1): 9–38.

Frater, G. (2001) *Effective Practice in Writing at KS2: Essential extras*. London: Basic Skills Agency.

Graham, L. and Johnson, A. (2012) *Children's Writing Journals* (revised edn). Leicester: UKLA.

Graham, J. and Kelly, A. (eds) (2010) *Writing Under Control: Teaching writing in the primary school*. London: David Fulton.

Grainger, T. (2005) 'Short, sweet and potent: Short stories in literacy learning', *The Primary English Magazine*, 10 (5): 25–9.

Grainger, T., Goouch, K. and Lambirth, A. (2003) '"Playing the game called writing": children's views and voices', *English in Education*, 37 (2): 4–15.

Grainger, T., Goouch, K. and Lambirth, A. (2005) *Creativity and Writing: Developing voice and verve in the classroom*. Abingdon: Routledge.

Graves, D. (1983) *Writing: Teachers and children at work*. London: Heinemann.

Hall, K. (2003) *Listening to Stephen Read: Multiple perspectives on literacy*. Maidenhead: Open University Press.

Hayes, J.R. and Flower, L. (1980) 'Identifying the organization of writing processes', in L. Gregg and E. Steinberg (eds), *Cognitive Processes In Writing*. Hillsdale, NJ: Lawrence Erlbaum. pp. 3–30.

Hill, D. (2001) 'The National Curriculum, the hidden curriculum and equality', in D. Hill and M. Cole (eds), *Schools and Equality: Fact, concept and policy*. London: Kogan Page. pp.95–117.

Ivanic, R. (2004) 'Discourses of writing and learning to write', *Language and Education*, 18 (3): 220–45.

King, C. (2000) 'Can teachers empower pupils as writers?', in J. Davidson and J. Moss (eds), *Issues in English Teaching*. Abingdon: Routledge. pp.23–42.

Lankshear, C. and Knobel, M. (2003) *New Literacies: Changing knowledge and classroom learning*. Maidenhead: Open University Press.

Latham, D. (2002) *How Children Learn to Write: Supporting and developing children's writing in school*. London: Paul Chapman.

Marsh, J. and Millard, E. (2003) *Literacy and Popular Culture in the Classroom*. Reading: National Centre for Language and Literature.

Marsh, J. and Millard, E. (2006) *Popular Literacies, Childhood and Schooling*. Abingdon: Routledge.

McCormick Calkins, L. (1986) *The Art of Teaching Writing*. Portsmouth, NH: Heinemann.

Medwell, J., Strand, S. and Wray, D. (2009) 'The links between handwriting and composing for Y6 children', *Cambridge Journal of Education*, 39 (3): 329–44.

Medwell, J., Wray, D., Poulson, L. and Fox, R. (1998) *Effective Teachers of Literacy: A report of a research project commissioned by the TTA*. Exeter: University of Exeter.

Meek, M. (1988) *How Texts Teach What Readers Learn*. Stroud: Thimble Press.

Mercer, N. (2000) *Words and Minds: How we use language to think together*. Abingdon: Routledge.

Merchant, G., Dickinson, P., Burnett, C. and Myers, J. (2006) 'Do you like dogs or writing?: Identity performance in children's digital message exchange', *English in Education*, 40 (3): 21–38.

Myhill, D. (2009) 'Becoming a designer: Trajectories of linguistic development', in R. Beard, D. Myhill and J. Riley, J. (eds), *International Handbook of Writing Development*. London: Sage. pp.402–415.

Olson, D. (2009) 'The history of writing', in R. Beard, D. Myhill and J. Riley, J. (eds), *International Handbook of Writing Development*. London: Sage. pp.6–17.

Packwood, A. and Messenheimer, T. (2003) 'Back to the future: Developing children as writers', in E. Bearne, H. Dombey and T. Grainger (eds), *Classroom Interactions in Literacy*. Maidenhead: Open University Press. pp.144–155.

Pennac, D. (1994) *Reads Like a Novel*. London: Quartet Books.

Rosen, M. (1998) *Did I Hear You Write?* London: André Deutsch.

Sedgwick, M. (2011) Unpublished talk given at UKLA conference, University of Chester, July.

Sharples, M. (1999) *How We Write: Writing as creative design*. Abingdon: Routledge.

Smith, F. (1998) *Joining the Literacy Club: Further essays into education*. Portsmouth, NH: Heinemann.

Stainthorp, R. (2002) 'Writing is hard', *Psychology of Education Review*, 26: 3–11.

Vygotsky, L.S. (1986) *Thought and Language*. Cambridge, MA: MIT Press.

Wilson, R. (2002) *Raising Standards in Writing: Strategies for immediate impact on writing standards*. Wakefield: Andrell Education.

Wyse, D. (1998) *Primary Writing*. Buckingham: Open University Press.

Yarrow, F. and Topping, K.J. (2001) 'Collaborative writing: The effects of metacognitive prompting and structured peer interaction', *British Journal of Educational Psychology*, 71 (2): 261–82.

## Children's literature referred to in the text

Andreae, Giles and Wojtowycz, David (2010) *Commotion in the Ocean*. London: Orchard Books.
Donaldson, Julia (2008) *The Snail and the Whale*. London: Macmillan.
Donaldson, Julia (2008) *Tiddler: The storytelling fish*. London: Alison Green Books.
Galloway, Ruth (2003) *Smiley Shark*. Wilton, CT: Tiger Tales.
Pullman, Philip (ed.) (2004) *The Firework Maker's Daughter*. New York: Yearling.

# Index